MINDFULNESS-BASED SUBSTANCE ABUSE TREATMENT FOR ADOLESCENTS

Mindfulness-Based Substance Abuse Treatment for Adolescents is a group-based curriculum incorporating mindfulness, self-awareness, and substance-abuse treatment strategies for use with adolescents dealing with substance use. The evidence-based, how-to format provides a curriculum for professionals to implement either partially, by picking and choosing sections that seem relevant, or in full over a number of weeks. Each session comes equipped with clear session agendas, example scripts and talking points, what-if scenarios that address common forms of resistance, and optional handouts for each session. Sections cover the major principles of working with adolescents—relationship building, working with resistance, and more—along with a full curriculum. The book is a natural fit for psychotherapists, but addiction counselors, school counselors, researchers, mentors, and even teachers will find that *Mindfulness-Based Substance Abuse Treatment for Adolescents* changes the way they work with young people.

Sam Himelstein, PhD, is a licensed psychologist in the state of California and a Behavioral Health Clinician at the Alameda County Juvenile Justice Center. He is also the author of *A Mindfulness-Based Approach to Working with High-Risk Adolescents*.

Stephen Saul, MS, is a mental health clinician who works with addiction and marginalized populations via individual, group, and family therapy. He focuses primarily on serving incarcerated and underprivileged adolescents and young adults in San Mateo County, California.

"Himelstein and Saul offer a rich and highly practical guide while providing much more than a how-to book. Clearly based in research, personal mindfulness practice, and years of clinical experience, here is a raw, honest, fearless program that promises to engage adolescents from all backgrounds. Deeply rooted in both mindfulness practice and science, the program skillfully integrates meditation, skits, role-plays, psycho-education, metaphors, acronyms, stories, poems, and even formal debates, while offering clinicians a reliable structure and guidance balanced with trust in one's own clinical expertise and personal mindfulness practice. This is the resource so many of us have been seeking, and this is a program that will undoubtedly change the course of countless young lives. A deep bow to my colleagues."

—Sarah Bowen, PhD, assistant professor of psychology at Pacific University in Portland, Oregon, and author of *Mindfulness-Based Relapse Prevention: A Clinician's Guide*

"Imagine taking the extensive experience of someone who has helped a range of high-risk youth, combining this with the ancient practice of mindfulness training, and then weaving these together beautifully with steps proven by science to help enhance emotional well-being and reduce self-destructive behaviors. This is the magnificent mixture you have in your hands in Himelstein and Saul's important guide, which offers step-by-step group lessons to support the healthy development of a resilient and insightful mind."

—Daniel J. Siegel, MD, author of *Brainstorm: The Power and Purpose of the Teenage Brain* and *The Mindful Therapist: A Clinician's Guide to Mindsight and Neural Integration*

"If you are working with adolescents suffering from addiction, this is the book you need. Himelstein and Saul have done a stellar job of gathering and imparting the mindfulness-based treatment methodology. Read this book, be mindful, and serve the truth."

—Noah Levine, author of *Dharma Punx* and *Refuge Recovery: A Buddhist Path to Recovering from Addiction*

"A truly authentic, sensitive, savvy, and invaluable curriculum for transforming young lives and the lives of those who are drawn to offer it to them."

—Jon Kabat-Zinn, author of *Full Catastrophe Living: Using the Wisdom of the Body and Mind to Face Stress, Pain, and Illness*

"Based on years of experience working with and listening to young people, Himelstein and Saul present a curriculum that is well-designed and user friendly, respectful of young people, and effective in building self-awareness, self-control, and community connection. An important resource for every professional in the substance abuse field. Highly recommended!"

—Paul Kivel, educator, activist, and coauthor of *Helping Teens Stop Violence, Build Community, and Stand for Justice*

"*Mindfulness-Based Substance Abuse Treatment for Adolescents* is a pioneering manual that weaves together science and clinical wisdom from the fields of mindfulness, psychotherapy, and addiction treatment. It is an invaluable resource for mental health professionals and teachers, and offers a unique and highly effective approach to treatment of substance abuse. I highly recommend this book."

—Shauna Shapiro, PhD, professor at Santa Clara University and author of *Mindful Discipline* and *The Art and Science of Mindfulness*

"Among the ever-growing number of resources for those privileged to share mindfulness with youth, this book stands out as an absolutely exquisitely crafted resource! The authors are extremely generous— sharing their wisdom, acknowledging the wisdom of the reader, and, most importantly, acknowledging the wisdom of the youth we serve. The book is grounded in research and provides nuanced guidance. Every chapter supports the reader in creating authentic connections with substance-using teens and sharing potent skills that they will actually use. The detailed notes to the facilitator and 'what if' scenarios are invaluable resources for readers committed to inspiring youth to choose to make meaningful changes in their lives."

—Amy Saltzman, MD, author of *A Still Quiet Place: A Mindfulness Program for Teaching Children and Youth to Ease Stress and Difficult Emotions* and director of the Association for Mindfulness in Education

"Himelstein and Saul have created a thoroughly detailed and researched compendium of how to apply mindfulness effectively in working with young people grappling with the complex issues of substance use and abuse. Their curricula beautifully weave experiential exercises, didactic information, and process-oriented techniques from multiple forms of learning, both through relationship building between adults and adolescents and among the adolescents themselves. In the spirit of the best pedagogy, the authors are able to train the trainers with the skill and finesse grounded in the solid foundation of their own clinical, teaching, and mindfulness practice and experience.

—Larry Yang, Buddhist meditation teacher

MINDFULNESS-BASED SUBSTANCE ABUSE TREATMENT FOR ADOLESCENTS

A 12-Session Curriculum

by Sam Himelstein and Stephen Saul

Routledge
Taylor & Francis Group

NEW YORK AND LONDON

First published 2016
by Routledge
711 Third Avenue, New York, NY 10017

and by Routledge
27 Church Road, Hove, East Sussex BN3 2FA

Routledge is an imprint of the Taylor & Francis Group, an informa business

© 2016 Taylor & Francis

The right of Sam Himelstein and Stephen Saul to be identified as authors of this work has been asserted by them in accordance with sections 77 and 78 of the Copyright, Designs and Patents Act 1988.

Library of Congress Cataloging-in-Publication Data
Himelstein, Sam.
  Mindfulness-based substance abuse treatment for adolescents : a 12-session curriculum / by Sam Himelstein and Stephen Saul.
     pages cm
  Includes bibliographical references and index.
  1. Teenagers—Substance use. 2. Substance abuse—Treatment. 3. Mindfulness-based cognitive therapy. I. Saul, Stephen. II. Title.
  RJ506.D78H56 2015
  616.86 00835—dc23
  2015002930

ISBN: 978-1-138-81252-9 (hbk)
ISBN: 978-1-138-81254-3 (pbk)
ISBN: 978-1-317-60705-2 (ebk)

Typeset in Stones Sans and Stones Serif
by Apex CoVantage, LLC

I, SH, dedicate this book to the many people who have supported me in my personal and spiritual journeys, from my parents and ancestors, to my clients and colleagues, to my wife Alicia and sons Solomon and Malakai. This book would not be possible without all of you. Your teachings and grace shine through me in this work.

I, SS, dedicate this book to my supportive family, my devoted wife Jennifer, and most cherished daughter, Avery. With love.

CONTENTS

TRAINING AND RESOURCES INFORMATION

Go to www.centerforadolescentstudies.com for:

Training:

- Get fully trained and certified in this curriculum to be able to implement it to the best of your ability!

Downloadable Resources:

- All handouts from every session
- All meditations from every session for practice and examples
- The slideshow from session 6 (and more)

Join our online community and contribute to the evolution of this work!

INTRODUCTION

This Mindfulness-Based Substance Abuse Treatment (MBSAT) curriculum integrates best practices from the fields of mindfulness, psychotherapy, and addiction treatment as applied to working with adolescents. The impetus for creating this program was simple: we wanted to provide mental health professionals, teachers, and other facilitators who provide group-based substance abuse treatment with a methodology for connecting with adolescents on an authentic level and with the necessary curricula to foster greater self-awareness and greater regulatory capacity over unhealthy behaviors (e.g., substance use, violence, etc.). While we first developed this curriculum for incarcerated youth, we have piloted it in educational, community-based, and inpatient and outpatient substance abuse centers. The curriculum is intended for adolescents broadly defined, and we've experienced engagement and receptivity among youth from diverse socioeconomic, ethnic, and gender backgrounds. Our hope is that adults facilitating this program ultimately deepen their ability to foster self-awareness and choicefulness and to reduce unhealthy behaviors—such as substance use—among the young people with whom they work.

Adolescent substance use and abuse indeed merits public attention. While some illicit drug use has decreased or remained stable in recent years, alcohol still remains the drug most widely used by teenagers, and daily use of marijuana increased significantly in 2010 (Johnston, O'Malley, Miech, Bachman, & Schulenberg, 2014). Furthermore, there were approximately 170,000 juvenile arrests in 2011 related to drug abuse, drunkenness, and driving under the influence (Puzzanchera, 2013). Thus, there is no shortage of need for innovative, engaging, and evidence-based substance abuse treatment and education for adolescents. Mindfulness has been growing in popularity at an exponential rate over the past decade. As an intervention, mindfulness has shown efficacy for both youth populations (Biegel, Brown, Shapiro, & Schubert, 2009; Burke, 2010; Himelstein, Hastings, Shapiro, & Heery, 2012a; 2012b) and addiction populations (Bowen, Chawla, & Marlatt, 2011; Bowen et al., 2009) and, thus, is a key component of this curriculum.

What Is Mindfulness?

The practice of mindfulness has most recently been popularized by its introduction from the Buddhist spiritual tradition. Upon close examination, however, it is evident that there are many spiritual traditions that have contemplative practices that mirror or are similar to mindfulness. Mainstream mindfulness was popularized in the early 1970s by Jon Kabat-Zinn (1990; 2013). The mainstream definition of mindfulness, to which we ascribe here in part, is often defined as being aware of the mental, emotional, and physical phenomena that arise in the present moment, with that awareness accompanied by an attitude of nonjudgment or acceptance fostered in its practice (Kabat-Zinn, 1990; 2013). Mindfulness can be practiced formally via meditation (i.e., assuming a meditative posture, focusing on an object within awareness, such as the breath or body, for a distinct period of time), or can be practiced informally when doing most daily activities (i.e., developing the above qualities while brushing your teeth, talking with friends, or when in verbal conflict). Thus, mindfulness can be thought of as the mental/ emotional attitude one has toward one's experience in this manner: as thoughts, sensations, and emotions arise in experience, the practitioner of mindfulness trains her or himself to be dis-identified with that experience. This doesn't suggest ambivalence or aversion to experience, but rather the acceptance and nonjudgment of experience.

Building on the above definition, we suggest here that mindful awareness is related to the practice of authenticity. Himelstein (2013) suggests that the term *authentic self-awareness* refers to the idea that it takes a certain level of authenticity to observe the full range of human experience in the moment—from the thoughts, emotions, and sensations that arise on the conceptual level to the biases, unconscious tendencies, and defense mechanisms that often go unobserved. The ability to be honest with oneself in the moment is related to the ability to be aware of a full range of one's experiences in the moment. Mindfulness practice enhances this ability, and we believe these two characteristics of such awareness are intimately intertwined.

Mindfulness as an Intervention for Addiction With Youth Populations

Mindfulness as an intervention has gained empirical support over the last four decades for its characteristic effects of enhancing psychological well-being and decreasing psychological distress with chronic pain patients (Kabat-Zinn, 1990; 2013), health care providers (Shapiro, Astin, Bishop, & Cordova, 2005), prison populations (Himelstein, 2011a; Samuelson, Carmody, Kabat-Zinn, & Bratt, 2007), and college students (Oman, Shapiro, Thoresen, Plante, & Flinders, 2008), to name a few of the social sectors in which it has been studied. Of particular interest has been the research conducted with addiction populations (Bowen et al., 2006; Bowen et al., 2009; Simpson et al., 2007), and youth populations (Black, Milam, & Sussman, 2009; Burke, 2010).

Literature: Mindfulness With Youth Populations

Still in its early years, mindfulness as an intervention for youth has shown promising results over the past decade. Studies have investigated the impact of mindfulness as an intervention for children and adolescents (Black et al., 2009; Burke, 2010) outpatient psychiatric populations (Biegel et al., 2009), incarcerated youth (Himelstein et al., 2012a, 2012b; Leonard et al., 2013), and substance-abusing youth (Himelstein, 2011a, 2011b; Robinson, Benjamin, & Anderson, 2014).

Two literature reviews (Black et al., 2009; Burke, 2010) investigated the feasibility of mindfulness-based interventions with children and adolescents. Black et al. (2009) systematically reviewed 16 empirical meditation studies from 1982–2008 that investigated the impact of sitting meditation on psychological, psychosocial, and behavioral outcome with youth. Although not all studies reviewed employed mindfulness-based interventions (some taught Transcendental Meditation), results showed promising evidence for the feasibility of sitting meditation interventions with young people, with median effect sizes ranging from .27 to .70 for psychosocial and behavioral outcome (Black et al., 2009). Furthermore, Burke (2010) conducted a literature review similar to the above, but focused exclusively on mindfulness-based interventions. A total of 15 studies were found via electronic databases (one with preschool-aged children, six with elementary school children, and eight with high school students). Results showed a variety of effect sizes, ranging from −.2 (nonsignificant) to 1.4 (significant). Despite the promise shown from the above two reviews, the authors of both conclude that research with more advanced methodological designs is needed for the field to advance.

One study that did incorporate a randomized clinical trial (the current staple of advanced research designs) with youth was Biegel et al. (2009). Biegel and colleagues randomly assigned 102 adolescent psychiatric outpatients to either Mindfulness-Based Stressed Reduction (MBSR) or a waitlist-controlled group. Participants ranged in age from 14–18 and were mostly young women. Study measures were obtained at pretest, posttest, and 3-month follow-up. The 10-item perceived stress scale (PSS-10), the State and Trait Anxiety Inventory (STAI), the 10-item Rosenberg Self-esteem Scale (SES), and six of the nine subscales of the Symptom Check-list-90-Revised (SCL-90-R) served as self-report measures at all assessment points. Licensed professionals who were blinded to condition before and after the treatment phase also took Global Assessment of Functioning (GAF) assessments for the scoring of study participants.

Results showed that, relative to controls, MBSR participants showed significant decreases over time in state and trait anxiety ($p < .05$), perceived stress ($p < .05$), and four of the six psychopathology indicators assessed by the SCL-90-R ($p < .05$). Self-esteem also significantly increased within participants receiving the MBSR intervention ($p < .05$). Relative to controls, MBSR participants showed significant improvements in GAF scores over time from pretest to posttest and pretest to follow-up ($p < .0001$).

Other research with diverse youth populations has also shown promising evidence that mindfulness as an intervention can be effective in increasing psychological well-being. Himelstein et al. (2012a, 2012b) investigated the impact of a 10-session of mindfulness-based curriculum on incarcerated male youth. Measures of self-regulation (Healthy Self-Regulation Scale), mindfulness (Mindful Attention Awareness Scale), and perceived stress (Perceived Stress Scale, 10-item version) were administered to 32 participants before and after the intervention. Results showed that perceived stress significantly decreased and self-regulation significantly increased from pretest to posttest. While there were no significant changes in mindfulness, scores did move in psychologically enhancing directions (Himelstein et al., 2012a). Furthermore, qualitative data (Himelstein et al., 2012b) corroborated quantitative data, and participants suggested the mindfulness intervention to have helped with behavioral regulation, stress management, and improving psychological well-being. While the above studies are rife with limitations (no control group; small numbers of participants), they point toward the feasibility of mindfulness as an intervention with diverse adolescent populations.

Leonard et al. (2013) was able to circumvent the limitations to the above studies, in part. Leonard and colleagues randomly assigned dormitories housing a total of approximately 267 incarcerated youth to either a mindfulness intervention or an active control intervention (ranging from 3–5 weeks in length). Participants were given the Attention Network Test, a cognitive computerized test that measures executive control, at baseline and at a 4-month follow up. Results showed that, while both groups' executive control decreased, participants from the mindfulness intervention group decreased to a significantly lower degree. This suggests that mindfulness may function as a protective factor to executive control when the testee is in extremely stressful environments (e.g., in correctional settings).

While there is still much needed advancement of research in the field of mindfulness employed with youth, it is clear that mindfulness as an intervention is feasible and points toward increased psychological well-being broadly defined. This result mirrors those found in over 40 years of research with adult populations.

Literature: Mindfulness With Addiction Populations

Promising advancements have also been made with mindfulness as an intervention for substance-abuse and addiction populations. Early studies showing efficacy for mindfulness as an intervention for substance use included intensive retreat interventions delivered within the prison system (Bowen et al., 2006; Simpson et al. 2007). Bowen et al. (2006) conducted a Vipassana meditation study (in a 10-day intensive mindfulness retreat) with prisoners in a correctional setting in the Pacific Northwest. A total of 305 inmates initially volunteered to participate in the 10-day Vipassana course. Of those participants, 173 completed posttest measures. Measures on a multitude of scales assessed daily drinking and drug use, impulse control, thought suppression, psychiatric symptoms, and optimism prior to participation in the Vipassana course. Follow-up assessments were conducted at 3 and 6 months after completion of the 10-day course. Results showed a decrease in the use of alcohol, marijuana, and crack cocaine at the 3-month follow-up assessment ($p < .05$). Furthermore, decreases in psychiatric symptoms and increases in optimism and internal locus of control related to alcohol consumption were also significant, at $p < .05$ (Bowen et al., 2006).

In a secondary analysis of the data from Bowen et al. (2006), Simpson et al. (2007) investigated the impact of the same 10-day Vipassana course on measures of daily alcohol and drug use, impulse control, and post-traumatic stress disorder (PTSD) symptoms prior to and 3 months after completion of the course. As congruent with participant results in the Bowen et al. (2006) study, Vipassana course participants revealed significant differences that did not manifest for the control groups. Decreases in the use of alcohol and drugs ($p < .001$) 3 months after course completion suggest that the 10-day Vipassana course may, in fact, have been found to be beneficial in reducing substance use in prison populations.

Research has also been conducted on the impact of mindfulness with addiction populations in studies conducted using less intensive modalities. The Mindfulness-Based Relapse Prevention (MBRP; Bowen et al., 2011) program is an 8-week intervention based in modalities that included Kabat-Zinn's (1990; 2013) Mindfulness-Based Stress Reduction (MBSR), Segal, Williams, and Teasdale's (2013) Mindfulness-Based Cognitive Therapy (MBCT), and Marlatt's Relapse Prevention (RP). Bowen et al. (2009) conducted a randomized controlled trial with 168 participants who had recently completed intensive inpatient or outpatient treatment for alcohol and other drug disorders. Participants were randomly assigned to either an 8-week MBRP course or a standard aftercare group. Surveys regarding substance use were administered before, after, and at 2- and 4-month follow-ups to the intervention. Of particular interest was the 4-month follow-up outcome data that suggested that participants in the MBRP group demonstrated significantly greater decreases in drug cravings than did those in the control group. Furthermore, while both groups exhibited overall reductions in days of alcohol and drug use, participants in the MBRP group demonstrated significantly fewer days using substances than did the control group.

Other studies have also shown promising effects of mindfulness as an intervention for substance-abusing populations. Zgierska et al. (2008) investigated the impact of MBRP on 19 alcohol-dependent participants and found reductions in alcohol consumption, craving to use alcohol, depression, anxiety, and stress. Brewer et al. (2009) found that mindfulness meditation reduced psychological and physiological responses to stress, as measured by skin conductance and heart rate, in participants with cocaine- and alcohol-use disorders. The results of the above studies are consistent with those found in literature reviews highlighting mindfulness meditation's effectiveness on substance use with adult populations (Zgierska et al., 2009).

Finally, mindfulness-based interventions have been piloted also with youth dealing with substance-use disorders (Himelstein, 2011b; Himelstein, Saul, Garcia-Romeu, & Pinedo, 2014). These studies suggest the feasibility of using mindfulness as an intervention with substance-abusing youth. Himelstein (2011b) conducted a study investigating the impact of a mindfulness-based intervention on self-regulation, attitudes toward drugs, and impulsiveness in 60 incarcerated male youth mandated to participate in substance-abuse treatment. Results showed that impulsiveness significantly decreased and perceived risk of drugs significantly increased from pretest to posttest.

Himelstein et al. (2014) conducted a grounded theory study to develop methodology for effectively teaching mindfulness to adolescents. Ten participants were taught various mindfulness meditations over a 10-week period and were interviewed extensively about their preferences, opinions, and experiences related to mindfulness meditation. Although the primary aim of the study was to develop a method for teaching mindfulness to youth that was grounded in actual data, results also revealed that participants suggested that self-regulation, decision-making, and decreased substance use were experienced as a result of mindfulness practice. These results and those of the other related study (Himelstein, 2011b) will be examined in more detail in our chapter on curriculum development and research. While the above studies are limited in many ways, they do suggest the feasibility of using mindfulness as an intervention with adolescents dealing with substance-abuse issues.

As has been summarized in the above report of related research, there are a number of key aspects of the intervention results that have been found to suggest why mindfulness can be beneficial as a treatment intervention for adolescents dealing with substance-abuse issues:

- An increased ability to manage strong emotions
- Reduced impulsiveness
- Reduced stress
- Decreased cravings to use drugs
- Ability to observe drug cravings without reacting
- Decreased stress
- Increased overall well-being
- Increased risk in the perception of drug use
- Decreased drug use

The above benefits are critical skills needed for adolescents attempting to reduce the frequency of substance use or other unhealthy behaviors. Below, we review the key assumptions we hold foundationally in encouraging the dissemination of this curriculum.

Key Assumptions Regarding Use of This Curriculum

As this is a curriculum that incorporates both mindfulness and substance-abuse treatment and education, there are some key assumptions that are necessary to explain upfront. The first is that you, the reader/facilitator, have an interest in the use of mindfulness as an intervention to help adolescents gain greater awareness and control of themselves and their substance-use behavior. There are a slew of treatment approaches for dealing with the issue of adolescent substance abuse. This program is offered to the facilitator who is passionate about incorporating mindfulness into substance-use work with young people because she or he understands on an experiential level the power of mindful self-awareness. The facilitator we are so addressing probably either already has a personal mindfulness practice or, at the very least, is eager to start one. This is the facilitator for whom we intentionally wrote this curriculum.

The second assumption is closely related to the above. It is the assumption that you will have a working knowledge of mindfulness as a practice prior to your facilitating of this curriculum. We are not suggesting that you need be considered an *expert* in the field of mindfulness in order to facilitate this program. It is even acceptable to use it if you consider yourself a novice practitioner. What is important, however, is that you have a working knowledge of the field of mindfulness: its practice on an experiential level, the conceptual underpinnings of the belief that it can be beneficial to young people generally, why it is an important component in substance-abuse treatment; and, of course, that you have an eagerness to develop your own practice and to help facilitate the mindful path for others (especially for young people). Below, we will review in greater detail the foundational importance, for the facilitator of this program, of having a personal mindfulness practice.

The third assumption is that you hold a working knowledge concerning illicit substances, substance-abuse treatment, and the health effects of substances. We cannot fit within these pages detailed information about which drugs are stimulants, which produce damaged livers, which affect your brain and how, and other such related information. Know that, when a facilitator is working with young people, questions of that nature will inevitably arise. When we facilitate session 6 of this curriculum, the session in which we review the effects of drugs on the brain, our participants always ask a number of questions regarding particular drugs (e.g., Is it true that ecstasy leaves holes in your brain?). What's important is that you either have an answer to most of these questions or, at the very least, know where to find those answers. It is critical when facilitating this curriculum that you will be able to insert the information about drugs via informal questions and answers that will inevitably arise as a function of young people's curiosity. We recommend that, if you do not feel comfortable generally with substance-related material, you will consult texts that disseminate information on the topic in order to strengthen your ability to skillfully facilitate this curriculum.

Fourth, and the most important of all our assumptions, is the idea that you, the facilitator, are paramount to the effectiveness of this curriculum. The content of the curriculum that you will find in these pages is, in our opinion, of very high quality. However, no curriculum comes to life unless a skilled facilitator is at its helm guiding it to fruition. Manualized programs that over-rely on the content of their curriculum rather than on the skill of their facilitators ultimately suffer in the quality and prevalence of positive outcomes for their clients. Because of our experience regarding differences among factors of program implementation, we understand that no two human beings will facilitate this curriculum in the very same way. This concern about implementation may sound paradoxical, given that this book presents as a step-by-step manual for implementing this curriculum, but the idiosyncrasies unique to each individual related to personality, temperament, interests, and opinions really do affect how individuals facilitate—and that's okay. Our intention isn't to clone facilitators and simply have them memorize the talking points and scripts from this program. It is for facilitators to authentically integrate the information and practices within this book into their substance-abuse group programs offered to young people. The unique way in which a facilitator shows up to implement this program will, of course, have an impact on its success, and, thus, the importance of a facilitator's personal practice regarding formal mindfulness meditation, daily mindfulness, and relational mindfulness are significant factors in successfully implementing this program.

Personal Practice

As has been stated above, you, the facilitator, are the most important factor in this curriculum. The extent of your personal formal mindfulness practice is a strong variable in your ability to facilitate skillfully. The personal practice and skill level of the facilitator is positively correlated with the receptivity, engagement, and, ultimately, the outcomes for the young people who participate in the program. Following suit with other mindfulness-based programs (Bowen et al., 2011; Broderick, 2013; Kabat-Zinn, 1990; 2013; Segal, Williams, & Teasdale, 2013), it is imperative that the facilitators of this program have a personal practice in mindfulness meditation. If you are new to the practice of mindfulness meditation, we suggest participating in a 5- to 10-day silent meditation retreat in the Vipassana or Insight traditions.

This will give you the experience of becoming intimate with the contents of your mind; the nature of how mental, emotional, and physical phenomena arise and pass away, the instability of the conditions that comprise what we call the *self*, deep states of concentration, and other elements comprising such meditation traditions. This personal experience will equip you with the tools to provide support for others in their path of meditation, via your personal disclosures about meditative experiences that can be accessed in these practices and your responses to participants' questions. As our esteemed colleagues in the MBRP program states "Supporting others in the practices comes from one's own lived experience and history of having encountered similar struggles. It cannot come from simply 'understanding' a treatment manual or attending a brief workshop" (Bowen et al., 2011, p. 10). We couldn't agree with Bowen's statement more enthusiastically than we are suggesting here. We further suggest

Figure 1.1

that, while in the process of facilitating this curriculum, you maintain a consistent mindfulness meditation practice, if you don't already have such an ongoing practice. Whether you meditate for 5, 10, 15, 30, or more minutes per day, it is essential to continue such a practice while facilitating this curriculum as a way to ensure that you will approach the sessions themselves with personally grounded intentional mindfulness.

Daily Mindfulness

Living mindfully throughout the day is also of central importance. Retreats can help bring insights about the mind and reality on deep levels, but it is daily practice that contributes to how we show up as human beings in all of our interactions: for instance, in relationships with others, at work, in school, and with ourselves throughout the day. This is the consistent commitment to bringing mindful awareness to the present moment, to what we're doing throughout the day. As daily practice is maintained, your ability to foster your own mindfulness during the curriculum sessions will increase. This is an essential element to facilitating this curriculum effectively. We recommend approaching each session as a meditation: setting the intention to practice mindfulness throughout the session and resolving to notice the reactions that arise within you, to pause and practice skillful speech with your adolescent clients or students, and to commit to modeling mindfulness for the group. A practice we strongly recommend is taking 5–10 minutes before each session to meditate and to set an intention to embody mindfulness. We've found that this simple practice prior to starting our sessions has immensely increased our ability to show up as models of mindfulness.

Relational Mindfulness

Beyond the formal meditation training and experience the facilitator possesses and the building on the commitment to daily mindfulness, there is another skillset that it is imperative to practice while facilitating this curriculum: *relational mindfulness*. Relational mindfulness is the practice of bringing mindful awareness to the relationships we create with the youth in the group. Himelstein (2013) suggested that practicing authenticity, within oneself and with others, intentionally attempting to immediately begin to forge human-being connections (rather than presenting first with a problem-solving approach), and understanding the limitations of our control of others' behavior (i.e., the stance one holds on behavioral change) are all aspects of relational mindfulness. It is especially true of working with adolescents that their red flags get raised when an adult attempts to tell them what to do, is inauthentic, or attempts to *fix* their problems without connecting authentically first. Substance-abuse therapists and facilitators often enter relationships with adolescent clients and students with the preconceived notion that the adolescent *needs to stop* doing drugs. This often creates a person-made barrier in the relationship because simply posturing from authority and preaching abstinence has proven woefully ineffective with adolescents, especially those already using drugs. Such an approach doesn't take into account the complexities of why adolescents use drugs in the first place. For example, we have met hundreds of youth who smoke marijuana and drink alcohol for the purpose of dealing with traumas they've experienced in their lives. Upon first query from the facilitating adult, they may simply state that they use drugs for fun, but, when an authentic, trusting relationship is built, defenses come down, and deeper levels of awareness become conscious, at which point the individual may disclose some of her or his underlying reasoning for using drugs in the first place. Thus, the facilitator's stance on behavioral change (e.g., either operating from the conviction that the youth needs to stop using drugs or, in contrast, first engaging the individual in a human connection) will no doubt influence the development of the facilitator's relationship with the group.

Another aspect of relational mindfulness that is critical for facilitating this curriculum is how you deal with resistance. Resistance can take many shapes and forms in a group of adolescents (i.e., traditional aggressive, humorous, ambivalent, etc.), and it will arise over the course of the program. The way in which you respond to that resistance will determine your ability to model relational mindfulness. If, when resistance arises, you become tense, aggravated, and unskillful and respond by yelling or asserting your authority in some way, impasses with the youth may arise. We are not suggesting it is abnormal to get frustrated while doing this work; we simply suggest that the quality of how you respond depends on your ability to be mindful in the moment: mindful of your own reactions, biases, countertransferences, and so forth, and then skillfully respond to the situation. In session 1 of the curriculum, for example, the last listed agreement to be made with the group is the agreement regarding a refocusing technique for when the group gets off-track or steps outside of the bounds of the agreements. The facilitator simply requests, "Can we all please refocus?" or simply rings the meditation bell and asks, "Can we all please take a breath and be quiet?" This is a technique that we stumbled upon when facilitating a session with a group of 20 incarcerated male youth who had just been released from 24-hour lockdown. The energy was so rambunctious that nobody was listening to us. One of us simply asked of the group, "Hey fellas, can we please be quiet? . . . Can we please refocus?" This was said softly, with no frustration evident in the tone, approximately 15 times. Fifteen times! The reader may think that's a great number of requests. However, it took only approximately 45 seconds until the youth started regulating themselves. This is when we decided to start implementing this as the last agreement in our first session, and, to this day we've never had to ask the group to refocus more than 3–4 times. The critical factor of its success, however, is not raising your voice when practicing this refocusing technique. The technique is often needed when some form of resistance has arisen. It is then the facilitator's job to refocus the group back within the bounds of the agreements (and potentially process the resistance). If the facilitator isn't getting the feedback he or she wants (the group listening and responding to the refocusing technique), it is very easy to become frustrated and raise the volume of one's voice. The practice of daily and relational mindfulness in such instances is the awareness of that frustration when it first arises inside of oneself, the practice of nonjudgmental awareness of the situation, and the choice to continuously implement the refocusing technique with a soft, nonattacking voice tone and volume. This is a process embedded in relational mindfulness and is critical to the skillful implementation of this curriculum. The refocusing technique will be reviewed in the description of session 1 of this curriculum, and we recommend also consulting Himelstein (2013) for a more in-depth analysis regarding relational mindfulness.

Formal mindfulness practice—either practiced via meditation or used in a daily mindfulness exercise—and relational mindfulness are both components key to the successful facilitation of this curriculum. Put more simply, it is imperative that you continue to work on your own personal growth in order to become or continue to be an effective group facilitator. The more open you are to being honest with yourself and to being present with discomfort in uncomfortable situations and learning from them, the more likely it is that you will continue to grow and to better serve the people with whom you work. Commitment to personal growth via all the forms of mindfulness described above results in this curriculum's (or any for that matter) flowing through you and affecting the young people with whom you work in the most authentic sense.

References

Biegel, G. M., Brown, K. W., Shapiro, S. L., & Schubert, C. M. (2009). Mindfulness-based stress reduction for the treatment of adolescent psychiatric outpatients: A randomized clinical trial. *Journal of Clinical and Consulting Psychology, 77*, 855–866.

Black, D. S., Milam, J., & Sussman, S. (2009). Sitting-meditation interventions among youth: A review of treatment efficacy. *Pediatrics, 124*, 532–541.

Bowen, S., Chawla, N., Collins, S., Witkiewitz, K., Hsu, S., Grow, K., . . . Marlatt, G. A. (2009). Mindfulness-based relapse prevention for substance use disorders: A pilot efficacy trial. *Substance Abuse, 30*, 205–305.

Bowen, S., Chawla, N., & Marlatt, G. A. (2011). *Mindfulness-based relapse prevention for addictive behaviors: A clinician's guide*. New York, NY: Guilford Press.

Bowen, S., Witkiewitz, K., Dillworth, T. M., Chawla, N., Simpson, T. L., Ostafin, B. D., . . . Marlatt, G. A. (2006). Mindfulness meditation and substance use in an incarcerated population. *Psychology of Addictive Behaviors, 20*, 343–347.

Brewer, J, Sinha, R., Chen, J. A., Michalsen, R. N., Babuscio, T. A., Nich, C., . . . Rounsavile, B. J. (2009). Mindfulness training and stress reactive in substance abuse: Results from a non-randomized, controlled stage I pilot study. *Substance Abuse, 30*, 306–317.

Broderick, P. C. (2013). *Learning to breathe: A mindfulness curriculum for adolescents to cultivate emotion regulation, attention, and performance*. Oakland, CA: New Harbinger.

Burke, C. A. (2010). Mindfulness-based approach with children and adolescents: A preliminary view of current research in an emergent field. *Journal of Child and Family Studies, 19*, 133–144.

Himelstein, S. (2011a). Meditation research: The state of the art in correctional settings. *International Journal of Offender Therapy and Comparative Criminology, 55*, 646–661.

Himelstein, S. (2011b). Mindfulness-based substance abuse treatment for incarcerated youth: A mixed-methods study. *International Journal of Transpersonal Studies, 30*, 1–10.

Himelstein, S. (2013). *A mindfulness-based approach to working with high-risk adolescents*. New York, NY: Routledge.

Himelstein, S., Hastings, A., Shapiro, S., & Heery, M. (2012a). Mindfulness training for self-regulation and stress with incarcerated youth: A pilot study. *Probation Journal, 59*, 151–165.

Himelstein, S., Hastings, A., Shapiro, S., & Heery, M. (2012b). A qualitative investigation of the experience of a mindfulness-based intervention with incarcerated adolescents. *Child and Adolescent Mental Health, 17*, 231–237.

Himelstein, S., Saul, S., Garcia-Romeu, A., & Pinedo, D. (2014). Mindfulness training as an intervention for substance-user incarcerated adolescents: A pilot grounded theory study. *Substance Use and Misuse, 49*, 560–570.

Johnston, L.D., O'Malley, P. M., Miech, R.A., Bachman, J.G., & Schulenberg, J.E. (2014). Monitoring the future national results on drug use: 1975–2013: Overview, key findings on adolescent drug use. Ann Arbor: Institute for Social Research, University of Michigan.

Kabat-Zinn, J. (1990). *Full catastrophe living: Using the wisdom of your body and mind to face stress, pain, and illness*. New York, NY: Dell.

Kabat-Zinn, J. (2013). *Full catastrophe living: Using the wisdom of your body and mind to face stress, pain, and illness* (rev. ed.). New York, NY: Bantam Books.

Leonard, N.L., Jha, A.P., Casarjian, B., Goolsarran, M., Garcia, C., Cleland, C.M., Gwadz, M.V., & Massey, Z. (2013). Mindfulness training improves attentional task performance in incarcerated youth: A group randomized controlled interventional trial. *Frontiers in Psychology, 4*, 1–10.

Oman, D., Shapiro, S.L., Thoresen, C.E., Plante, T.G., & Flinders, T. (2008). Meditation lowers stress and supports forgiveness among college students: A randomized controlled trial. *Journal of American College Health, 56*, 569–578.

Puzzanchera, C. (2013). *Juvenile arrests in 2011*. Office of Juvenile Justice and Delinquency Prevention National Report Series Bulletin (NCJ 244476).

Robinson, J.M., Benjamin, O.L., & Anderson, K.G. (2014). When you see it, let it be: Urgency, mindfulness, and adolescent substance abuse. *Addictive Behaviors, 39*, 1038–1041.

Samuelson, M., Carmody, J., Kabat-Zinn, J., & Bratt, M.A. (2007). Mindfulness-based stress reduction in Massachusetts correctional facilities. *Prison Journal, 87*, 254–268.

Segal, Z.V., Williams, J.M.G., & Teasedale, J.D. (2013). *Mindfulness-based cognitive therapy for depression* (2nd ed.). New York, NY: Guilford.

Shapiro, S.L., Astin, J.A., Bishop, S.R., & Cordova, M. (2005). Mindfulness-based stress reduction for healthcare professionals: Results from a randomized trial. *International Journal of Stress Management, 12*, 164–176.

Simpson, T.L., Kaysen, D., Bowen, S., MacPherson, L.M., Chawla, N., Blume, A., . . . Larimer, M. (2007). PTSD symptoms, substance use, and Vipassana meditation among incarcerated individuals. *Journal of Traumatic Stress, 20*, 239–249.

Zgierska, A., Rabago, D., Chawla, N., Kushner, K., Koehler, R., & Marlatt, A. (2009). Mindfulness meditation for substance use disorders: A systematic review. *Substance Abuse, 30*, 266–294.

Zgierska, A., Rabago, D., Zuelsdorff, M., Coe, C., Miller, M., & Flemming, M. (2008). Mindfulness meditation for alcohol relapse prevention: A feasibility pilot study. *Journal of Addiction Medicine, 2*, 165–173.

CURRICULUM DEVELOPMENT AND RESEARCHED OUTCOMES

This curriculum was developed as a comprehensive mindfulness-based substance-abuse treatment program geared toward adolescent populations. The term *mindfulness-based* can characterize a variety of practices and techniques. Some mindfulness-based curricula focus heavily on formal mindfulness and ask participants to meditate for large portions of each session. Others focus more on developing informal mindfulness and allow for a variety of group activities and experiences. Something that hasn't been researched extensively, especially in youth and adolescent populations, is the proportion of formal meditation time spent in session as compared with time spent in other group activities and its effect on the outcome of mindfulness-based programming. While we haven't researched the outcomes of every portion or activity of our curriculum, we have conducted a fair amount of formal process research regarding the components of this curriculum in that respect.

When the authors of this curriculum first started working together, we were facilitating two separate groups per week, each with a cohort of about 8–10 adolescents. We were very adventurous with our experimentation and had one goal in mind: to try to develop an effective method for engaging adolescents in group-based substance-abuse treatment that emphasized mindfulness-based practices. We meticulously dissected different methods for engaging young people in this work. In one of our two groups, for example, we offered no formal curriculum and facilitated a pure process group. The group was seated in a circle of chairs, and we simply processed a variety of topics together without any agenda. Concurrently, in our other group, we set the chairs up with desks facing forward as in a classroom and took a much more educational approach. We found through our anecdotal experience, as one might think, that neither of these extreme approaches was well suited for adolescents and that a mix of process-based and didactic-based methods is what would work best. Suffice it to say that we put great effort into figuring out both the major components of the curriculum and the subtle aspects of the curriculum (e.g., chair configuration for differing activities). Through meticulous anecdotal trial and error, formal process, and outcome research, and by means of building upon existing curricula and evidence-based practice, this curriculum was molded over a period of about five years. There are many curricula we have pulled from, and, where identifiable, we pay homage in a humble manner to those sources. Other aspects were either created by us or retooled to be appropriate for adolescent populations, and, of course, were influenced by youth participation and feedback.

Below, we review the general components of group-based curricula to contextualize the specific components of this curriculum, which follow. Finally, rather than citing our research in detail throughout reviewing the components of the curriculum, we have a "research" section that follows the curriculum description and that outlines the process and outcome research we have conducted.

General Components of Group-Based Curricula

Most group-based curricula are comprised of *experiential* activities, *didactic* (psycho-education) presentations, and *process*-based activities. Experiential activities include those that offer an actual experience for the adolescent—a personal encounter with the subject matter of the group program. These activities include formal meditation, emotionally charged activities that tend to influence the arising of emotions, games, and any other activity that elicits actual experience rather than just participation by thinking or talking about experience. Didactic activities, on the other hand, can be characterized for this curriculum as the dissemination of information that the group participants may not already have: for example, in defining mindfulness, reviewing the techniques of meditation, disseminating the facts about how different types of drugs interact with the brain, and so forth. Process-based activities include both the processing of direct experience and the processing of stimulating discussion topics. Examples of this include the processing of the experience of meditation after it has been completed, the processing of strong emotions as they arise, and the discussion of curriculum topics such as the pros and cons of substance use.

In actuality, these three types of activities overlap and, to counteract boredom and disinterest, should all be used when facilitating groups with adolescents. We have found, both anecdotally and through our process research, that balanced proportions of experiential, didactic, and process-based activities equate to higher adolescent engagement and receptivity.

MBSAT Curriculum Components

A working knowledge of the above general components of group-based curricula will contextualize for the facilitator the components of this MBSAT program. Such components include mindfulness meditation, informal mindfulness activities, mindfulness-based concepts, emotional awareness activities, and substance abuse education and relapse-prevention strategies.

Mindfulness Meditation

The formal meditation taught within this curriculum is nothing novel. There is no reason to reinvent the wheel for practices that, frankly, have been considered sound for thousands of years. The mindfulness meditations we teach in this curriculum include variations of the following activities: 1) mindfulness of the breath, 2) mindfulness of bodily sensations, 3) the noting or labeling technique, and 4) compassion-based meditations. We have sequenced these meditations over the 12 sessions in a format in which each meditation (with the exception of the noting meditation) builds upon itself over 2–3 sessions. Further, our research (Himelstein et al., 2014) suggested that tangible meditations with easy-to-follow instructions are best suited for adolescents who are starting meditation practice for the first time.

Thus, as the tangible aspect of this type of meditation is prominent in its bodily connection, mindfulness of the breath starts with mindfulness of deep breathing (session 1), used prior to the dissemination of the traditional teaching of mindfulness of the breath (session 3; i.e., being aware of the breath and not manipulating it to be deep). The Bodyscan series, another tangible meditation, follows the mindfulness of the breath series and builds upon itself by starting with a basic Bodyscan (session 4) and progressing toward a nonmoving Bodyscan with an emphasis on nonjudgment and acceptance of all sensations (session 7).

Following the Bodyscan series is the practice of noting, or labeling. The practitioner maintains a constant awareness of the present moment and *notes* his or her primary experience from a metacognitive point of view (i.e., noting *sensation, thinking,* and *emotion* within awareness). This practice is taught in session 8, which focuses on triggers and emphasizes the skill of becoming aware of and noting drug triggers.

Finally, the last series of mindfulness meditations focus on compassion-based meditation. Compassion practices are taught in a sequence in which the practitioner first focuses on compassion toward a family member or loved one (session 9), then toward a member of her or his peer group (session 10), and, finally, toward her or his community as a whole (session 11). The final session weaves these practices together

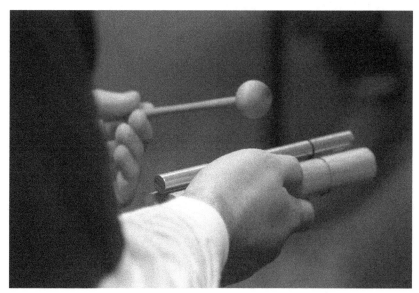

Figure 2.1
Photo courtesy of MBA Project. Reprinted with permission.

and adds the practice of self-compassion. Our goal was to offer a plethora of mindfulness meditations in the hopes that each participant would identify the meditation that best suited her or his individual needs and, hopefully, would continue practicing that meditation long beyond the 12th session of the curriculum.

Informal Mindfulness Activities

Informal mindfulness techniques employ the qualities of mindfulness without requiring a formal meditation. The informal mindfulness techniques within this curriculum were developed in-house; however, variations of these activities can be found across a multitude of other published curricula. These activities include 1) the mindful-check-in, 2) the STIC acronym, 3) the mindful eating activity, and 4) the refocusing technique.

Starting in session 2, we introduce the *mindful check-in* practice, a practice in which participants take a breath, pause, and then state how they feel in the present moment. This is done, in some form, in most of the groups listed in reference to this curriculum, and, after session 6, youth oftentimes don't even need to be reminded to take the deep breath. They simply pause, breathe, and check in with how they're really feeling prior to actually disclosing their subjective experience.

In session 3, the group is taught the cognitive acronym *S.T.I.C.*, which stands for *Stop*; *Take a breath*; *Imagine the future consequences*; and *Choose*. Cognitive acronyms have been utilized in cognitive and behavioral therapy for many years and have caught on in the mindfulness-based world, as well (e.g., SOBER = Stop, Observe, Breath, Expand, Respond, from the MBRP curriculum). We wanted to create a cognitive acronym that was both easy to understand and empowering of young people to choose their responses. Thus, STIC was born, and, after much piloting and feedback from youth, it was solidified in the curriculum.

Mindful eating has been a staple in mindfulness-based curricula since Jon Kabat-Zinn introduced his raisin exercise (Kabat-Zinn, 1990; 2013) in the MBSR program, in addition to its having being practiced in Buddhist traditions for thousands of years. Mindful eating is a wonderful way to practice mindfulness in daily life, because people normally eat every day. Furthermore, young people tend to appreciate the diversity of these approaches to learning the same concept. Session 7 incorporates mindful eating with small chocolate bars (or another small snack of your choice) and focuses on cravings associated with foods and drugs.

Finally, informal mindfulness can be facilitated via the process-level of the curriculum. In session 1, group agreements are highlighted, and the last listed group agreement is the refocusing technique. This is a technique (see session 1 for greater details) to counteract disruption of process when the group gets off-track and needs to be redirected to the topic at hand. Redirecting the group is simply like redirecting the mind when focusing on a particular object during meditation. It can be done without judgment and with integrity, and can be used as a teaching moment. For example, when youth are talking over each other or the energy in the group is really high in some way (e.g., rambunctious or playful), we simply ask the group to refocus in a soft tone and sometimes ring the meditation bell. Rather than simply returning to the content we were supposed to be covering in that moment, we often state to the group that the consciousness of the group wanders just as do our individual minds and that it is important to practice not getting frustrated or think that something's wrong when it happens (and that is a deep truth you as the facilitator need to accept!). We then invite everyone to take a few breaths in the moment and remind them that mindfulness can be practiced at any time (i.e., not just in formal meditation), before to returning to the curriculum content.

Mindfulness-Based Concepts

Mindfulness-based concepts include the teaching of the underlying philosophy and value of the practice of mindfulness. For example, in session 1, we define mindfulness via an adapted version of Rosenberg's (1998) lion mind vs. dog mind metaphor. In session 3, we discuss the differences between reacting versus responding and the value of the latter and in session 4, the role of delusion in drug use is overviewed. Session 5 includes mindfulness-based concepts regarding the major tones underlying different emotions (e.g., pleasant, unpleasant, and neutral), session 7 includes content related to the deep truth that craving causes suffering, and session 11 reviews content about mindfulness and the external environment. The purpose for the presentations of the above mindfulness-based concepts is to further contextualize the practice for youth, and we believe they are successful in that respect.

Emotional Awareness Activities

Emotional awareness activities are those that either educate about or elicit strong emotions. Rather than completely reinventing the wheel, we've adapted some exercises that have been used in esteemed youth programs across the country. The *tree of emotions* exercise is a metaphor in which the part of the tree above ground is conceptualized as the emotions we show in public and the roots below ground are those we keep in private. This exercise is conducted in session 5 and is an activity that builds upon the "Man/Woman Box" that was highlighted in the Making The Peace curriculum from the Oakland Men's Project (Kivel & Creighton, 1997), Challenge Day, and the Mind Body Awareness (MBA) Project. The "stand if" and "deep disclosure" activities of session 5 are also adapted from the above programs and elicit actual emotions of empathy, compassion, and others. We have adapted these activities to cater specifically to adolescents dealing with substance use and bow deeply to those who pioneered them with many other groups of young people over the years. Although emotional awareness activities can also be conceptualized as informal mindfulness activities (e.g., mindfulness of emotions) and mindfulness-based concepts (e.g., education about emotional experience) we felt it necessary to distinguish this category of exercises, given their unique propensities toward fostering trust, group cohesion, and deep disclosure.

Substance-Abuse Education and Relapse-Prevention Strategies

Finally, as this curriculum is geared toward adolescents dealing with substance-abuse issues, a core component of the program is related to substance-abuse education and relapse-prevention strategies. All of the relapse prevention strategies incorporated in this curriculum have been included above, as

Table 2.1 Overview of the 12 Sessions

Session 1	Introduction to the Program
Session 2	Mindfulness of Drugs and Their Health Effects
Session 3	Reacting vs. Responding
Session 4	Mindfulness of Delusion
Session 5	Emotional Awareness
Session 6	The Brain and Drugs
Session 7	Mindfulness of Cravings
Session 8	Mindfulness of Triggers
Session 9	The Family System and Drugs
Session 10	Mindfulness of the Peer System
Session 11	Mindfulness of the External Environment
Session 12	Closing Ceremony

the primary tool for preventing substance relapse is, in this curriculum, mindfulness practices, which include the mindfulness meditations and the informal mindfulness techniques (specifically the mindful check-in and the STIC acronym). The substance-abuse education activities have long been used in the field of substance-abuse treatment and include the categorization of major substance categories, the identification of the specific drugs that comprise them, and their major health effects (session 2); the distinguishing of the advantages and disadvantages of substance use (e.g., in discussions of the pros and cons of drug use) in session 4, the effects of general drug use on the brain in session 6, and identifying and understanding the role of triggers in drug use in session 8.

Beyond The Self: Integrating Family, Peer Group, and Community

A factor of this curriculum that distinguishes it from other programs is that we spend three sessions identifying and contemplating the relationship and reciprocal effects of drug use on the major systems that adolescents commonly interact with: the family (session 9), the peer group (session 10), and the external environment (session 11). Short of having an actual family-based intervention—which programs have a multitude of evidence supporting their effectiveness in reducing drug use with adolescents, we wanted to make sure that at least the concepts of family, peer, and external environmental systems were taken into account in this group curriculum, given the prominence they have in most adolescents' lives. In Table 2.1 below is an outline of the 12 sessions in chronological order:

A Deep Bow to Mindfulness-Based Relapse Prevention

We believe it is important to recognize the work and curriculum of the MBRP team, as they published a seminal work on integrating mindfulness with addiction populations (Bowen et al., 2011). While this curriculum isn't based directly in MBRP itself, we are filled with gratitude for the pioneering work they've completed and will continue to offer. Probably the primary difference between this curriculum and MBRP's is that this program is designed specifically for adolescents. Adolescents are much more interested in the educational aspects of substance abuse, such as effects on the brain, the major drug categories and their effects on the body, and so forth. Adults who are addicted for years may be more concerned with the bottom line of figuring out how to get clean. Not that the two populations don't have an interest in both of the above outcomes, but adolescents often don't have the information that some adults may already have since adults have oftentimes been using drugs for a long period of time. Therefore, this curriculum is proportioned around substance-abuse education, relapse-prevention strategies, mindfulness practices, and emotional awareness techniques, as have been described above, to provide a response to adolescent drug abuse that is custom-fitted to the addressing of the specific needs of the adolescent population.

Research on This Curriculum

In the introduction of this book, we reviewed some of the major research studies on the impact of mindfulness on both youth and other addiction-presenting populations. Research we have conducted on this curriculum has primarily been feasibility and process research, with one pilot randomized controlled-outcome study. If you are interested in the research supporting mindfulness as an intervention for youth populations, addiction populations, or both, we urge you to review the reference sections and consult the cited studies for an in-depth analysis of the effect of mindfulness on youth and other substance-abusing populations.

Our first study of this curriculum (Himelstein, 2011) investigated the effects of an adapted, 8-week version of this program on a group of 60 male youth who had been mandated to substance-abuse treatment while incarcerated at a juvenile detention camp in the greater San Francisco Bay Area. Self-reported impulsiveness, perceived drug risk, and healthy self-regulation assessments were administered before and after the 8-week adapted intervention and a total of $N = 48$ completed both sets of measures. Paired t-tests revealed a significant decrease in impulsiveness at posttest ($p < .01$) and a significant increase in perceived drug risk ($p < .05$) (i.e., with participants in the program ranking risky drug behavior as more dangerous after completing the protocol). No significant differences were found regarding healthy self-regulation at posttest, although scores changed in psychologically enhancing directions. Although this study is significantly limited (i.e., had no control group), it points toward the feasibility of using mindfulness as an intervention for adolescents dealing with substance-abuse issues and lends credence to the idea that mindfulness partnered with substance-abuse treatment could have the potential to increase for the program participants their degree of perceived risk associated with drug use.

As we continued to research the program and tweak details (e.g., 8 vs. 10 vs. 12 sessions), we wanted the actual mindfulness practices we taught in the curriculum to follow a conceptual map grounded in data and not simply presenting theory. Thus, we developed a grounded theory for teaching mindfulness to adolescents (Himelstein et al., 2014). The grounded-theory approach is a qualitative research approach that incorporates actual data from research participants as a basis on which to form a method or theory (Corbin & Strauss, 2014). We recruited 10 participants from a juvenile detention camp to participate in this study. The juvenile detention camp housed male offenders in dormitory-like settings and youth were rewarded with home passes on weekends for good behavior. Participants were taught numerous forms of meditation (mindfulness of the breath, deep breathing, the Bodyscan, informal cognitive mindfulness techniques, etc.) and interviewed extensively about their experiences meditating, their preferences with each meditation, and their real-life benefits. We found that adolescents tended to prefer tangible and easy-to-follow meditations when starting out in the program, such as mindfulness of deep breathing, the Bodyscan, and easy-to-follow-and-remember techniques such as the STIC acronym in the protocol of this curriculum. These results were used to indicate to us how best to retool the meditation sequence throughout the entire curriculum.

Beyond the sequence and approach to teaching meditation to adolescents that was derived from the results of this study, the final major theme that was identified was the potential for the reduction of relapse and recidivism. One youth, who recently was on a home pass, spoke about his experience using the techniques he learned in the program to abstain from drug use and AWOLing:

> I ain't gonna lie. I was supposed to not come back to camp, and I was supposed to hit the blunt [marijuana], when I was in the house. 'Cause my boy, when we got back to the house, he was

out there rolling a blunt. I ain't gonna lie, once I seen him in the wheelchair, I already knew I was gonna do something; drink, or something . . . I used STIC. I kinda looked at him (takes a deep breath while talking), and I took a deep breath, and just calmed down, sat down, and I was like, "Damn man, it's good to see you." But at the same time I was really thinkin' about the blunt. He was like, "You gonna smoke?" I was like, "Nah, I'm good." He was like, "Fool, what the fuck? Since when do you say no?" I felt more me, doing me. I'm like, "Nah I'm good" . . . You feel me? (Himelstein et al., 2014, pp. 566–67).

The above quote describes a situation in a program participant's life in which he encountered a friend who had been recently hospitalized and put in a wheelchair due to gun violence. The participant describes how, overcome with emotion when seeing him for the first time, he wanted to use marijuana and alcohol to deal with his emotions. He described using our STIC technique and breathing mindfully while his friend smoked marijuana right in front of him. This participant chose to come back to the detention center and finish his sentence rather than running away. The above results and quote exemplify the power of mindfulness practice for young people struggling with substances and strong emotions. The research this represents, however, is not without limitation. This was a small, pilot qualitative study, and it would be a stretch to extend its results to the general population of adolescents.

In a larger grounded theory study we investigated the experiences and opinions of 40 incarcerated adolescents via eight focus groups (Himelstein, Saul, & Garcia-Romeu, 2015a). Focus groups were conducted following eight cohorts of 4–6 participants who completed our group-based, mindfulness and substance abuse intervention. Participants were asked about their experiences and preferences specifically regarding their receptiveness to the overall intervention, drug education, and relapse prevention strategies (not including mindfulness meditation). Focus groups were audio-recorded and transcribed verbatim. Corbin and Strauss's (2014) grounded theory approach was utilized to develop a theory for how to effectively facilitate group-based substance abuse interventions with adolescents. Results revealed that participants felt open to learning drug education information and actually attempting relapse prevention strategies when facilitators fostered authentic relationships and weren't over-concerned with forcing behavioral change (i.e., reducing drug use). More specifically, adoption of a harm-reduction as opposed to an abstinence only approach was found to facilitate more openness to treatment. Additionally, participants reported that authentic relationships contributed to a positive atmosphere, which included freedom of expression. Freedom of expression was reported to contribute to participant receptivity of drug education information and relapse prevention strategies, which in turn contributed to participants actually attempting to use relapse prevention strategies in life experiences.

One participant described how the facilitators not "forcing" recovery fostered authentic relationships:

I like how [the facilitators] really didn't preach like other programs. [Other programs] just be talking and talking at you, and you don't pay attention . . . [the facilitators] here weren't mean to us. They gave us respect. They didn't ever really disrespect us, even though sometimes we got out of hand (Himelstein et al., 2015a).

Another participant described how authentic relationships with the facilitators lead to freedom of expression and in turn more receptivity to drug education:

You get to act like yourself here [during the group sessions]. You can just be yourself and say what you want. You're free to be yourself. And that helps to learn stuff about drugs; about cocaine and about marijuana. I learned how it actually affects you in your future and how it causes brain issues (Himelstein et al., 2015a).

One of the participants also explained how he used the informal STIC technique to not run away during his home pass (from a juvenile detention center):

> I enjoyed STIC cause it helped me a lot with decisions, you think before you act and it helps you, like, you just don't act on impulse . . . I had a chance to leave my house. I didn't. I thought about it. I just imagined, I imagined getting pulled over by the cops. Just for going out for the night. So, I just stayed home (Himelstein et al., 2015a).

While the above results are primarily concerned with the process of implementing this intervention rather than the outcomes among participants, it is clear via the quote above that some of the relapse prevention strategies utilized positively affected study participants. What is clearer is that it is important to put effort into developing a therapeutic atmosphere based in authentic relationships for client receptivity (to both drug education and relapse prevention strategies) to result. This is why so much emphasis is placed on building authentic relationships in this curriculum.

Finally, we have conducted one pilot randomized clinical trial where we recruited 44 participants from a juvenile detention camp (Himelstein, Saul, & Garcia-Romeu, 2015b). All participants who were in the group-based intervention were also given one-on-one sessions and randomized to either a treatment as usual (TAU) condition where they received conventional therapy or the treatment condition where they received mindfulness meditation training with psychotherapy. Mindfulness meditation was stripped from the group-based intervention to isolate it as an intervention and determine its effectiveness as a curriculum component. Pretest and posttest measures on locus of control, attitude toward drugs, self-esteem, decision-making, and mindfulness were administered prior to and upon completion of the intervention, which lasted 10–12 weeks. Further, averages of behavioral points (points that youth in the detention camp were awarded daily for good behavior and lack of negative behavior and averaged weekly) were also assessed to determine if the mindfulness intervention impact behavioral regulation. We analyzed the entire sample's data as a whole (via paired t-tests) to test for overall group differences from pretest to posttest on the above self-report measures, and analyzed whether there were significant differences on any of the measures and behavioral points between the treatment and control group (via independent samples t-tests and mixed ANOVA statistical analyses).

On the sample as a whole (both treatment and control groups), self-report test results showed that both decision-making ($p < .01$) and self-esteem ($p < .05$) significantly increased from pretest to posttest. All other measures were found to be insignificant however moved in psychologically enhancing directions. Interestingly, change scores for the treatment group increased at a significantly higher rate than those of the control group ($p < .05$) for self-esteem, suggesting that mindfulness meditation coupled with psychotherapy may help foster self-esteem at a greater rate than psychotherapy alone. These results are supported by past research suggesting that mindfulness increased self-esteem for adolescent psychiatric outpatients (Biegel et al., 2009). Further, results showed that the treatment and control group's behavioral points were significantly different from pretest to posttest ($p < .05$), with the treatment group's behavioral points increasing and the control group's behavioral points decreasing. This suggests that the mindfulness intervention may have played a role in increasing behavioral regulation for study participants.

The above study, however, is not without limitation. The sample size was small and the study took place in a juvenile detention camp where participants interacted with each other outside of treatment. This may have skewed results and thus should be interpreted with caution.

Evidenced-Based Treatment

Regardless of the limitations and pilot nature of the above studies, what's clear from our work and the multitude of research (with more advanced designs) that has investigated the impact of mindfulness with youth and addiction populations is that there is value in mindfulness as an intervention for young people dealing with substance abuse issues. Further, some of the above studies provide data that fit within the *commonly unknown* criteria for evidence-based practice. The Institute of Medicine (2001) and the American Psychological Association (2005) agree that one's choice of evidence-based practice is required to address three necessary aspects: 1) empirical research that indicate valid and generalizable results, 2) clinical expertise of the facilitators, and 3) client preference/values. All of these are represented with the latter two aspects represented to a higher degree in our qualitative studies. Our hope is that this curriculum continues to be researched with more advanced designs and, if necessary, evolves into a better curriculum based on data from the three aspects of evidence-based practice as described above.

A Continuous Evolution of Curriculum

We urge you to facilitate this curriculum in whatever way works best for you. Deploy this program and become your own expert. Adapt whatever you need to adapt to fit within the values of the specific subcultures with which you are working. The above-named components and conceptual map of the program comprise how we facilitated this intervention. Please understand that no two facilitators can facilitate this program exactly alike, especially given the emphasis on how important you, the facilitator, become in this work. It would be against our philosophy to suggest that this curriculum, as well as any other, is beyond the necessity to evolve. You will inevitably find ways of expressing the ideas within these pages more skillfully and more appropriately for the young people you are working with—and that's okay. Your own life experience will play a large part in how you present certain concepts and practices. Our intention in writing, implementing, researching, and disseminating this curriculum is to help facilitators teach young people transformational techniques to take control of their substance abusing and other unhealthy behaviors. We know by your being interested in this manual—and in this work generally, for that matter—that you have your own wisdom to offer. We hope you will take this curriculum and integrate it with your own wisdom and practices to reach as many adolescents as possible. Please make sure that, prior to reading the curriculum, you extensively review the "Using This Curriculum" chapter that follows here.

References

American Psychological Association. (2005). *American Psychological Association statement: Policy statement on evidence-based practices in psychology.* Washington, DC: APA.

Biegel, G.M., Brown, K.W., Shapiro, S.L., & Schubert, C.M. (2009). Mindfulness-based stress reduction for the treatment of adolescent psychiatric outpatients: A randomized clinical trial. *Journal of Clinical and Consulting Psychology, 77,* 855–866.

Bowen, S., Chawla, N., & Marlatt, G.A. (2011). *Mindfulness-based relapse prevention for addictive behaviors: A clinician's guide.* New York, NY: Guilford Press.

Corbin, J.M., & Strauss, A. (2014). *Basics of qualitative research: Techniques and procedures for developing grounded theory* (4th ed.). Thousand Oaks, CA: Sage.

Himelstein, S. (2011). Mindfulness-based substance abuse treatment for incarcerated youth: A mixed-methods study. *International Journal of Transpersonal Studies, 30,* 1–10.

Himelstein, S., Saul, S., & Garcia-Romeu, A. (2015a). *Does mindfulness meditation increase effectiveness of substance abuse treatment with incarcerated youth? A pilot randomized clinical trial.* (Manuscript submitted for publication)

Himelstein, S., Saul, S., & Garcia-Romeu, A. (2015b). *Group-based substance abuse treatment with adolescents: A grounded theory study.* (Manuscript submitted for publication)

Himelstein, S., Saul, S., Garcia-Romeu, A., & Pinedo, D. (2014). Mindfulness training as an intervention for substance-user incarcerated adolescents: A pilot grounded theory study. *Substance Use and Misuse, 49,* 560–570.

Institute of Medicine. (2001). *Crossing the quality chasm: A new health system for the 21st century.* Washington, DC: National Academy Press.

Kabat-Zinn, J. (1990). *Full catastrophe living: Using the wisdom of your body and mind to face stress, pain, and illness.* New York, NY: Dell.

Kabat-Zinn, J. (2013). *Full catastrophe living: Using the wisdom of your body and mind to face stress, pain, and illness* (rev. ed.). New York: NY: Bantam Books.

Kivel, P., & Creighton, A. (1997). *Making the peace: A 15-session violence prevention curriculum for young people.* Alameda, CA: Hunter House.

Rosenberg, L. (1998). *Breath by breath: The liberating practice of insight meditation.* Boston, MA: Shambhala.

USING THIS CURRICULUM

Our goal in developing and researching this curriculum was twofold: 1) to offer a comprehensive mindfulness-based group substance-abuse treatment intervention for professionals working with adolescents, and 2) to offer a resource for numerous interventions, both mindfulness-based and drug education-based, for professionals wishing to simply incorporate a few activities into their existing curriculum. We realize that these two goals are on opposite ends of the spectrum in regard to curriculum fidelity, but it is our deepest wish to help broadly to improve the treatment and education of youth dealing with substance abuse, and we know that everyone that buys this book isn't going to want to implement (or won't be able to implement, for logistical reasons) this curriculum in full. This book is about improving the lives of young people who are dealing with substance use and abuse, anger management, aggression, trauma, and many more such factors inhibiting healthy development. Therefore, we humbly submit this program. If you wish to obtain help to be fully trained in the curriculum, as has been stated in offerings on our resource page, we do offer that support. However, we hope you don't think that, because you buy this book, you need to implement the curriculum word-for-word. That's not how group practice with adolescents works, in reality. As with any two groupings of individuals, one cannot assume that preferences and problems to be addressed will be uniform in their presentation because the demographics and such are equivalent.

If you wish to implement this curriculum as it is disseminated within these pages, we bow deeply to your efforts in furthering this program. We have worked for countless hours in refining, researching, and implementing this program and appreciate your commitment to its utility. The progression of the 12 sessions follows a sound conceptual map that teaches youth mindfulness and other contemplative practices, drug education, and emotional and behavioral management, and gets them thinking about the key issues and situations that adolescent youth continuously deal with and that, more often than not, involve drugs and drug use (consult the previous chapter for in-depth review of the curriculum components to assess a fit for your group). Below, we have elucidated numerous sections that are a part of every session's text. Reviewing these clarifications will help you correctly interpret what the curriculum is suggesting be done in a given activity.

Interpreting the Curriculum Text

The Face Sheet

The face sheet is the first page of each session chapter. It includes the session summary, the materials needed to facilitate the session (if any), the amount of formal meditation time, the session's learning objectives, and the session's agenda. The agenda contains the chronological order for activities in the session and, in parentheses next to each item, is the suggested chair configuration. These

Session Summary

As the introduction to the entire program, the first session serves the purpose of orienting participants to the structure of the curriculum, setting agreements and expectations for behavior and effort, and answering any logistical or structural questions the youth may have. The majority of this session is spent building the groundwork for a therapeutic culture that has the potential to result in trust, receptivity, and disclosure. Introductory mindfulness concepts and meditations are presented and youth are asked what they want to learn from the program.

Materials Needed

- Meditation bell
- Session 1 Handouts (Optional)

Formal Meditation Time

- Five minutes

Learning Objectives

- Review the structure and logistics of the program
- Set group agreements
- Define and practice mindfulness
- Discuss what youth participants may want to learn from the program

Group Agenda (Chair Configuration)

1. Informal Greeting (N/A)
2. Introduction to the Group (Circle)
3. Group Agreements and Expectations (Circle)
4. Defining Mindfulness (Circle)
5. Mindfulness of the Breath (Circle)
6. Group Poll: Learning Interests of the Youth (Circle)
7. Homework and Closing (Circle)

Session 1 example face sheet

configurations reflect only how we have, in implementing the curriculum components, traditionally configured the chairs; however, we hope you will feel free to mix and match these suggested plans to create what feels comfortable to you and acceptable to your clients.

Talking Points and Example Scripts

You will find talking points and example scripts virtually throughout every session. We wanted to provide as many tools as possible so that it would be easier to get a clear sense of how we have facilitated the dialogues and activities in the curriculum. The talking points comprise the essential content for each discussion topic or activity or any plan of action. ***These are what you should pay most atten-tion to***. The example scripts are included to give you a real sense for how we typically deliver the talk-ing points for any given activity. The scripts are intended as a guideline only. ***We strongly urge you to not simply read from these scripts word for word. Develop your own voice***. The goal would be for you to develop your own voice and disseminate the information in a way that feels most authentic and natural to you. We simply wanted to add these scripts into the curriculum because we've received feedback that it helps gives readers a clear sense of the information that needs to be disseminated. An example is as follows:

Talking Points

- Ask the group, "What's the difference between rules and agreements?"
- Ask, "What happens when you break a rule?"
- State that it is simply a conversation that occurs when an agreement is broken in this protocol.

Example Script

Facilitator: Okay, so one of the most important things in getting this group to work is what we call group agreements. Before we get into the specifics, who can tell me what the difference between an agreement and a rule is? . . . That's right, an agreement is something we all agree to and a rule is oftentimes created by the teacher or facilitator without talking to the participants . . . What happens when a rule is broken? . . . Right! When you break a rule you usually get punished. That's why we want to stay away from rules. With an agreement, if you step outside the bounds of the agreement, it's just more like a conversation will happen, like, "I thought we agreed to this. Are you still okay with that agreement?" It's like a reminder conversation. Does that make sense? . . . That's what we want to do in this group, agree to a set of agreements rather than call them rules. Let's discuss some specific agreements that might be good for this group.

Talking points and example script from session 1

When reading each script, you may notice that there are questions asked followed by statements as if the question was answered. This is because the talking points and scripts in real time are more of a call and response with the group rather than a straight monologue. Whenever you see three consecutive dots " . . . " that means that there is a pause, either after a question was asked or at another appropriate time. This means it is okay to actually pose the question to the group at that point and field the participants' responses.

Notes to the Facilitator

Notes to the facilitator are included throughout the descriptions of the sessions and are meant to remind you of certain concepts, principles, and practices. They will be bolded and out of the normal text format. Make sure to pay close attention to these notes, as they may be differentiated by impor-tance: may simply read *Note*, or may be represented as *Important Note*, to signify greater importance. An example is below:

NOTE

Make sure that you have the circle of chairs already set up prior to the youth entering the space.

And

IMPORTANT NOTE

It's imperative to understand that the agreements will need to be re-activated whenever a group participant steps outside of their bounds. Thus, think of the agreements as something that could be discussed at any time throughout the curriculum, not just in the first session.

Example notes to reader

What-if? Scenarios

What-if? Scenarios are scenarios that have arisen in our groups many times and have, thus, been incorporated into the protocol. Contemplating them in advance may be helpful in dealing with them as they arise. They will also be bolded and out of the normal text format so as to be easily identifiable. There are actually many What-if? Scenarios for any given activity, and, rather than exhausting all of them (because of page limitations) we have added the most common scenarios and our responses to them. An example is below:

WHAT IF?

The first or second volunteer doesn't take the deep breath or just checks in with "cool" or "good," etc.? Whenever a group member doesn't follow the instructions of the activity, it's important to remember that it's okay to remind him or her of the correct behavior. You don't want to stop everyone every time if s/he doesn't take the breath (choose your interventions wisely), but if the first or second participant doesn't take the breath or checks in vaguely, simply remind him or her gently of the protocol and ask that s/he try again. The first and second volunteers are the tone-setters. If you don't catch this early on, you will have potentially gone through a whole mindful check-in without anyone taking the deep breath.

What if? Scenario example from session 2

Meditation Scripts

Meditation scripts are exactly the same as the talking points and example scripts described above but have to do specifically with the meditations taught within this curriculum. The talking points and example script are almost identical to regular scripts, but we wanted to review some key elements important when teaching meditation. You'll see text bolded and within brackets, at times. That means you as the facilitator are being instructed to do something (e.g., *Place your hand on your belly*). The three consecutive dots described above (. . .), suggest a pause in speech. This is so the meditator can have some time to himself or herself without your speaking. An example is on the page opposite:

You can also download all meditations for your use, as is described in the resource and training section. While it is acceptable to play the recordings of these meditations during your facilitation of the curriculum, we encourage you to develop your own voice as a facilitator and practice teaching yourself. The downloadable meditations are provided more to give you a sense of how we facilitate each meditation than to take from you that self-training by which you can own the process.

Talking Points

- Instruct the youth to sit in a comfortable position.
- Have the youth place one of their hands on their stomachs.
- Briefly educate them on the difference between a breath into the stomach and a breath into the chest.
- Invite the youth to close their eyes (but don't demand it).
- Instruct the youth in the mindfulness of deep breathing exercise.
  - Keep awareness on breath.
  - Focus on the breath filling up the stomach.
  - Feel the stomach expand and contract with the hand.
  - Whenever the mind wanders, bring it back to the stomach and breath.

Example Script

*Facilitator: Okay, now it's time to practice some formal meditation. We've been talking about mindfulness all during this session and now we're going to formally practice it. This exercise is going to be short, only five minutes or so, and I'll guide you through it the whole way. I want to invite everyone to put one hand on the belly like this **[place your hand on your belly]**. Does everyone know the difference between breathing into your belly and breathing into your chest? When you breathe into your belly, you fill it up like this on the inhale **[show example]**, and when you breathe into your chest, you fill your chest up with air like this **[show example]**. For this meditation, we're going to practice breathing into our bellies. Keep your hand on your belly for the whole meditation. It's good to sit in an upright position, so you can breathe naturally, and it's also good to close your eyes during meditation so you don't get distracted. However, if you don't feel comfortable closing your eyes, just keep them open and focused on the floor a couple feet in front of you. When I ring the bell, take a deep breath into your belly and a deep breath out and wait for further instructions.*

[Ring bell]

Breathing in, and breathing out . . . Take slow, deep breaths in, and take slow, deep breaths out . . . Feel your belly slowly filling up with air as you breathe in, and slowly deflating as you breath out . . . If your mind starts to wander off, and think of something else other than the breath, just gently redirect it back to your breathing, taking slow and deep breaths in and slow and deep breaths out . . . This is the practice, just breathing in slow and deep, and breathing out slow and deep . . . Feel the movement of your belly with your hand . . . Breathing in deep, and breathing out deep . . . The breath is like an anchor on a ship. Just as the anchor keeps the ship in place in the ocean, the breath anchors our awareness to our body, to this present moment. Breathing in deep, and breathing out deep . . . And if the mind wanders, again, there's no need to get frustrated, or annoyed, or to think you're doing anything wrong. It's the nature of the mind to wander. Just gently redirect your mind back to your breathing, taking deep breaths in and deep breaths out.

. . . In a moment I'm going to ring the bell, and when I do I want to invite you to shift your awareness from your breathing to your ears and your hearing sense, and see if you can listen to the bell until you can't hear it any longer. . . .

[Ring bell]

When you feel comfortable, you can slowly open your eyes, and come out of the formal meditation, expanding your awareness from your inner world to encompass the rest of the group.

Meditation script example from session 1

Session Handouts

At the end of each session there are one or more "handouts." These are either worksheets referenced in the text for youth to complete, meditation scripts for you to print and have on hand for quick reference, or other handouts referenced in the text. They are at the end of each session for easy consultation and printing if desired.

Logistics to Consider When Facilitating

When facilitating this program, there are a number of logistics to consider. These include facilitating open vs. closed cohort groups, the number of participants you admit to your group, how long each group should be, cofacilitation, and whether you implement this curriculum in part or in full.

Open vs. Closed Cohorts

If you have a choice in facilitating either open or closed cohort groups, we recommend closed cohort groups (i.e., having a specific number of youth and not admitting any new youth for the duration of the 12 sessions). The curriculum is designed to build upon itself in both content and group cohesion, and, when new youth are constantly admitted every few weeks, it is difficult to maintain group cohesion. This isn't to say that, if you have no control over your group's limitation and can only facilitate an open group, you are doomed. On the contrary, we facilitated open and rolling groups for years. It can be done with integrity, and great benefit can result for the youth. Just know that you will need to become skilled at facilitating the group agreements (see session 1) concisely when new youth enter and that it will be more difficult to build group cohesion.

Figure 3.1

Group Size

If you are facilitating this group in a clinical, counseling, or AOD (alcohol and other drug) setting, we recommend that you admit 6–12 participants. Program sessions whose number of participants are higher than 12 run the risk of youth being able to "hide" and not participate as much, and group sizes less than six run the risk of the youth feeling at times too highlighted and under the microscope. You may or may not have control over this choice of group size. If you're teaching this as a class in an afterschool program or school-based setting, you may have 20–30 youth in your class. This isn't the ideal atmosphere, but can, in fact, work.

We have implemented this program in an educational setting with 25 youth participants and simply relied more heavily on our classroom management skills (e.g., maintaining agreements, using the refocusing technique).

Group Length

This curriculum is designed for sessions to be implemented for 90 minutes at a time. However, we understand that you may have no control over the length of the sessions and only have 60–75 minutes available. Additionally, if you work in a school-based setting, you may only have a class period (45 minutes) available. If you cannot use the full 90 minutes, it is okay to break up one session over a couple of sessions' time. When we implemented this curriculum in an educational setting, it was in an afterschool program with 25 students who attended twice per week for an hour. Because it was a school (and not a correctional or inpatient) setting, that would mean we would really only have about 50 minutes per class, as we would have to account for student tardiness. Thus, we implemented the curriculum over 24 classes and spread one session's content over two classes.

Cofacilitation

If you have the resource of a cofacilitator or co-teacher available, we highly recommend that you cofacilitate. If you cannot (and, at times, in both of our careers, we have each facilitated groups alone), you can still facilitate this curriculum to a high quality of effect. We simply recommend having someone you can consult with on the various issues that arise. Many situations are inevitably better handled when two facilitators can speak with each other and offer feedback. Himelstein (2013) suggests the following benefits of cofacilitation:

- Sharing the group consciousness load
- Feedback sessions
- Processing after the group
- Scanning of the group (while the other facilitator presents)
- Self-care

Please review Himelstein's (2013) work on the benefits of cofacilitation for an in-depth review.

A La Carte vs. Entrée

When you are looking at the menu of activities within this book, it is really up to you whether or not you implement this curriculum in full or in part. We recommend implementing it in full, given how much thought we've put into its particular sequence; however, we also understand that this isn't possible at

Figure 3.2
Courtesy of iStockphoto, reprinted with permission.

times. You may have an existing group structure in which it would be too difficult to implement the curriculum in full (e.g., an outpatient substance abuse group that is open and rolling with new youth constantly), or simply be merging this curriculum with another (e.g., anger management). In such cases, use your best discernment to implement the activities of interest into your group. Any of the activities within this curriculum can be highlighted and implemented into another curriculum if need be.

Working With Youth of Diverse Ethnic and Gender Backgrounds

Finally, if you plan on facilitating this curriculum with youth of diverse ethnic and gender backgrounds it is extremely important to consider the diversity issues that may arise. As you traverse through facilitating this program with young people, it is important that you take into account their specific subcultural, ethnic, gender, and socioeconomic status. It is recommended that you attempt to adapt this program to them rather than the other way around. Use your best discernment, judgment, and intuition. Your own cultural competency will be of extreme importance, and that is another practice that falls within the personal practice and relational mindfulness categories. Substance use and addiction are heavily interrelated with some of the socioeconomic issues related to some communities, and it is important to understand that such issues may arise in conjunction with substance abuse treatment and education. Please do not ignore or invalidate those issues. Make sure you pay close attention to them and weave them into the curriculum as needed.

If you, the facilitator, happen to be of Caucasian descent and are working primarily with youth of color (which happens to be the case in many treatment and intervention settings, at least), we urge you to review Kivel's (2011) work on deconstructing racism and oppression. We wish you mindful awareness, skillfulness, compassion, and love as you work with young people in such need. Please remember to join our online community and contribute to the evolution of this work!

References

Himelstein, S. (2013). *A mindfulness-based approach to working with high-risk adolescents*. New York, NY: Routledge.
Kivel, P. (2011). *Uprooting racism: How white people can work for racial justice*. Gabriola Island, BC: New Society.

12-SESSION CURRICULUM

SESSION 1

INTRODUCTION TO THE PROGRAM

Session Summary

As the introduction to the entire program, the first session serves the purpose of orienting participants to the structure of the curriculum, setting agreements and expectations for behavior and effort, and answering any logistical or structural questions youth may have. The majority of this session is spent building the groundwork for a therapeutic culture that has the potential to result in trust, receptivity, and disclosure. Introductory mindfulness concepts and meditations are presented and youth are asked what they want to learn from the program.

Materials Needed

- Meditation bell
- Session 1 Handouts (optional)

Formal Meditation (Time)

- Mindfulness of Deep Breathing (5 minutes)

Learning Objectives

- Review the structure and logistics of the program
- Set group agreements
- Define and practice mindfulness
- Discuss what youth may want to learn from the program

Session Agenda (Chair Configuration)

1. Informal Greeting (N/A)
2. Introduction to the Program (Circle)
3. Group Agreements and Expectations (Circle)
4. Defining Mindfulness (Circle)
5. Meditation: Mindfulness of Deep Breathing (Circle)
6. Group Poll: Learning Interests of the Youth (Circle)
7. Homework and Closing (Circle)

1. Informal Greeting

The introduction to the first group may be the first time you meet the youth you'll be working with. It's important that the youth feel welcomed into the program and that you ***distinguish*** this program from status-quo treatment or education. The first introduction doesn't actually happen once everyone is sitting down in a circle, but rather upon the first greeting as the youth enter your treatment room or classroom. You (or you and your cofacilitator) are the introduction to the program. If you are the only facilitator, wait by the entrance of the space where the program will take place and introduce yourself as the youth enter the space. If you have a cofacilitator, he or she can wait by the circle of chairs and do the same.

NOTE

Make sure that you have the circle of chairs already set up prior to the youth entering the space.

2. Introduction to the Program

Once all the youth are sitting in the circle, begin to formally introduce the program. Use the talking points and example script below as guidelines for introducing the program.

IMPORTANT NOTE

Remember! Simply use the talking points and example scripts as guidelines. We highly urge you not to read the script word for word, but rather develop your own voice.

Talking Points

- Formally re-introduce yourself.
- State the curriculum's philosophy on change (e.g., not there to change them, are there to build self-awareness and real relationships).
- Review the content, activities, and logistics of the program.

Example Script

Facilitator: *Welcome. As I said before, I'm Sam, and this is my partner Stephen. We just want to take a few moments and give you a little information about this program. We'll have time for questions throughout the session. I do this work because I'm passionate about serving young people, and really believe that youth can make a difference in this world. I BELIEVE that, with training, you can take control of your lives and be successful, whatever that means to you.* **[At this point Stephen would introduce himself and disclose a similar mission statement]**. *We just want to tell you a little about this program. The first thing is that we know there are a lot of programs that just tell you drugs are bad and you shouldn't do them. This isn't one of those programs. We're not here to tell you what to do. We're not here to try and change you. We believe you have the ability to change yourself if you choose to do that. What we're here to* *do is connect and build REAL relationships. We're also here to offer information and some transformational practices that have changed our lives. So our focus isn't on changing you or telling you to stop doing drugs, that could be too presumptive of your experience and reasoning, we're just here to connect, offer information that you might be interested in, and help you develop a higher self-awareness so that you can live as consciously as possible. Any questions about that piece? . . . Just to give you a sense of what this group is going to be like, sometimes we're going to sit in a circle like this, sometimes we'll sit in a half circle, and sometimes we might even sit classroom style. Over the years we've found that switching it up can be a good thing, so we don't want to do one thing for too long. Each of the groups will have a different theme: learning about drugs, drugs in the community, how to deal with drug cravings, emotional regulation, and more. One of the most important things is that, over time, our goal is to come together and connect as a group. We want you all to eventually feel comfortable enough talking about serious and deep things. Sometimes it will be playful in here, and sometimes it will get deep. On those group sessions that generally get deep, we'll let you know ahead of time that they are coming, but we really want to encourage you to fully participate. Any questions about the logistics of the program?*

Oftentimes, when we'd state this at the start of a group we see signs of an actual sense of a relief from the youth. Most youth (especially those who are mandated to treatment), do not want to change their behaviors. Furthermore, the youth will appreciate your reviewing a brief "lay of the land" and answering any questions related to the logistics of the program.

3. Group Agreements

Reviewing the group agreements and actually getting the youth to *agree* to them is the most important aspect of this first session. It gives the youth an expectation of what's okay and not okay in regard to behavior and sets the stage to develop a therapeutic culture in which trust and disclosure can result. What's most critical is to have an actual dialogue and not simply "list off" the agreements as though you're reviewing a checklist. The first step in this process is to discuss what agreements are and how they're distinguished from "rules" that are based on a model of punishment (e.g., when a rule is broken, the rule-breaker gets punished). Alternatively, agreements are "agreed upon" by everyone in the group (i.e., not set in a top-down fashion), and, when agreements are fragmented by behaviors contrary to them, a conversation occurs. Presenting the agreements has two steps: 1) distinguishing rules vs. agreements, and 2) presenting and agreeing to specific behaviors.

Step 1: Distinguishing Rules vs. Agreements

Use the following talking points and example script as a guide when facilitating step one.

Talking Points

- Ask the group, "What's the difference between rules and agreements?"
- Ask, "What happens when you break a rule?"
- A conversation occurs when an agreement is broken.

Example Script

Facilitator: Okay, so one of the most important things in getting this group to work is what we call group agreements. Before we get into the specifics, who can tell me what the difference between an agreement and a rule is? . . . That's right, an agreement is something we all agree to and a rule is oftentimes created by the teacher or facilitator without first talking with the participants . . . What happens when a rule is broken? . . . Right! When you break a rule, you usually get punished. That's why we want to stay away from rules. With an agreement, if you step outside the bounds of the agreement, it's just more like a conversation will happen, like, "I thought we agreed to this. Are you still okay with that agreement?" It's like a reminder conversation. Does that make sense? . . . That's what we want to do in this group, agree to a set of statements rather than call out rules. Let's discuss some specific agreements that might be good for this group.

Step 2: Presenting and Agreeing to the Preferred Group Behaviors

After the distinguishing between agreements and rules, you can then begin the process of presenting the agreements. Below is a list of agreements regarding behavior principles that are suggested for use in this curriculum.

- Confidentiality
- Respect
- One Mic Agreement
- Skillful Speech
- Skillful Listening
- Authenticity
- No Violence
- Group Refocus

The above, in our experience, have generally been the most important agreements to be made in order for cohesiveness and trust to develop. You might ask the youth if they can think of any other agreements, as it can be powerful to involve them in decision-making processes in regard to such major aspects of the group experience.

Agreement 1: Confidentiality. It is important to inform youth of the limits of confidentiality to which the facilitators can be bound in these agreements and that it be explained immediately after circling up and discussing the logistics of the program. Youth must be informed that, if they discuss material related to their hurting themselves or others, or, for instance, physical/mental/emotional abuse toward minors or elders, that such material can be reported to the appropriate authorities. Use the talking points and example script below to guide this conversation.

Talking Points

- Limits of confidentiality include hurting self, hurting others, and abuse.
- Other than comments in that category, all information is confidential.

Example Script

Facilitator: Who knows what the word confidentiality means? . . . Anybody ever heard of the Vegas rule? "What happens in Vegas stays in Vegas?" That's sort of how confidentiality works here, as well. It means that the information that we share in here will stay confidential. Now, before we say anything else, we have to let you know that there are only a few instances where we'd have to break confidentiality. Has anyone ever been in therapy in which this is the case or think they know when those instances are? That's right! If you plan to hurt yourself, hurt someone else, or if you report child or elder abuse, we'd have to let someone know. Now, it's important to clarify a few things about these instances. Just because we'd have to report these instances doesn't mean you're not allowed to state them. Some people may want to report child abuse in their house to get help so it can stop. Some may want to report that they're feeling as if they want to hurt themselves because they really need help. It's okay when that happens; just know that we're obligated to report those instances to the appropriate authorities. We'll let you know when you're talking about something that sounds like a report, so we can deal with it together. As for hurting others, this only has to do with the future. So if you came in here and said that you beat someone up yesterday, we wouldn't report on that. It is only if you had a concrete plan to beat someone up in the future that we'd have to report that. Does that make sense? . . . Other than in these instances, everything in here is confidential. Here's a test question: If you come to the next group and state that you got really high the past week, would we have to report that? Does it fall within those three main instances I just spoke about? Right! It doesn't. Now, we're probably going to speak with you about getting really high and use it to deepen our treatment, but we wouldn't break confidentiality. Does that make sense to everyone? . . . Another aspect of confidentiality is concerning our own personal information as individuals in a group. So, just as we said we only have to report on those three instances above, that means we won't report on anything else. We'll respect your confidentiality. But another important aspect of the group is that we respect each other's confidentiality, as well as being able to have our own respected. There are going to be times during the group when we share things about our lives and we don't want anyone going around talking about other peoples' business. As a general agreement, we ask that, if someone asks you about your experience in the group, you just talk about your own experience and not anyone else's or any information someone else has said that is personal. If we keep to this confidentiality agreement, our group cohesiveness will grow and the group will be better. Does that make sense to everyone? . . . Can we all agree to this first agreement of confidentiality?

Make sure you get actual acknowledgements from the youth after presenting the agreement of confidentiality. Don't simply "talk at" the youth.

Agreement 2: Respect. This agreement is disseminated to the group via a discussion concerning each one's personal definition of *respect*. The purpose is to get everyone's voice in the room and to define respect as a group. Again, simply listing "respect" as an agreement and not fully discussing it only glosses over this agreement and takes away from the essence of the activity. Remember that you're not only discussing respect as a concept, but also discussing *how* everyone will respect each other in the group, which is an important component necessary for therapeutic culture to develop.

Ask for a volunteer to start and share his or her personal definition of respect. After he or she is finished, choose in which direction the circle will go. Make sure to share your personal definition of respect, as well, but only after all the youth have shared. Once everyone has shared their definitions, briefly summarize what everyone said and get actual agreement that everyone will abide by this agreement.

WHAT IF?

A group member shares a definition of respect that will not contribute to a therapeutic environment and/or that perpetuates violence? Honor the youth's personal definition and ask to alter it solely for the purposes of the group and nothing more. Refer to "Dealing with Definitions of Respect" at the end of this session's chapter for a specific example.

Agreement 3: One Mic. The one mic (short for microphone) agreement gives the group an expectation for how each will be expected, by agreement, to speak and listen to each other. The agreement essentially gets youth to agree to the practice of one group member speaking at a time, while everyone else listens. Use the talking points and example script to present and discuss this agreement.

Talking Points

- One mic means that one person speaks at a time, while everyone else listens.

Example Script

Facilitator: Anyone ever heard of the "one mic" concept? . . . It's like the person who's talking has a metaphorical microphone, and that when whoever's talking, everyone else listens. We do this so that that person can feel he or she will be fully heard and listened to, so that when you or you are talking **[point to a few people in the group]**, *you feel listened to and heard, as well. Does that make sense? . . . Can we all agree to the agreement of one mic? When one person's talking, everyone else listens and doesn't talk over him or her?*

Make sure to get acknowledgment and agreement from the group.

Agreement 4: Skillful Speech. The next agreement, skillful speech, is closely linked to the one mic agreement. It's the agreement that group participants will mindfully speak and not simply blurt out whatever comes to them. Use the talking points and example script below as a guide from which to present and discuss this agreement.

Talking Points

- Skillful speech is thinking about what you want to say prior to saying it.
- Skillful speech is not simply blurting out what's on your mind.
- Skillful speech can be facilitated by taking a breath prior to speaking.

Example Script

Facilitator: When we're in this group, one of the main practices we want to push is how we actually talk with each other. This agreement is called "skillful speech." What do you all think that means? . . . The conventional definition of skillful speech is to be aware of what you want to say prior to saying it, and then say it. Sometimes we all blurt words out because of reaction or we're triggered, and that's not skillful speech. Skillful speech is when we think about what we want to say before saying it; that's what makes it skillful. If you're ever in a situation where you do get triggered and need to still practice skillful speech, take a deep breath and collect yourself prior to talking and it will help you speak skillfully. Can we all agree to this? To practice skillful speech?

Agreement 5: Skillful Listening. Skillful listening is also closely linked to skillful speech and the one mic agreement. It is the agreement that group participants will practice giving their undivided attention when other youth are speaking. Use the talking points and example script below as a guide when presenting this agreement.

Talking Points

- Skillful listening includes present moment awareness.
- Skillful listening includes presence with body language.
- You can refocus your mind on your breath if it wanders to help stay present to the speaker.

Example Script

Facilitator: And what do you all think skillful listening is? . . . Skillful listening is listening in a specific way so that the person talking actually feels more heard than if the listening was unskillful. We can practice this in a number of ways, and I want to encourage you all to practice this in a few specific ways. First, is that we engage in actual listening. When we're listening skillfully, we're actually listening to the person talking, not daydreaming or thinking about something that's not happening in the here and now. To do that you need to keep your attention in the present moment and focused on the person talking. If you're someone who has trouble focusing, and your mind wanders, just take a deep breath or two and that will ground your attention back into the here and now. Now, what if my attention is on the speaker but I'm sitting like this **[model body language that suggests disinterest]**? How do you think that plays into listening? . . . It can come off as disrespectful at times. Sure, sometimes people are tired and we don't want to read too far into their body language, but it is also good to practice attentive listening with our bodies, as well. And the way to do that is to orient our bodies and eyes toward the speaker. Those components, the listening to the speaker, keeping your awareness in the present moment with attentive body language, comprise skillful listening. Can we all agree to practice skillful listening while in this group?

Agreement 6: Authenticity. The next agreement is simple but profound: we ask the group participants to practice authenticity. Authenticity begets authenticity and an explicit goal of the curriculum is to create an authentic atmosphere. Use the talking points and example script below to present this agreement.

Talking Points

- Authenticity invites support from the group.

Example Script

Facilitator: The next agreement we like to practice is simple. Be authentic when you're in here. Like a lot of us like to say, "Keep it real." That means when you feel a certain way, like angry or hurt, you own it. You are real about it and don't try to hide from it. When we do that, we learn to communicate and support each other in a whole different way. And that's what this group is about. Can everyone agree to that?

Agreement 7: Nonviolence. The agreement of keeping an attitude of nonviolence, both physically and verbally, is especially important to get the group to agree to. Whether you're working in correctional settings with rival gang members or young people who perpetrate relational aggression, it's important to present this agreement explicitly. Use the talking points and example script below to discuss this agreement.

Talking Points

- The group couldn't remain confidential and without the presence of extra staff (from correctional or other treatment settings) if violence were to occur in the group.
- The violence we are talking about refers to both physical and verbal aggression.

Example Script

Facilitator: One of the last agreements we want to present is really, really important. That is, when we're in this circle, for this hour and a half each week, it is extremely important that we all commit to *practice nonviolence. That's the main reason we can conduct this group confidentially without extra staff in here. Because there's no fights. If you ever feel the need to fight, if you're ever that angry, just pull me or my cofacilitator to the side and ask us to take you on a walk outside. One of the things we'd hate is if you got into more trouble, from being in a fight, as a result of being in this group. So, that's why it's so important to practice nonviolence, so that we can maintain the safety of the group. If there were to be fights here, we wouldn't be able to conduct this group without an extra staff person in here. Does that make sense? . . . Does violence happen only on the physical level? . . . We can be really nasty with our words. And the agreement of nonviolence goes beyond just physical violence for this group time, as well. This agreement means that we want to practice nonviolence, or peacefulness, while talking to each other, like in skillful speech, and how we interact with each other at any time. Does that make sense? . . . Can we all agree to this? . . .*

Agreement 8: Refocusing. The refocusing technique is a process-based group-management skill to help both refocus discussions/activities and re-activate the agreements when necessary. If you add other agreements to your list for your group, it is highly encouraged to still present this agreement last, as it presents the fact that the youth will at some point step out of bounds of the agreements, and this is the method you as the facilitator will use to either reactivate the agreements or get back on track. The basis of this technique, when the group is off-track, for example, and talking over one another, is to gently remind the group to "please refocus and take a breath." This MUST be done in a nonjudgmental, nonaggressive tone, and, therefore, rests on the facilitator's ability to be mindful to his or her own internal experience with nonreactivity. One can easily get decentered and announce "PLEASE REFOCUS AND TAKE A BREATH" in a harsh tone that conveys a command rather than a gentle request. Use the talking points and example script to present and discuss this agreement, and remember to practice mindful speech when employing this technique throughout the program.

Talking Points

- We'll get off-track at times as a group, and that's normal.
- The refocusing technique is a way to respectfully get back on track.
- When we're off-track, I'll just simply ask everyone to settle in and take a breath.
- I will never raise my voice or have a harsh tone.
- I will always speak to you respectfully.

Example Script

Facilitator: *Okay, the final agreement is one of the most important ones. We all know that, even though we agreed to these agreements, we will at times step outside their bounds. Sometimes we'll talk over each other and not speak skillfully. Sometimes we'll be off-track laughing when we're supposed to be doing something else. That's just normal because we're human beings. What's important is that we have a built-in method that is respectful of everyone for getting back on track and for re-activating the agreements when we step out of their bounds. We like to call it the "refocusing" technique. That is, when we're all laughing and off-track, or if everyone is talking over each other, I'll gently say, "let's refocus and take a breath." Or "can we all settle in and take a breath." I will NEVER raise my voice. I will ALWAYS speak with skillfulness and dignity to you. This is just the way we'll get back on track when we're off-track. Is that okay with everyone? It's important we all agree.*

What makes this practice actually work is the ability of the facilitator to employ it without raising her or his voice. If you as facilitator get agitated or frustrated, it is not the end of the world. However, this is where your mindfulness practice is VERY important. Bring your awareness to your breath and body, take a few breaths, think of what you're about to say, and then mindfully and with intention ask the group to refocus as described above. Think of this as its own mindfulness practice that you will employ over and over again as needed.

NOTE

Your agreements with your group may vary depending on setting. For example, in school- and/or community-based settings, you might have an agreement to not use cell phones or other technologies while in session. You can also ask the youth to come up with their own agreements they'd like to add.

Wrapping Up the Agreements

At this point you will have reviewed and discussed all of the agreements with your group members. Although you will inevitably need to re-activate the agreements throughout the program (whenever a member violates an agreement), you have laid the groundwork for a therapeutic group atmosphere. It can be skillful to summarize the agreements to solidify their purpose. Use the talking points and example script below as a guide.

Talking Points

- The agreements serve the purpose of building a therapeutic atmosphere.
- We'll probably need to re-activate the agreements at times.

Example Script

Facilitator: *So, as we have talked about for this last portion of time, the agreements serve the purpose of helping the group become cohesive, so we can be authentic and really build together. We want this hour and a half to be different from a regular class. We want it to be a place where you will eventually feel comfortable coming to because you know it will be a place to learn, to practice, and to discuss things you might not feel comfortable discussing elsewhere. Does that make sense to everyone? . . . This is why we have agreements, and not rules. It's also important to know that we'll probably bring these up throughout the program. We're all only human, so sometimes we might make mistakes and violate the agreements. And, because they're not rules, we aren't going to punish anyone for that, but we will send out a gentle reminder to stay within the bounds of the agreements for the sake of the group. Is that okay with everyone? . . .*

If you prefer, you can have all the youth in your group sign and date the agreement page that can be found in the handouts at the end of this session's chapter. This helps some groups stay more accountable.

IMPORTANT NOTE

It's imperative to understand that the agreements will need to be re-activated whenever a group participant steps outside their bounds. Thus, think of the agreements as something that could be discussed at any time throughout the curriculum, not just at the first session.

4. Defining Mindfulness

Once you've presented and discussed the agreements, define the term *mindfulness* with the group, as it is the foundational practice of the program. We define mindfulness in a two-step process: 1) the lion mind vs. dog mind metaphor, and 2) a standard, simple definition.

Step 1: Lion Mind vs. Dog Mind Metaphor

The lion mind vs. dog mind metaphor is an adapted metaphor from Larry Rosenberg's (1998) book, *Breath by Breath*. The metaphor compares the state of mind between a dog and a lion in relation to how a bone is perceived when waved in each of their faces. Make sure you have a meditation bell striker, pen, or pencil to mimic the holding of a bone. Use the talking points and example script below as a guide to presenting this metaphor.

Talking Points

- Ask the group what a dog would do if you waved a bone in his face and threw it 5 yards away.
- Ask the group what a lion would do in the same situation.
- Explain that the dog's reality is consumed by the bone, and that it, therefore, has little to no autonomy.
- Explain that the lion's reality is the opposite. The lion has more choice and autonomy because the bone is viewed as a small part of reality, not the whole of reality.
- Make an analogy of the bone with strong emotions.
- Close by relating the *king of the jungle* metaphor with regulating the *inner jungle* of the mind and heart.

Example Script

Facilitator: Who knows what the word mindfulness means? . . . We like to start by defining mindfulness with a metaphor. This one's called the lion vs. dog mind metaphor and it will exemplify what the state of mindfulness is. Let's say that this is a bone [**wave the meditation stick or pen around briefly**] *and let's say I'm standing in front of a dog. If I wave the bone from left to right, what do you think the dog will do? . . . Right, probably the dog's eyes will follow the bone. And let's say I threw the bone 5 yards over there to the right. What do you think the dog will do? . . . Right. 9 times out of 10, the dog is going to go after that bone. That's what dogs do. Now, let's say that, for some reason—I have no idea why I'd ever be in this situation—but let's say that, for some reason, I'm standing in front of a lion. And I wave this bone from left to right and then I throw it over there 5 yards to the right. What do you all think will happen? . . . Right. The lion could eat me. The lion might eat me. The point is that there's a fundamental difference between the states of mind of the dog and of the lion. When I wave this bone in the dog's face, the dog can't see anything besides the bone. When I wave it to the right, the dog's eyes go to the right. When I wave it to the left, the dog's eyes go left. When I throw it over there, the dog goes after it. The bone is the whole of the dog's reality. So if I control the bone, I control the dog's reality. But, with the lion, it's different. When I wave the bone to the left and to the right, the lion's eyes don't track the bone. They stay glued right on me. When I throw the bone 5 yards to the right, the lion doesn't move, and his or her eyes stay glued on me. I imagine that if the lion thought like a human being, he would think, "Doesn't this stupid person know that I can just eat him?" The point is that the lion isn't fooled by the bone. He can see that the bone is being held by a hand that's connected to a person. The bone isn't the whole of the lion's reality! It's just a small object within the lion's reality. And because of that, the lion has much more choice in how to respond. He could go after the* *bone, he could go after me, but it's his choice. That's the difference between him and the dog. The dog just reacts and has no choice. So, if you think of the bone as a metaphor for something like anger, or stress, or any strong emotion, when the bone, anger, is tossed into your reality, if you react with the dog mind, all of your reality is consumed by the anger. All you know is anger and, in turn, you become its puppet. It controls you, rather than you controlling it. But with the lion mind, you'd become aware of the anger as it arises, and your attitude would be much different. You might think, "Oh, this is anger," or, "this is what it feels like to be angry," knowing that this bone will not last forever and that you have a choice in how to respond to it. That's the lion mind, and that's why there's so much power in the practice of mindfulness. Does that make sense? . . . Good. One last question. Who is the king of the jungle? . . . That's right, the lion's the king of the jungle. So think of this group being about learning about the inner jungle of our minds and our hearts. To walk the path of mindfulness and transformation is to be the king or queen of our own inner jungles of the mind and heart. This will be the main underlying theme of this group: learning and practicing mindfulness, learning and practicing the lion mind.*

Step 2: Standard Definition of Mindfulness

After presenting the lion mind metaphor, follow up with the standard definition of mindfulness with the group. We define **mindfulness** as being aware of any mental, emotional, or physical phenomena in the present moment with an attitude of acceptance. You can also use Jon Kabat-Zinn's (1990) standard definition: paying attention, on purpose, in the present moment, with an attitude of nonjudgment. Make sure to also discuss the differences between mindfulness meditation and informal mindfulness. Use the talking points and example script below for presenting the standard definition of mindfulness.

Talking Points

- Present conventional mindfulness definition.
- Differentiate between formal mindfulness (meditation) and informal mindfulness (daily mindfulness).
- Use the weight-lifting metaphor.

Example Script

***Facilitator:** Okay, good. I'm glad you all understand the lion vs. dog mind metaphor. That metaphor exemplifies the practice of mindfulness, which, as we said, is what this whole program is about. I just want to give you a more standard definition so that you can think of it another way, if you like. Mindfulness is the practice of being present to your mental, emotional, and physical activity. So for example we all have thoughts, experience emotions, and feel sensations. Mindfulness is about being present to those experiences—not really judging or trying to avoid them, just being present to them and watching them, sort of like you watch a TV in a somewhat dis-identified manner. That's the practice of mindfulness. By practicing with our thoughts, emotions, and sensations like this, it gives us more choice, so we're not reactful to them. Now, there's a difference between mindfulness and meditation. Meditation is when you formally close your eyes and focus your awareness on a mental object, which we'll try out in a little bit. But you don't need to do all that to be mindful. You could be employing those concepts, being present to what arises in you without judgment, right now as you listen to these words come out of my mouth. That's called informal or daily mindfulness, it's where we can bring mindfulness into anything we do. Think of it like working out for your mind. When you go to the gym, you lift weights right? Oftentimes people do this to get strong. But when you do something that relies on strength, let's say picking up a box of books and carrying them to another room, you don't think, "let me lift some weights right now." You just pick up the box and carry it. So mindfulness meditation is like going to the gym and lifting weights, while informal mindfulness is like* *utilizing that strength in our daily activities, like moving boxes. Does this make sense? . . . Does anyone have any questions about this? . . .*

If anyone in the group has any questions about the definition of mindfulness, spend a few minutes in discussion prior to moving on to the next activity.

5. Meditation: Mindfulness of Deep Breathing

After defining mindfulness, facilitate the first formal meditation. This curriculum starts with mindfulness of deep breathing because it often provides youth with a here-and-now positive result of feeling calm and relaxed (Himelstein et al., 2014). This is a simple meditation and should be taught for 3–5 minutes. This exercise is composed of two steps: 1) mindfulness of deep breathing, and 2) processing the meditation.

Step 1: Mindfulness of Deep Breathing

Use the talking points and example script below as a guide to facilitating this meditation.

Talking Points

- Instruct the youth to sit in a comfortable position.
- Have the youth place one of their hands on their stomachs.
- Briefly educate them on the difference between a breath into the stomach and a breath into the chest.
- Invite the youth to close their eyes (but don't demand it).
- Instruct the youth in the mindfulness-of-deep-breathing exercise.
  - Keep awareness on breath
  - Focus on the breath filling up the stomach
  - Feel the stomach expand and contract with the hand
  - Whenever the mind wanders, bring it back to the stomach and breath

Example Script

Facilitator: *Okay, now it's time to practice some formal meditation. We've been talking about mindfulness all during the session and now we're going to formally practice it. This exercise is going to be short, only five minutes or so, and I'll guide you through it the whole way. I want to invite everyone to put one of their hands on their belly like this* **[place your hand on your belly]***. Does everyone know the difference between breathing into your belly and breathing into your chest? When you breathe into your belly you fill it up like this on the inhale* **[show example]***, and when you breathe into your chest you fill your chest up with air like this* **[show example]***. For this meditation, we're going to practice breathing into our bellies. Keep your hand on your belly for the whole meditation. It's good to sit in an upright position, so you can breathe naturally, and it's also good to close your eyes during meditation so you don't get distracted. However, if you don't feel comfortable closing your eyes, just keep them open and focused on the floor a couple feet in front of you. When I ring the bell, take a deep breath into your belly and a deep breath out and wait for further instructions.*

[Ring bell]

Breathing in, and breathing out . . . Take slow, deep breaths in, and take slow, deep breaths out . . . Feel your belly slowly filling up with air as you breathe in and slowly deflating as you breath out . . . If your mind starts to wander off, and think of something else other than the breath, just gently redirect it back to your breathing, taking slow and deep breaths in and slow and deep breaths out . . . This is the practice: just breathing in slow and deep, and breathing out slow and deep . . . Feel the movement of your belly with your hand . . . Breathing in deeply, and breathing out deeply . . . The breath is a like an anchor on a ship. Just as the anchor keeps the ship in place in the ocean, the breath anchors our awareness to our body, to this present moment. Breathing in deep, and breathing out deep . . . And if the mind wanders, again there's no need to get frustrated, or annoyed, or to think you're doing anything wrong. It's the nature of the mind to wander. Just gently redirect your mind back to your breathing, taking deep breaths in and deep breaths out . . . In a moment I'm going to ring the bell, and when I do I want to invite you to shift your awareness from your breathing to your ears and your hearing sense, and see if you can listen to the bell until you can't hear it any longer . . .

[Ring bell]

When you feel comfortable you can slowly open your eyes, and come out of the formal meditation, expanding your awareness from your inner world to encompass the rest of the group.

Step 2: Processing the Meditation

Once the meditation is complete process the experience for a few minutes, using the following discussion questions:

- What was it like for you during that meditation?
- How do you feel after it?
- Was it easy or hard? Why?
- Other questions?

During the above discussion present the idea that, as a group, you'll practice formally meditating for a longer period during each successive group session. That is, at every group session, you'll add an extra minute or two on until the last group, where you'll be meditating for approximately 15–20 minutes. Present this to the group and have them agree to it as the "meditation agreement" of the program.

IMPORTANT NOTE

Some groups will gravitate more toward formal meditation and others won't. If you feel it's appropriate to add more time to formal meditation earlier than this curriculum suggests, simply use your best judgment.

6. Group Poll: Learning Interests of the Youth

The final activity of the first session is to take a brief poll on what the youth may want to learn about during the course of the curriculum. It's a good way to get a pulse on where youth are in regard to the idea of recovery and drug use.

Simply ask youth in the group if there's anything they'd like to learn about or take away from the program. This could include learning the effects of a specific drug on the body, drug policies, or how to combat the urge to use drugs. We've heard everything from "I want to learn how to control my urge to use drugs," to "I want to know exactly what happens in my brain when I'm high off weed," to "I want to know more about why there's more people of color who get locked up for drug use." As the participants disclose what they'd like to learn, pay close attention, because this will influence your presentation of how drugs impact brain physiology during session 6.

Figure 4.1
Photo courtesy of MBA Project, reprinted with permission.

7. Homework and Close-Out

To finish the first group session, ask the group if anyone thinks they'd ever be comfortable teaching the meditation they have just learned. Prime the group with the idea that, at about half-way through the program, you want to start teaching them how to actually teach meditation, as a way to practice leadership but also so that they can develop skills that could be useful down the road. Encourage the youth to practice mindfulness of deep breathing at least 2–3 times before the next session. Thank the group for their participation and end the first session.

SESSION 1 HANDOUTS

Dealing With Definitions of Respect

When dealing with a youth's personal definition of respect that doesn't fall within the bounds of a therapeutic environment, it is extremely important to both honor the youth's definition and also to ask to alter it for the sake of the group. Consider the example below of (a real experience in one of our groups) a youth defining her personal definition of respect after other participants shared generally conventional definitions:

> **Youth Participant:** *For me, respect is about fear. I gain respect by showing you that I'm stronger, better, and not to be messed with. That's how you gain respect where I'm from. That's what respect is for me.*

What should you do when a group member responds like this? How do you honor her personal definition but circumvent the fact that that particular attitude of respect probably won't contribute to a therapeutic and trusting atmosphere? What's most important in a situation like this is to honor the youth's definition but then to ask if it is okay to alter the definition solely for the purposes of the group. The example below exemplifies this:

> **Youth Participant:** *For me, respect is about fear. I gain respect by showing you that I'm stronger, better, and not to be messed with. That's how you gain respect where I'm from. That's what respect is for me.*
> **Facilitator:** *It really seems like you learned that way of respect based on where you're from. Is that right?*
> **Youth Participant:** *Yeah, that's just how it is where I'm from.*
> **Facilitator:** *Yes, and it makes sense that you learned respect that way. I'm sure it would've been dangerous to think of it any other way.*
> **Youth Participant:** *Exactly. That's how you gotta survive where I'm from.*
> **Facilitator:** *Thanks so much for sharing that. It seems like you've been through a lot and that definition has served in your favor. One question I have for you is, is there any reason that you feel the need to employ that definition in this circle, with the particular youth right here and now?*
> **Youth Participant:** *What do you mean?*
> **Facilitator:** *Well, do you feel like you need to show that you're stronger and not to be messed with right here with us in this circle?*
> **Youth Participant:** *Well, I don't know. No not really, I guess that's just what I'm used to thinking.*
> **Facilitator:** *Yes, of course. That makes a lot of sense. And I want to be clear in that I'm not asking you to forget about your personal definition of respect; it has obviously served a necessary role for you. What I am wondering is for this 1.5 hours, just once a week, would you be willing to alter your definition, again just for this short time, to one that is more conducive to a therapeutic group like this? (NOTE: I would at this point summarize some of the other definitions from other youth.)*
> **Youth Participant:** *Yeah, I didn't think about it like that. I'll give it a try, for sure.*

What transpired in the above transcript was an interaction we had with one of our group members that turned out to be very therapeutic for her and the group. We defined respect, honored the definition she grew up with, and then asked to simply alter it ONLY for the purpose and time frame of the group. This was very feasible for her and made for the start of a relationally corrective experience (in that she was starting to learn new models of respect).

Group Agreements

I, _____ agree to the following practices while participating in this program:

- Respect

- One Mic (not to talk while others are talking)

- Skillful Speech

- Skillful Listening

- Authenticity

- Nonviolence (both physical and verbal)

- To refocus when asked to

- Other group-developed agreement: _____

Name (Print): _____

Signature: _____

Date: _____

Mindfulness of Deep Breathing Script

Example Script

Facilitator: *Okay, now it's time to practice some formal meditation. We've been talking about mindfulness all during the group session, and now we're going to formally practice it. This exercise is going to be short, only five minutes or so, and I'll guide you through it the whole way. I want to invite everyone to put one of their hands on their belly like this* **[place your hand on your belly]**. *Does everyone know the difference between breathing into your belly and breathing into your chest? When you breathe into your belly you fill it up like this on the inhale* **[show example]**, *and when you breathe into your chest you fill your chest up with air like this* **[show example]**. *For this meditation, we're going to practice breathing into our bellies. Keep your hand on your belly for the whole meditation. It's good to sit in an upright position, so you can breathe naturally, and it's also good to close your eyes during meditation so you don't get distracted. However, if you don't feel comfortable closing your eyes, just keep them open and focused on the floor a couple feet in front of you. When I ring the bell, take a deep breath into your belly and a deep breath out and wait for further instructions.*

[Ring bell]

Breathing in, and breathing out . . . Take slow, deep breaths in, and take slow, deep breaths out . . . Feel your belly slowly filling up with air as you breathe in, and slowly deflating as you breathe out . . . If your mind starts to wander off, and think of something else other than the breath, just gently redirect it back to your breathing, taking slow and deep breaths in and slow and deep breaths out . . . This is the practice, just breathing in slow and deep, and breathing out slow and deep . . . Feel the movement of your belly with your hand . . . Breathing in deep, and breathing out deep . . . The breath is a like an anchor on a ship. Just as the anchor keeps the ship in place in the ocean, the breath anchors our awareness to our body, to this present moment. Breathing in deeply, and breathing out deeply . . . And if the mind wanders, again there's no need to get frustrated, or annoyed, or to think you're doing anything wrong. It's the nature of the mind to wander. Just gently redirect your mind back to your breathing, taking deep breaths in and deep breaths out . . . In a moment I'm going to ring the bell, and when I do I want to invite you to shift your awareness from your breathing to your ears and your hearing sense, and see if you can listen to the bell until you can't hear it any longer . . .

[Ring bell]

When you feel comfortable you can slowly open your eyes, and come out of the formal meditation, expanding your awareness from your inner world to encompass the rest of the group.

Session 1 References

Himelstein, S., Saul, S., Garcia-Romeu, A., & Pinedo, D. (2014). Mindfulness training as an intervention for substance-user incarcerated adolescents: A pilot grounded theory study. *Substance Use and Misuse, 49,* 560–570.

Kabat-Zinn, J. (1990). *Full catastrophe living: Using the wisdom of your body and mind to face stress, pain, and illness.* New York, NY: Dell.

Kabat-Zinn, J. (2013). *Full catastrophe living: Using the wisdom of your body and mind to face stress, pain, and illness* (rev. ed.). New York: NY: Bantam Books.

Rosenberg, L. (1998). *Breath by breath: The liberating practice of insight meditation.* Boston, MA: Shambhala.

MINDFULNESS OF DRUGS AND THEIR HEALTH EFFECTS

Session Summary

Session 2 focuses on awareness of major drug categories, specific drugs, and their health effects. Youth will learn about the major substance categories (i.e., stimulants, depressants, opioids, etc.), their physiological effects on the brain and body, and fatal drug combinations. This information will be presented via innovative activities and discussion. A new informal mindfulness activity will be presented and formal meditation will be practiced.

Materials Needed

- Meditation bell
- Session 2 Handout (optional)
- Sticky notes
- Markers
- Board/wall for sticky notes

Formal Meditation (Time)

- Mindfulness of Deep Breathing (5–7 minutes)

Learning Objectives

- Define major drug categories
- Review general psychological effects of major drug categories
- Discuss fatal drug combinations
- Practice mindfulness of deep breathing

Session Agenda (Chair Configuration)

1. Centering Meditation (Circle)
2. Mindful Check-In (Circle)
3. Drug Classifications Activity (Semicircle)
4. Fatal Drug Combinations (Semicircle)
5. Mindfulness of Deep Breathing (Circle)
6. Homework and Close-Out (Circle)

1. Centering Meditation

Beginning with the second session, each group session will begin with a brief, introductory centering meditation. It is best to use the meditation that was taught and practiced in the previous session, for continuity purposes. Use a truncated version of the "mindfulness of deep breathing" meditation script from the previous module. This centering meditation should be 1–3 minutes in length.

2. Mindful Check-In

The mindful check-in is a modified check-in in which participants first take a deep breath before disclosing how they feel in the present moment. The exercise encourages participants to actually think about how they're feeling prior to checking in and, thus, facilitates informal mindfulness. Participants are encouraged to stay away from using nondescriptive words such as "cool," "fine," and "okay," and this activity gets the youths' voices in the circle. In this initial presentation of the mindful check-in, there are two steps: 1) the mindful check-in, and 2) the processing of the deep breath.

Step 1: The Mindful Check-In

Use the talking points and example script below as a guide to facilitating the mindful check-in.

Talking Points

- Instruct the group as to what a general check-in is.
- Distinguish a mindful check-in by discussing the taking of a deep breath and checking in about the present moment.
- Emphasize that you'll process the meaning of the deep breath after everyone has checked in.
- State that youth should avoid words like "cool," "fine," and other nondescriptive words.

Example Script

Facilitator: Who knows what a check-in is?. . Right! It's when you talk about how you're feeling or what's going on with you. Remember, when you check-in, you can speak about your thoughts, what you're thinking about, your feelings, the emotions you are having, or your physical state of being, your sensations. What's different about this type of check-in, the mindful check-in, is that I ask that, prior to checking in, you take a deep breath in and let a deep breath out. Then, check in about any of those three above categories, but keep it in the present moment. Once everyone's finished we'll discuss the meaning and purpose of taking the deep breath. Also, try to avoid words such as "cool," "fine," "okay," and other nondescriptive words. Choose words that really describe how you feel. Does that make sense to everyone? . . . I'll go first and model what I'm talking about.

As the facilitator, model the mindful check-in and then have the youth to the left or right of you go next and continue around the circle until everyone has mindfully checked in.

Step 2: Processing the Deep Breath

Use the following talking points and example script as a guide to processing the significance of the deep breath.

Talking Points

- Ask, "What do you think the purpose of taking that deep breath was?" to start the discussion.
- Guide the discussion toward 3 major purposes for the deep breath: 1) the breath enables one to pause and become aware of one's experience, 2) the breath calms one down mentally, and 3) the breath calms the body down physiologically and activates stress-relieving endorphins.
- The mindful check-in is a way to practice informal mindfulness.

Example Script

Facilitator: Who can tell me why the deep breath is important? . . . That's right! When we take a deep breath, it gives us a little time to figure out how we're actually feeling in this moment. Remember, that's what mindfulness is about: knowing our experience right now. You all know how it is, someone asks us how we're doing and we often say "cool". . . "good" or whatever. But we don't often actually check in with how we really feel. That's what that deep breath is for—to give us time to really be aware of what's going on with us. What else? . . . Yes. The other piece to the deep breath is that is has a calming effect to it. Sometimes our minds have a lot going on, and it's always okay to just say that in a check-in, but, when you calm the mind for an instant, it can give you the time you need to verbalize what's going on with you. And, on top of that, taking a deep breath activates a stress-reducing system in your body called the parasympathetic nervous system. When you take the deep breath, this system activates the relaxation response, and that's why sometimes, when you breathe deeply for a while, you feel relaxed and less stressed out. All of these steps help us to really check in—in the present moment. We're going to be doing some form of this mindful check-in in every group. It's a way to practice mindfulness without having to close our eyes or perform formal meditation.

WHAT IF?

The first or second volunteer doesn't take the deep breath or just checks in with "cool" or "good," etc.? Whenever a group member doesn't follow the instructions of the activity, it's important to remember that it's okay to remind him or her of the correct protocol. You don't want to stop everyone every time if they don't take the breath (choose your battles wisely), but if the first or second participant doesn't take the breath or checks in vaguely, simply remind him or her gently of the instruction and ask to try again. The first and second volunteers are the tone-setters. If you don't catch this early on, you will have potentially gone through a whole mindful check-in without anyone taking the deep breath.

IMPORTANT NOTE

The mindful check-in is a great skill for youth to learn. It gives them the ability to mindfully check in without having to do any elaborate meditations. Besides teaching it as a great tool, we often use it as an assessment for how well the group can perform the mindful check-in without much prompting. This assessment will occur in group 6, on which occasion you won't give the youth the full instruction of the mindful check-in, but will simply say, "let's check in." If the better half of the group goes on to take the breath and do the mindful check-in as originally instructed, the technique is being internalized, and, if not, simply provide the full instructions.

3. Drug Classifications Activity

The drug classifications activity (and the following fatal drug combinations activity) spans the majority of the second session. This activity is designed to teach youth about the major drug categories and their physiological effects and is standard in drug treatment with youth. However, oftentimes this information is disseminated purely didactically, and we have found instead that it is important for youth to be engaged in the learning process.

There are three major steps to this activity: 1) the brainstorming of specific drugs that can be abused, 2) education of the major drug categories and their physiological effects, and 3) the friendly group competition of matching the specific drugs to the correct categories.

Step 1: Brainstorming Session

Immediately following the mindful check-in, have the youth rearrange the circle into a semicircle so they are oriented toward the wall or board on which you'll paste your sticky notes. State to the group that this session is about learning the many different drugs and their major categories and that you're going to start with brainstorming a number of different drugs and posting them on the wall or board. Use the talking points and example script below as a guide.

Talking Points

- State that this activity is about brainstorming different types of drugs.
- Restate that this isn't a "scared straight" activity.
- Instruct the youth to call out drugs they have done personally or know of.

Example Script

> ***Facilitator:*** *Today we're going to talk about drugs. We're going to talk about the specific drugs that make up the major drug categories and how they affect our bodies.* **Remember, our role here isn't to try and tell you not to do drugs! So, we're not doing this to try to scare you out of using drugs—we know that won't work anyway. Over the years, group members have just asked us about these types of things and reinforced this part of the curriculum, saying it was helpful for them.** *The first thing we're going to do is brainstorm as many drugs as we can think of. Each drug someone shouts out I will write on this sticky note and post it to the wall, okay? I want you to shout out drugs that you know of. They can be drugs that you've personally done, or drugs that you haven't done yourself but know of. Also, just because someone shouts out a drug doesn't mean that individual has done it personally, so let's leave those judgments out, okay? Who wants to start?*

You can either have the youth shout out drugs popcorn style or have them raise their hands. It may be better to have them raise their hands if you don't have a cofacilitator, so that you don't find yourself trying to write on the sticky notes too rapidly. If you have a cofacilitator, both of you can stand up and write the drugs on the sticky notes, which is slightly more conducive to participation that is not chaotic than is having youth call out drugs popcorn style. Use your best discernment here.

As the youth start naming drugs, make sure to stick the sticky notes on the wall or board in one smaller cluster so that they are visible to all youth. We usually stick them to the right of the board (where the major categories will be presented). The goal is to have a large collection of different drug names on the board with which to fill all major drug categories during the next activity.

If it seems as if there's a good amount missing from the wall, challenge the youth and guide them toward recalling different types of drugs. Also, make sure that not only traditional street drugs (e.g.,

Figure 5.1

marijuana, alcohol, cocaine, crack, heroine, etc.) are represented but that prescription drugs are named as well (Xanax, Oxy, etc.). Figure 5.2 represents a typical list we usually develop from the group that includes both prescription and nonprescription drugs:

• Marijuana	• Triple Cs
• Alcohol	• Promethazine and Codeine (Bo, Lean)
• Cocaine	• Cigarettes
• Crack Cocaine	• Salvia
• Ecstasy	• Mushrooms
• Methamphetamine (Crystal Meth)	• Acid
• Heroin	• Spice
• OxyContin	• Opium
• Valium	• Methadone
• Xanax	• Hash
• Peyote	• PCP

Figure 5.2

You don't need to have every drug ever named on the list; it's just important to have most of them, as above, so that the next two phases of this activity can be done effectively.

Step 2: Major Drug Category Education

Once you have enough sticky notes placed on the wall, the next step of this activity is to educate the group about the major categories those specific drugs comprise and their general physiological effects, which, in this curriculum, include the following:

- **Stimulants:** Also known as *uppers*, they stimulate the central nervous system, and one main physiological effect is an increased heart rate.
- **Depressants:** Also known as *downers*, they depress the central nervous system, and a main effect is a decreased heart rate.
- **Cannabinoids:** In their own category now, they were once classified with hallucinogens, and they can both stimulate and depress the central nervous system (increase and decrease heart rate).
- **Hallucinogens:** Oftentimes hallucinogens provide some form of extrasensory experience, even if subtle.
- **Opioids:** These are like very strong depressants, depressing the central nervous system, and are also used to reduce pain.
- **Other:** It is necessary to have this category, since some drugs that youth shout out will inevitably not fit into the above major categories (e.g., steroids, paint huffing, etc.).

See this session's handout, "Major Drug Categories," for the option of printing and distributing copies to the youth after this activity is finished.

To start this activity, place sticky notes with the names of each category from the above list across the wall/board in a row.

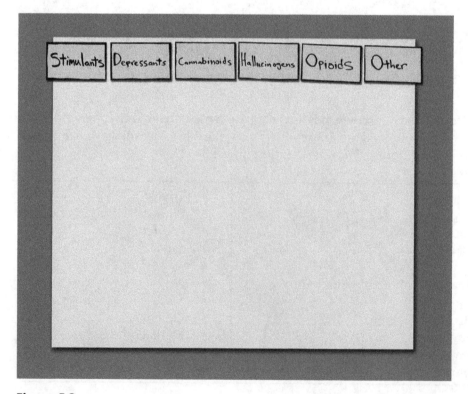

Figure 5.3

Begin by educating the group about the different major categories from the farthest left category to the farthest right. Use the talking points and example script below to facilitate this activity.

Talking Points

- State that you're going to educate the group about the major categories.
- Review each of the major categories.

Example Script

> **Facilitator:** *Okay, now we're going to learn about the major drug categories that all these drugs* **[point to the cluster of drugs]** *comprise. We're going to start with this one over here on the left. Stimulants. Has anyone in the group ever heard this term? . . . Right. "Uppers" is a term that's often used for this category. Does anyone know what happens in the body when you've taken a stimulant? . . . Right. Stimulants can do a lot of things to your body, and different drugs act slightly differently, but the major, general effect they all have is to stimulate your central nervous system and increase your heart rate. That's one of the reasons why people get so amped up when they're on stimulants. Just remember, stimulants, or "uppers," make your heart rate go up.*

Proceed to each category in the same fashion as above, and, when you're finished with them all, provide a brief summary before introducing the next activity.

IMPORTANT NOTE

Make sure you have a one-liner for each major category, as we did above, e.g.: "Just remember, uppers make your heart rate go up." This simplicity will help for information retention.

Step 3: Drug-Matching Competition

After you've reviewed the major drug categories and their general physiological effects, it's time to split the group into two teams and have them each attempt to match all the specific drugs written on the sticky notes to the major drug categories. This competition usually gets the energy of the group going pretty well and is a way to engage the group in a fun activity while also educating them about the correct alignment of specific drugs to their major categories. The basic premise of this activity is that you'll split the group into two, flip a coin to which group goes first, and then have that team attempt to put all the specific drugs written on sticky notes in the correct major drug category column. Have each group assign one "representative" to go up to the board/poster paper and actually place the sticky notes in the columns. Instruct the group that only one of them can be up there at a time, but that group members who are sitting down can help their representative. Give the teams approximately 4–5 minutes to complete the activity and time them (this makes it more like a competition and more fun). After the first group has finished, tally the amount of correct and incorrect matches. Do NOT disclose the number at this time. Next, place all the sticky notes back to the side in a cluster.

Repeat this whole process with the second team. Once the second team is finished, tally the amount of correct and incorrect matches, and in dramatic fashion, announce the winning team. Sometimes we have told the teams that the winning team could pick a snack for the facilitators to bring to the next session, as an incentive. Use your best discretion.

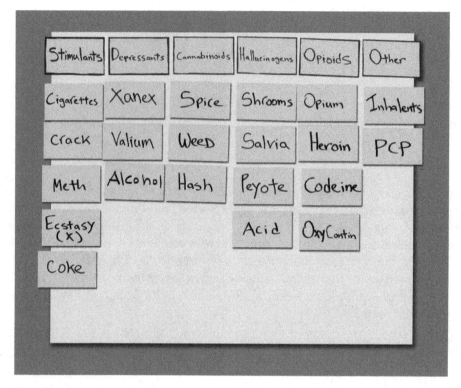

Figure 5.4

Correcting the board. After you've announced the winner, correct the incorrect matches on the board so the youth get accurate information regarding the correct matches. As the facilitator, go to the board and remove only the incorrect matches, putting them back to the side.

Then, one-by-one, review each one of the specific drugs that was incorrectly placed, asking the youth what they know about the drug and, based on either their personal experiences or experiences of people they've known, what category it should be a part of. If they don't know, you can disclose the answer; just make sure to explain the drug's general physiological effect when doing so.

4. Fatal Drug Combinations

The major message during this discussion/activity is that *too much of one drug category is not a good thing*. We usually start by asking the group, "What happens when you use one depressant with another depressant? What's the effect of that on your heart rate and central nervous system?" The basic message is that, when pairing depressants with depressants there is a higher risk for the central nervous system to slow down to the point where it's difficult for the person to breathe, and, when pairing stimulants with stimulants, there is a greater risk of heart attack.

Prior to starting this next activity, check the time. The next activity is this group's formal meditation and is important to balance with the drug education. If there are less than 30 minutes left you can simply ask the question, "Who knows which drugs become fatal when mixed with each other?" and have a discussion in which you educate the youth about the topic. If there are 30–45 minutes left in the group session, you can re-activate the two teams and ask them to place specific drugs in pairings that would be fatal and score the two teams in another competitive round. If you opt to pair the groups back up for another competitive round, educate the group about the different fatal effects only after both teams have participated. Whether you opt for the competitive round or proceed directly with discussion, use the discussion questions (and their corresponding answers) below as a guide to presenting the information on fatal drug combinations.

Discussion Questions

- What are some drugs that, when used in combination, lead to greater risk of overdose and death? (Too many different ones all belonging to one major category)
- What is the effect of having two depressants in your system? (Greater risk to CNS shutting down and heart/breathing stopping)
- What is the effect of pairing alcohol (a depressant) with an opioid? (Same as above, but usually a stronger chance)
- What is the effect of pairing two stimulants in your system? (Greater risk of heart attack)

WHAT IF?

A youth states to the group that s/he's done all those drug combinations and has never been harmed? This is actually not uncommon. We suggest educating the group that their intake pairing of contraindicated drugs doesn't automatically mean they're going to die. It means that the risk heightens and there is a greater chance. The risk for death occurs when mixing drugs excessively and/or consuming large quantities of each drug.

5. Meditation: Mindfulness of Deep Breathing

Facilitate "mindfulness of deep breathing" exercise from session 1. Consult session 1 for an example script. Remember to practice facilitating this meditation to develop your teaching skills.

6. Homework and Close-Out

Encourage the youth to reflect on the different drugs and their physiological effects that were reviewed in today's session. Invite the youth to practice the mindfulness of deep breathing at least four times between now and the next session. Remember to ask once again who might be willing to facilitate a meditation during session 6 and take note of who volunteers, if any. **If you facilitate alone, ask a volunteer to assist you in the opening role play of session 3.**

SESSION 2 HANDOUT

Major Drug Categories

- **Stimulants:** Also known as *uppers*, they stimulate the central nervous system, and one main physiological effect is an increased heart rate.

- **Depressants:** Also known as "downers," they depress the central nervous system, and a main effect is a decreased heart rate.

- **Cannabinoids:** In their own category now, they were once classified with hallucinogens, and they can both stimulate and depress the central nervous system (increase and decrease heart rate).

- **Hallucinogens:** Oftentimes hallucinogens provide some form of extra-sensory experience, even if subtle.

- **Opioids:** These are like very strong depressants, depressing the central nervous system, and are also used to reduce pain.

- **Other:** It is necessary to have this category, since some drugs that youth shout out will inevitably not fit into the above major categories (i.e., steroids, paint huffing, etc.).

SESSION 3

REACTING VS. RESPONDING

Session Summary

The third session begins with two facilitators (or a facilitator and a youth) performing a role-play scene exemplifying mental versus physical power and reactions versus responses. The overarching objective of this session is that youth learn and practice tangible techniques that can improve mindful decision-making. Session 3 alternates with the regular group format by starting with a role-play by the facilitators rather than a centering meditation and mindful check-in. This session incorporates mindfulness of the breath as taught traditionally and a cognitive acronym that facilitates informal mindfulness.

Materials Needed

- Meditation bell
- Session 3 Handouts (Optional)

Formal Meditation (Time)

- Mindfulness of the Breath (5–7 minutes)

Learning Objectives

- Define the difference between reactions and responses
- Discuss the relationship between cause and effect with regard to emotions and behaviors
- To practice and demonstrate proficiency in the STIC technique (informal mindfulness acronym)
- To demonstrate proficiency in mindfulness-of-the-breath meditation

Session Agenda (Chair Configuration)

1. Role Play: Mental vs. Physical Power (Semicircle)
2. Discussion: Reactions vs. Responses (Semicircle)
3. STIC Contemplation (Circle)
4. STIC Role Plays (Semicircle)
5. Meditation: Mindfulness of the Breath (Circle)
6. Mindful Check-In (Circle)
7. Homework and Close-Out (Circle)

1. Role Play: Mental vs. Physical Power

Before the youth enter the room, arrange the chairs in a half circle as if placed around a stage. After greeting the youth as they enter the space, explain that you and your facilitator (or another youth if you facilitate alone) are going to perform a role-play.

NOTE

Remember to think ahead about session 3, if you facilitate alone. At the end of the second session, you were to have asked a youth to volunteer to be your partner in the role play. You must now meet with him or her for a few minutes prior to the third session to explain and practice the role-play.

The role-play exemplifies mental versus physical power and has 4 steps: 1) presenting the initial skit, 2) processing the skit and developing its plot, 3) presenting the second skit, and 4) processing of the second skit.

Step 1: Initial Skit

The initial skit involves you (the facilitator as actor) walking on the sidewalk and passing by another person (your cofacilitator or youth volunteer) walking toward you on the same sidewalk. When your cofacilitator passes by, s/he verbally insults you, which prompts an automatic violent reaction in which you punch him or her (acting this out, of course). The idea is to get the group to contemplate who in that situation had more power and to define the differences between mental and physical power. While the "puncher" has physical power, the person who insulted the puncher has mental power by being able to prompt such a reaction. Prior to starting the skit, make sure that you prompt the youth for the skit by asking them to contemplate one main question: "Who has more power in this situation?" Use the talking points and example script below to set the stage for the exercise.

Talking Points

- State that you're about to perform a skit.
- Ask youth to contemplate who has more power in the situation.
- Describe the scene of the skit.

Example Script

> **Facilitator:** *Today's a little bit different. Instead of starting with a centering meditation and mindful-check-in, we're going to start with a role-play and skit. This skit involves me walking down the sidewalk, and my partner right here is walking down the same sidewalk toward me. That's all you need to know for now. The main thing we want you to do is contemplate, Who has more power? in this situation. Everyone got that? . . . Good. We need someone to yell, "Action!"*

Have one youth yell, "Action!" and slap together her or his hands as if s/he were a movie director, and then perform the skit in its entirety.

Step 2: Process Initial Skit

Immediately following the skit performance, pose the question to the group: "Who had more power in that situation?" Make sure to ask every group member. In our experience most youth (both men and women) will suggest that the person who punched the other had more power. Sometimes however, a youth will suggest that the person who got punched had more power because s/he manipulated the other person. This is actually the underlying point of the skit—that the person who got punched manipulated the puncher, but that isn't unveiled until after the second skit.

After you've processed the skit and asked the youth their opinions of who had more power in that situation, state to the group that you're going to re-perform the role-play but that, before doing so you are going to unpack the plot and context of the situation a bit more (basically, giving the group more information to judge who had more power in the situation). Use the talking points and example script below as a guide.

Talking Points

- Your character has just been released from prison and has two strikes.
- The other character knows that, if you hit him/her and get caught, you'll go back to prison for many years.
- The other character can see from his/her vantage point that there are police in a coffee shop that have a clear view of you both.

Example Script

Facilitator: *So let's return to the beginning of this story. Last time, I just walked down the street, this guy called me a bitch, and I hit him real fast. This time, I want to give you a little of the backstory of my character. I actually just got out of the pen. I was down for 10 years on my second strike. The person who's walking toward me on the same side of the street I've known my whole life. He doesn't really like me because I used to take all his drug business on the block. He knows I have two strikes and that, if he can get me to hit him, I'll go right back to the pen. He also knows that there are two police officers at the corner coffee shop behind me that I can't see, and that can see us both in clear view. He wants me off the block and back in the pen because he's got business plans and they don't involve me.*

NOTE

This story is geared mostly toward youth who are either incarcerated or youth who come from low-income communities where incarceration and drugs are prominent. Feel free to alter the story to meet the needs of your community.

Step 3: Second Skit

After explaining the backstory of the characters, perform the skit again physically, acting out the scene just as it was acted out in the initial skit (see above). Have another youth yell *Action!* and perform the role-play once more, virtually acting out the same scene as done in the initial skit.

Step 4: Processing of Second Skit

Once you've completed the second role-play ask the group, "Who had more power in that situation?" Oftentimes, the youth will consider the person who got punched to have more power after the plot is developed and more context is offered. Sometimes the group will be split as to who actually has the power. They might say, *"You have the physical power, but he has the mental power because he made you hit him and knew you were going back to jail."* You don't need to shy away from the fact that the assaulter does have physical power; however, the objective of the role-play is to exemplify the relationship between choicefulness and mental power. Wrap up the role-play by discussing the differences between mental and physical power and the complementary nature of mental power and choicefulness. Use the talking points and example script below as a guide.

Talking Points

- There is a difference between physical and mental power.
- One character had physical power, and the other mental power.
- True mental power comes from the ability to choose.

Example Script

Facilitator: Okay, so now after this second skit, who had more power? . . . Yes, the puncher did have physical power. But the one who got punched had the mental power, because he knew what buttons to press in me. He didn't want me around messing up his drug business, did he? So what did he do? He planned to entrap me and get me locked up again. He saw those two police officers in the cafe on the corner behind me. I couldn't see them. What did the police officers see? . . . Right. They just saw me punch him. That's it. They didn't hear what he said to me. So I'd be the one that gets arrested—all because this person knew what buttons to press in me, he knew how to control me mentally, and, in that sense, he had more power. Mental power and physical power both play different roles in our lives, but mental power is what we're going to focus on in this group today. Mental power has the potential to keep you out of jail, keep you from using drugs, and contribute to your being happy in life. And does anyone here know how I, the puncher, in that case could've retained my mental power instead of giving it all to him? . . . Yes. I could've chosen not to punch him! But that takes a lot of will power, and that's why it's called mental power. Because I really want to punch him, but, if I do, I know I could go back to jail. So it takes mental power to walk away from the insult. True mental power comes from the ability to choose a response rather than blindly reacting to situations, and that's the underlying theme of this whole program.

2. Discussion: Reaction vs. Response

Next, lead a discussion on the differences between a reaction and response. We define a **reaction** as blindly and immediately acting because of an internal or external stimulus (e.g., immediately punching someone who's insulted you without any forethought regarding the punch). We define a **response** as taking time to process the stimulus and *choosing* how to respond. This discussion is comprised of 1) defining the differences between reactions and responses and 2) presenting the copy machine metaphor.

Step 1: Defining Reacting and Responding

Start this discussion by asking the group what they think the differences between reactions and responses are. Use the talking points and example script as a guide to facilitating this discussion.

Talking Points

- Ask the question, "Who knows the difference between a reaction and a response?"
- Guide the discussion toward the above definitions of reactions verses responses.

Example Script

Facilitator: Who knows what the difference between a reaction and a response is? . . . Yes. A reaction is when you just react without thinking—like when I was walking down the street in the role-play, I got called a bad name and just hit the other guy. That's a reaction. A response is when there is time and space in between the stimulus—the thing that happens and causes us to react—and the behavioral action I choose and do. I have time to choose whether it's a good idea to hit the other guy. I have time to think about how I could go back to jail on my third strike. That's a response. A simpler way to think about it is, when you react, you don't think at all. When you respond, you think about what you're about to do. Do these definitions make sense to everyone? . . . That's what we're going to learn how to do today. We're going to teach you a technique that's easy to remember and going to help you stay out of trouble and have the ability to not simply do drugs without thinking about the consequences.

Step 2: The Copy Machine Metaphor

After defining reactions and responses, proceed with presenting the copy machine metaphor to solidify the youths' understanding. The copy machine metaphor is understood in this way: when one presses "copy" on the copy machine, it simply copies whatever document is in its feeder. When one is in a reactive mode, one acts like a copy machine. Once the button that is a trigger for a person is pushed, s/he simply acts out a certain unconsidered behavior. In the case of the role-play above, if one insults me (pushes my button) then, without thought, I react with violence. It followed then, that the person who insulted me in the example above held all the power; he knew how to push my button. This is another way to convey the differences between reactions and responses and the role mental power has in both. Use the talking points and example script below to guide this presentation.

Talking Points

- Ask, "Who knows how a copy machine works?"
- State that, as a machine, the copy machine only reacts. When its button is pushed, it behaves the same way, every time. It makes a copy.
- Relate the metaphor to the initial skit above.

Example Script

Facilitator: Anyone here know how a copy machine works? . . . It's simple. All of I have to do is put in whatever I want copied and push a button, and the copy comes out the other side. A copy machine doesn't think, "Oh I need to make this copy." It simply makes the copy without thinking. So, when I'm in a reactive mode, as in the last skit where I punched my partner, I'm acting like a copy machine: my button gets pushed by his insulting me, and I don't think, I just react, and, as we said above, that gives the other person all the mental power. He simply came up to me, pushed my button, and got the result he intended to have. He controlled me just as easily as someone can make copies on a copy machine. This is just another way to think of the differences between reacting and responding. Just remember to ask yourself, "How much control do I want to give this person who's antagonizing me? How much control do I want to give to drugs? How many copies of what got me into trouble do I want to make?"

Field any questions or comments from the youth about this metaphor and/or anything related to reacting versus responding.

3. STIC Contemplation

After concluding the discussion on reaction vs. response, have the youth rearrange their chairs into circle. The next activity involves teaching the group a cognitive acronym/informal mindfulness technique. Our acronym in this curriculum is: **STIC** (Stop, Take a breath, Imagine the future consequences, Choose); pronounced, "stick." The STIC Contemplation involves guiding the youth through a meditative contemplation within which they enact the STIC technique. For the purposes of this curriculum, guide the group through a scenario in which they are being offered drugs. Use the talking points and example script below as a guide.

Talking Points

- Tell the group members that you're going to teach them how to respond instead of react.
- Explain the STIC acronym: S = stop, T = take a breath, I = imagine the future consequences, and C = choose.
- When guiding the contemplation, remember to be descriptive.
- Explicitly have the youth recall times when they have been offered drugs.

Example Script

Facilitator: Okay, right now we're going to teach you this technique that will really help you to respond to your situations instead of reacting to them. It could keep you out of trouble and could even save your life. Does everyone know what an acronym is? It's when you take a number of words and just say the first letter of each word to remember it more easily. You all know of the CIA, right? It stands for Central Intelligence Agency, but most of the time we just say CIA because it's easier to say and remember. That's what the STIC acronym is: S, T, I, C. It stands for Stop, Take a breath, Imagine the future, and Choose. And we're going to take you through a contemplation in which someone is offering you drugs and you use this technique to respond, rather than reacting to the situation and thus making another copy of your conditioned behaviors. Everyone okay with that? . . . Get in a comfortable position. Keep your feet flat on the ground and close your eyes. This will help you to imagine better. But if you don't feel comfortable closing your eyes, that's fine. Just put your gaze on the floor toward a spot a few feet in front of you.

[Ring bell]

What I want you to do is begin to imagine the main person you do drugs and/or alcohol with. Who is it? Is it just one person or many friends? Or maybe it's just you. Now think of the place where you normally use. It might be in your backyard, at the park, or just on the block. What I want you to imagine is that your friend offers you to use your drug of choice; whether that be weed, cocaine, alcohol, or whatever. Then, before you respond to your friend, I want you to go through what's called the STIC technique. First, stop. That's what the S stands for. Then, take a breath. That's what the T stands for. And really take a breath right now in this moment, don't just imagine it. Then, imagine the future consequences. That's the I. Actually think about what the future consequences might be: you might get caught smoking, you might not, you may go to juvenile hall, etc. . . . After this, weigh the pros and cons of using. Is it worth it? Is it worth getting in trouble with your parents? Getting kicked out of school? Going to jail? Finally, choose. That's the C. Remember, we're not here to tell you how to live your life. If you want to use the drug, that's your choice. Just consciously choose instead of reacting. Imagine yourself making the choice. What happens next? Just notice . . . In a few moments, I'm going to ring this bell, and, when I do, I want you to slowly shift your awareness back to the present moment and open your eyes.

[Ring bell]

After finishing the contemplation, lead a short discussion using the following guiding questions:

- How was that contemplation? Could you visualize yourself there?
- How many of you went through the contemplation and still used the drugs in your mental scenario? How many didn't?
- Were you able to really imagine potential consequences of your actions? If so, was that hard? If not, what do you think got in the way?
- Do you think you could use this technique in real life? Why or why not?
- What real life situations could this be applied to in your life?
- What situations does STIC not apply to?

IMPORTANT NOTE

In our experience it's imperative to discuss the situations in which STIC doesn't apply. For example, if someone is attacking you, you shouldn't close your eyes and engage in STIC. The youth will have less faith in the technique if you present it as a silver bullet that works all the time. Be honest about where it can be applied and the youth are less likely to write it off.

Remembering STIC

After you've all been honest about applicable situations, begin to suggest some easy ways to remember the STIC acronym. Use the talking points and example script below as a guide.

Talking Points

- There's no use in an acronym if you can't remember to use it.
- Use the mnemonic device to suggest that the youth *STIC to their plan.*
- *STIC to your family.*
- Brainstorm other ways to prime memory.
- STIC is a place holder for deeper self-awareness and mindfulness.
- Practice STIC and you'll have a better chance of using it when it's needed.

Example Script

Facilitator: STIC is an acronym so that all you have to remember is STIC. Then you'll remember what it stands for: stop, take a breath, imagine the future, and choose. But, if you can't remember the acronym in one of those situations we talked about, STIC will be almost useless. For you to remember STIC in times when it's needed, what do you think you can do? **[Try and get the youth to think of their own ideas, then suggest some of your own.]** *We make plans when we come to a program like this, right? . . . Whether it's just getting through this program, or quitting drugs for good, or going to college and getting a high-paying job—at some point all of us come up with a plan when we come to counseling programs like this. And I'm sure that, if you've set a plan, you'd like to succeed in it, right? . . . So* **STIC** *to your plan. Every time you find yourself in a situation in which you might stray from your goal, like when you're in a situation that suggests to you to react—to use drugs, get in a fight, whatever, you can think of how to* **STIC** *to that plan. When you prime yourself to think of STIC, you're much more likely to use it. Or maybe you don't want to disappoint your mother any longer and want to be a good role model for your younger brother or sister. So, in that case,* **STIC** *to your family. There are many ways you can teach yourself to remember STIC. What are some other ways? At the end of this group session, we're going to hand out some business cards to everyone on which is the acronym STIC and what it stands for, but it's still good to think of as many situations as you can with which to practice visualizing yourself using STIC instead of instantly pushing the button to make a copy of former behavior. Anyone have any other ideas?*

[Have the youth brainstorm.]

One last thing. The whole point of this STIC technique is not for you to do this all the time in every situation that could elicit a reaction from you. It's just a placeholder until you develop enough mindfulness and self-awareness and can naturally pause and weigh the consequences before responding. Remember how we said a big part of this course is to learn mindfulness and become more self-aware? STIC helps us to get that process started. So before you go to sleep each night, think of a situation where you usually might react and visualize yourself doing the STIC technique. Go through all the steps. Practice at least once a day, and the next time we meet we'll talk more about it. If you at least remind yourself every day what STIC stands for, there's a much greater likelihood that you'll use it when the time comes. If you actually practice and visualize situations in which it could be used, as we just said, you'll have even more of a chance to use the technique when it's needed. Does this make sense to everyone? . . . We'll give you those business cards at the end of the session to take with you. Put them in your wallet or purse and keep them handy.

NOTE

Go to the end of this session's chapter for STIC handouts for the youth.

4. STIC Role-Plays

After you've facilitated the STIC contemplation, it is now time to have the group members literally practice the STIC technique in simulated role-plays that they can relate to. Rearrange the chairs back into a semicircle and create a stage-like area. Then ask for two to three volunteers depending on how many youth are in your group. Ask the group to think of a situation in which STIC could be applied. It doesn't have to be specifically about drugs. For youth who are incarcerated, a common role-play that's usually suggested is one in which a juvenile hall guard is yelling at someone disrespectfully and unjustly. For youth who aren't incarcerated, a common scenario is a teacher or parent yelling at someone. If no one offers a better role-play, use one of the above examples.

Next, ask one of the actors to volunteer to be the protagonist of the role-play. He or she will be the one who will practice the STIC role-play, while the other actors support him or her by playing the roles of trying to elicit a reaction. For example, in the above-suggested scenario of the youth in juvenile hall, the protagonist will be minding his or her own business when the other volunteer actor (playing the guard) starts to yell disrespectfully and unjustly at the protagonist. The protagonist then—letter-by-letter and out loud—practices STIC. S/he stops, takes a breath, imagines the future consequences (out loud for the sake of the group), and then chooses what to do.

Before the role-play commences, set up the scene by asking the volunteers to take it seriously and perform their best acting skills. Then say *Action!* and let the role-play develop. After the guard starts yelling, hold your hands together in the time-out hand gesture and pause the group. Ask the youth individually how he or she would really be feeling at that moment. The example below represents one used in many of our sessions in this exercise:

> **Facilitator:** *This guard's been yelling at you unjustly. How would you really feel right now and what would you usually do?*
> **Youth:** *I'd be pissed off and want to cuss his ass out, maybe even swing on him!*
> **Facilitator:** *Okay, let's play the rest of the scene out, but, when we say Action!, do the STIC technique* again. *Do every step and say each of them out loud so the rest of the group can hear, okay?*
> **Youth:** *Cool.*

After processing with the youth in the above fashion, restart the role-play and coach the youth through the STIC technique. Make sure the actor pronounces aloud every letter of STIC and its meaning. Make sure s/he actually takes a breath, weighs the future consequences of the present possible actions, and chooses how s/he will respond. After this is done, have the two actors switch roles and do it again. Then have them sit back down, call up two more actors, and do a different role-play. Repeat these steps with other volunteer actors, as time permits.

WHAT IF?

The youth are too playful and don't take the STIC role-plays seriously? We've had many youth who joke around during the STIC role-plays. Oftentimes a group member will be playful and, in a skit similar to the above, choose to fake hit the other person in the skit and then erupt in laughter. We'd then engage that individual and make the point that if it was hard for him or her to employ STIC in role-play scenario, then it would probably be exponentially harder in real life. This is a way to not take away from the playfulness of the group but also highlight just how difficult it can be to practice this technique. Most youth get the point and ask to practice again.

5. Meditation: Mindfulness of the Breath

After finishing the STIC role-plays, rearrange the chairs back into a tightly knit circle and tell the group that it's time to practice the formal meditation for this group. This meditation builds on those of the first two sessions in that it suggests not the taking of deep breaths practiced initially but rather the observing of the breath as it is in the moment (a more standard mindfulness of the breath). Remind the group that the STIC technique is a placeholder for mindfulness and self-awareness. Use the talking points and example script below as a guide for this meditation and consult the end of this session for a printable script.

Talking Points

- The STIC technique is a placeholder for one's use until higher mindfulness is developed.
- We've learned deep breathing over the last two groups, now we'll just focus on our breathing as it is in the present moment.

- Facilitate mindfulness of the breath.
  - Bring attention to the breath.
  - Notice where it's easiest to sense the breath, in the nostrils, belly, or chest.
  - When the mind wanders, bring it back to the breath.
  - Use metaphor of breath as an anchor.
  - Repeat steps as necessary.

Example Script

Facilitator: *Remember folks, that the STIC technique is just a tool that will help you to develop mindfulness. After a long time practicing, you won't have to go through all the steps of STIC to get the benefit of responding vs. reacting. You will just start to do it naturally. Another way to cultivate it is to formally practice meditation, which we've done over the last two groups and which we're about to do now. In the last two groups we've practiced deep breathing. Today we're just going to observe the breath as it is, whether deep or not. What I encourage you to do is to sit up straight, but don't strain yourself, keep your feet flat on the floor, and close your eyes. If you don't want to close your eyes, though, that's okay. Just look at the floor a few feet in front of you. At the sound of the meditation bell, what I want to encourage you to do is to bring all of your awareness and attention to your breath . . .*

[Ring bell]

Breathing in and breathing out, just notice your breath . . . Notice where you can feel your breath most easily. It might be in your nostrils with the actual touch of the air, or it might be in your stomach or chest. Just choose whatever place it is easiest to keep your awareness on . . . Breathing in, and breathing out. Just notice the breath . . . This is slightly different from the breath protocol in our previous meditations. Instead of breathing deeply on purpose, just breathe naturally. If you're breathing deeply, just notice that you're doing that naturally. If you're breathing shallowly, just notice that you're breathing that way naturally, not by a deliberate intervention. It's just about noticing the breath as it is occurring during this meditation . . . And you might notice that your mind wanders away from the breath. That's completely normal. No need to get frustrated, or annoyed, or think you're doing anything wrong. Whenever that happens, just gently bring your awareness back to your breath and refocus . . . Think of your breath as an anchor. Just as a ship uses an anchor to stay in one place in the sea or the ocean, the breath is like an anchor to the body, to the present moment. It keeps us here and now, rather than floating off into the ocean of imagination . . . simply breathing in, and breathing out . . . In a few moments I'm going to ring the bell. When you hear the sound of the bell, I encourage you to become aware of how you're feeling right now in this present moment. You could become aware of sensations and physical activity or of feelings and emotional activity, or even just what's going on in your mind. Do your best to stay with whatever experience you are feeling, so you can share it during the mindful check-in.

[Ring bell]

6. Mindful Check-In

Immediately following the above meditation, facilitate a mindful check-in to process the youth's experience. Remind the youth to take a deep breath and to pause prior to disclosing how they feel. Consult session 2 for full details of the exercise. The differences in this session include that you don't need to process the relevance of taking the deep breath moving forward (as is done in session 2) and that, depending on time available to your group, you can ask the youth to summarize how they're feeling by reporting quickly and sequentially around the circle in 2–3 words (if short on time) or to check in at their own leisure (if time permits).

7. Homework and Close-Out

Encourage the youth to practice mindfulness of the breath and the STIC technique as many times as they can prior to the next group session. Distribute the STIC business cards and remind the youth that they should be thinking about potentially facilitating a meditation a few group sessions out. Gauge any interest from potential volunteers for this future participation in your group's facilitation.

SESSION 3 HANDOUTS

STIC Printout

Figure 6.1

STIC Business Cards

S.T.I.C.
Stop→Take a breath→ Imagine future consequences→ Choose

S.T.I.C.
Stop→Take a breath→ Imagine future consequences→ Choose

S.T.I.C.
Stop→Take a breath→ Imagine future consequences→ Choose

S.T.I.C.
Stop→Take a breath→ Imagine future consequences→ Choose

S.T.I.C.
Stop→Take a breath→ Imagine future consequences→ Choose

S.T.I.C.
Stop→Take a breath→ Imagine future consequences→ Choose

Figure 6.2

Mindfulness of the Breath Meditation Script

What I encourage you to do is to sit up straight, but don't strain yourself, keep your feet flat on the floor, and close your eyes. If you don't want to close your eyes though, that's okay. Just look at the floor a few feet in front of you. At the sound of the meditation bell, what I want to encourage you to do is to bring all of your awareness and attention to your breath . . .

[Ring bell]

Breathing in and breathing out, just notice your breath . . . Notice where you can feel your breath most easily. It might be in your nostrils with the actual touch of the air, or it might be in your stomach or chest. Just choose whatever place it is easiest to keep your awareness on . . . Breathing in, and breathing out. Just notice the breath . . . This is slightly different from the breath protocol in our previous meditations. Instead of breathing deeply on purpose, just breathe naturally. If you're breathing deeply, just notice that you're doing that naturally. If you're breathing shallowly, just notice that you're breathing that way naturally, not by a deliberate intervention. It's just about noticing the breath as it is occurring during this meditation . . . And you might notice that your mind wanders away from the breath. That's completely normal. No need to get frustrated, or annoyed, or think you're doing anything wrong. Whenever that happens, just gently bring your awareness back to your breath and refocus . . . Think of your breath as an anchor. Just as a ship uses an anchor to stay in one place in the sea or the ocean, the breath is like an anchor to the body, to the present moment. It keeps us here and now, rather than floating off into the ocean of imagination . . . simply breathing in, and breathing out . . . In a few moments I'm going to ring the bell. When you hear the sound of the bell, notice the sound until you can't hear it any longer or until the sound is gone before opening your eyes.

[Ring bell]

SESSION 4

MINDFULNESS OF DELUSION

Session Summary

The fourth session blends drug education and self-awareness. Group members are encouraged to contemplate *why* they actually use the drugs that they do. Youth are encouraged to think beyond the simple reasons of "it feels good," and such, which are often delusions (simple false beliefs), and to seriously contemplate the potential underlying reasons for drug use. A number of activities, including a poem, debates about the pros and cons of drug use, individually focused activities, and group discussion highlight this session. A new formal meditation, the Bodyscan, is introduced and practiced during this session.

Materials Needed

- Meditation bell
- Poster paper
- Tape
- Markers
- Pencils or pens for the youth
- Session 4 Handouts (optional)

Formal Meditation (Time)

- Bodyscan (6–8 minutes)

Learning Objectives

- Discuss the role of delusion in drug use
- Discuss pros and cons of substance abuse generally
- Discuss pros and cons of substance use personally
- Practice the Bodyscan meditation

Session Agenda (Chair Configuration)

1. Centering Meditation: Mindfulness of Breath (Circle)
2. Poem: "The Perfect High" (Circle)
3. Mindful Check-In (Circle)
4. Debate: Pros and Cons of Substance Use (Semicircle)
5. Personal Pros and Cons of Substance Use (Spread Across Room and Circle)
6. Meditation: Bodyscan (Circle)
7. Homework and Close-Out (Circle)

1. Centering Meditation

Begin session four by facilitating a mindfulness-of-the-breath centering meditation. Use the script from the previous chapters as a guide. You should provide approximately 1–3 minutes for this centering exercise.

2. Poem: "The Perfect High"

"The Perfect High" is a poem by Shel Silverstein about a boy who is consumed with finding the best high in the world and who embarks on a search to find a guru who supposedly knows how to obtain the perfect high, but who is severely disappointed when he hears that the high is "inside oneself." One of the underlying concepts of the poem is that the main character is under the delusion that the perfect high, an analogy to true happiness, can be found via external means (i.e., drug use). The poem is a great teaching tool to highlight the role of delusion in drug use. This activity has two steps: 1) the reading of "The Perfect High," and 2) the processing of the moral of the poem.

Step 1: The Perfect High

State to the group that you are going to be reading a poem and that they should contemplate the moral of the story and its underlying meaning. "The Perfect High" can be easily searched via the Internet and downloaded. Due to permission restrictions, we were unable to include the full text poem in this curriculum.

Step 2: Processing the Underlying Meaning of "The Perfect High"

After reading the poem, facilitate a discussion with the youth on the moral and underlying meaning of the poem. Use the discussion key below (also at end of session's chapter for printing) as a guide and make sure to elicit answers from the youth.

Table 7.1 Discussion Key for "The Perfect High"

Discussion Questions	Answer Key
1. What happened when Roy finally reached Bubba Fats?	Bubba Fats told Roy the high was "within himself."
2. Why do you think Roy was offended by Bubba Fats's answer?	He had searched for 14 years only to hear that the high wasn't actually an external drug, but an internal search for happiness. He was also frustrated because the high he was educated about wasn't something that was a quick high, it would have to be obtained by years of meditation practice.
3. What did Bubba Fats ultimately do at the end of the story?	He told Roy a lie to send him away.
4. What was the main, take-home point of the story?	That the perfect high is something that's found within. That it's easy to get hooked on searching for the perfect high, or happiness, through external sources.
5. Who knows what a delusion is? And how it played a part in this story?	A delusion is generally defined as a false belief that one has a strong conviction about. It kept Roy in the mindset that the perfect high, or true happiness, was something to be found outside of himself, when in fact it was really something that he should be looking for within.

The last discussion question asks about the role of delusion in the poem. **Delusion**, defined here simply as a lack of awareness of one's underlying intentions in choosing to use drugs, is of central importance to bring into presence during this discussion. This is the underlying concept that guides session 4, and our objective is to help youth deepen self-awareness about why they do the drugs they do (or engage in other behaviors).

NOTE

It's important to ask the group about delusion and its role in the poem's story. Oftentimes, youth will think of the DSM psychosis symptom of delusion and get it confused with hallucination. It's critical to clarify the difference between a delusion and a hallucination and to normalize the nonpsychotic version of delusion (e.g., lack of awareness of behavior/motivation/intention) as something that all people deal with.

---

3. Mindful Check-In

After processing the above poem, facilitate a mindful check-in using the example script from the previous sessions. Remember, you don't need to continually process the significance of the deep breath but you can encourage youth to continue to practice that element of the exercise.

4. Debate: Pros and Cons of Substance Use

The next activity is the *meat* of this session and is an innovative method by which to review the pros and cons of substance use. The idea of this activity is to get the youth thinking about why people do drugs. We must face it: if there weren't positive consequences for doing drugs, people wouldn't do them. The goal of this activity is to highlight those pros and cons as objectively as possible to prime the youth to start thinking of their own personal pros and cons for using drugs.

This activity has 3 steps: 1) splitting the group into teams and defining a debate, 2) a brainstorm session (on the pros and cons of substance use), and 3) the actual debate.

Step 1: Splitting Into Teams and Defining A Debate

Start this step by defining to the group what a debate is. Make sure to drill home the point that this is a debate; that no matter what one's belief is, in a debate, one should always try to make one's points cleanly. Use the talking points and example script below to guide you in presenting this activity:

Talking Points

- Define *debate*.
- Highlight the idea that debating is a skill; one should strive to present one's points clearly in support of the side one is assigned, no matter what one's personal opinion may actually be.

Example Script

> *Facilitator:* Who knows what a debate is? . . . A debate is when you and someone else, or two teams, develop calculated arguments about the points they're trying to make. Anyone ever seen that movie The Great Debaters *with Denzel Washington? It's like that. No matter what your personal opinion is, whichever side of the debate you're assigned to, you develop skillful arguments to support it. That's what we're gonna do here today. We're going to split into two teams and debate the pros and cons of drug use. One team is going to be "for" drugs, and the other "against," debating its negative consequences. After we split into two teams, we'll take some time to brainstorm your main arguments. Does that make sense? . . .*

Next, split the group into two teams. Once that's done, flip a coin to see which team will get to choose whether they will debate *for* or *against* substance use. The team that didn't win the coin flip and thus didn't get to choose their side of the debate will be allowed, as a consolation, to choose whether their team speaker presents their arguments first or second.

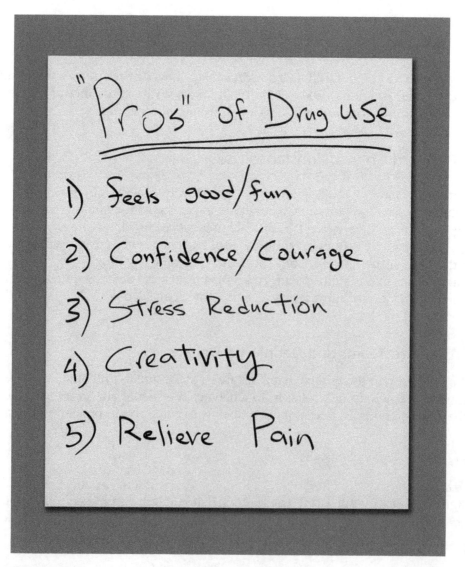

Figure 7.1

Step 2: Brainstorming Session

After the teams have been split equally, send one group to one side of the room (have them circle up with a few chairs around a table or individual desks) and the other to the other side of the room. If there are two facilitators, each of you can accompany a group and help them brainstorm the points for their argument. If there is only one of you, you can oscillate back and forth while supervising.

Once the groups are split, give each team a large piece of poster paper and have each team select someone to write everything down. Instruct the group to come up with 10 major points to support their side of the debate. Encourage each group to give concrete examples for each major point. Allow about 10–15 minutes to brainstorm the 10 major points.

After completing the brainstorming session, have each group select a group member to be their representative *speaker* and actually engage in the debate in front of both groups.

Step 3: The Debate

Remember, as a consolation, the team that lost the coin flip will get to choose whether their speaker debates first or second. Rearrange all the chairs into a semicircle around the area in which the presentations/debates will take place. Have one group sitting in one half of the semicircle and the other group

Figure 7.2

sitting in the other half. Prior to starting the debate, educate the group members about the *ground rules* of the debate so that they are clear. Use the talking points and example script below as a guide to presenting this phase of the activity.

Talking Points

- Only the speaker may present debate arguments.
- Two major ways to evaluate debate: what you say, how you say it.
- Will have roughly five minutes to complete debate.
- Other team and its speaker must stay quite during presentations.
- If time permits, might be able to have a rebuttal session.

Example Script

Facilitator: Remember folks, only the primary speaker can present his or her team's debate points. Speaker, once you get up there, remember that there are two ways you'll get graded on your debate: what you say—the actual content and whether it's good—and how you say it—how good your delivery is, how convincing you are, the examples you use. Also, you will have approximately five minutes to get all your points across. When one person is up there presenting, we all need to remember the "one mic" agreement. So no heckling from the other team. Does that make sense to everyone? . . . Finally, if we have time, we may be able to have a rebuttal session, where each team gets a chance to rebut the other team's primary presentation.

When ready with the first team, tape their talking points from the brainstorm session to the wall or easel behind them and start the debate. Use your own distraction to evaluate which team presents a more clear, better-supported debate. Sometimes we have sweetened the deal and announced that whomever won could pick the snack or the topping on the pizza for the last day of the group. If the debate goes faster than planned (should be about approximately 10 minutes), let each team rebut each other. Once the debate (and rebuttals, if time permits) is completed, summarize the major points from each group and proceed with the next activity.

WHAT IF?

The group is extremely riled up after this activity and it's difficult to get them to settle down for the next, introspective activity? This happens quite often, actually. The youth oftentimes will have a very fun time debating and the energy will get very high. If this is the case, first acknowledge the group's enthusiasm for the activity and state that it's very normal for their energy to be so high. Next, state that part of the skills they're learning while in this program is to regulate and manage themselves when activated emotionally. Contract with the group by asking them to practice managing themselves in this activated state by taking a few deep breaths in and out. We have also done some light mindful movement to slowly taper the energy prior to deep breathing. Most importantly, emphasis how this is a time to practice being present and mindful to one's physiological, emotional, and mental state, and that this practice can be helpful to the development of each individual's ability to be non-reactive in more serious emotionally charged states (e.g., reactive anger).

5. Personal Pros and Cons of Substance Use

This activity takes the pros and cons conversation one step further: to the personal level. While the prior activity presents the idea on a general level (to prime the youth and avoid singling anyone out), this activity highlights the potential delusions youth subscribe to in regard to their own drug use (i.e., a youth's saying s/he uses drugs because it's fun when, in fact, s/he uses drugs to numb painful emotions).

Spread the youth out across the room so they have privacy and aren't distracted during this activity. This exercise includes three steps: 1) personal pros and cons of substance use contemplation, 2) personal pros and cons worksheet, and 3) group discussion.

Step 1: Personal Pros and Cons of Substance Use Contemplation

Start this contemplation by centering the group with a few moments of mindfulness of the breath, proceeding then with the below contemplation (also found at the end of this session). Use the talking points and example script below as a guide for facilitating this contemplation.

Talking Points

- Start by inviting youth to contemplate their breath (mindfulness of the breath).
- Guide youths' awareness to their own drug use.
- Ask, "What are your personal pros and cons of drug use?"
- Encourage youth to be authentic.

Example Script

Facilitator: *For this contemplation we're going to start with some mindfulness of the breath. And then I'll guide you in some specific things to think about. It's good to let your eyes close, so you can visualize with your imagination, but if you don't feel comfortable, it's okay to keep them open. When I ring this bell, just start off by taking a few deep breaths in and a few deep breaths out.*

[Ring bell]

Breathing in, and breathing out. Let your awareness rest with your breath . . . You might notice that your mind takes a while to settle down, or sometimes it doesn't settle down at all . . . That's okay. If the mind wanders away from the breath, just simply bring it back, breathing in, and breathing out . . . I want to now invite you to start contemplating your own drug use. We debated about the pros and cons of substance use on a general level, but what are your personal pros and cons? Do you smoke weed to have fun? Do you smoke to relieve stress? Think of the drug that you most often use and then think of all the pros and cons for using that drug. Maybe one pro is that the drug helps you relax, and maybe one con is that it's against the law and gets you incarcerated when caught. Maybe a pro is that it makes you feel positive, and a maybe a con is that it makes you more temperamental, reactive, and quick to get in fights . . . Just visualize your past experiences. Think of the drug that you most often use. Remember the last time you used it and why you used it. Remember, whatever comes up is okay. No need to censor anything . . . All the while just keep breathing in, and breathing out, using your breath like an anchor, to not let you get too lost in imagination . . . When you really, really think to yourself: "What are the reasons I use this drug?" Just notice what comes up and be authentic with yourself. This contemplation isn't about shaming or finding anything wrong with you, it's about being real with yourself; it's about learning the nature of the delusions we hold ourselves under when it comes to drug use . . . In a few moments I'm going to ring the bell, and, when I do, you can slowly let your eyes open and come out of the formal contemplation.

[Ring bell]

Step 2: Personal Pros and Cons Worksheet

After finishing the personal pros and cons contemplation, pass out the Personal Pros and Cons of Drug Use worksheet that can be found in the back of this session. The worksheet simply asks the youth to list his or her pros and cons of drug use in the traditional decisional-T format. Allow approximately 7–10 minutes for this portion of the exercise.

NOTE

If desired, an alternative method for engaging this content is to simply stay in a circle and discuss personal pros and cons of substance use openly. Some groups that are more intimate early may be able to do this. Use your intuition and best judgment.

Step 3: Group Discussion

After completing the worksheet, have the youth rearrange their chairs into a circle. Remind the youth that sharing what they wrote down on their worksheet is encouraged, but optional. Give everyone the opportunity to share.

When closing this activity remember to highlight the concept of delusion. Youth will oftentimes discuss pros for substance use that are unhealthy and it's important to facilitate thinking about what particular delusion they might be working under that perpetuates continued use (e.g., using drugs to deal with pain and trauma). Again, this isn't to shun, shame, or scare young people out of using drugs; it is just simply an attempt to help youth to develop and deepen their self-awareness.

6. Meditation: Bodyscan

After finishing the Personal Pros and Cons of Substance Use activity, proceed into the formal meditation of the group. You'll be teaching them a new meditation today. For the first three groups, you've presented, practiced, and developed the general mindfulness-of-the-breath protocol. This is often used as an introductory meditation. Next, you're going to teach the group the Bodyscan meditation—a meditation in which you'll guide the youth through systematically observing (from head to toes and toes to head) the different sensations of the body. Use the talking points and example script below as a guide for facilitating this meditation. You can find this meditation at the end of this session's chapter, as well.

Talking Points

- Alert youth to the introduction of a new meditation protocol.
- Direct youth into a comfortable posture with eyes closed (if comfortable).
- Alert youth that the meditation will be mostly guided and ask them to follow along with your instructions.
- Alert youth that the meditation will be slightly longer than the last few, approximately 6–8 minutes.
- Facilitate the Bodyscan meditation.
  ○ Start with mindfulness of the breath.
  ○ Systematically scan sensations from feet to head and back.

Bodyscan Script

Facilitator: We'll start this meditation similarly to the way we've been practicing it up until this point. That is, get in a comfortable position, let your eyes close if you feel comfortable with that, and then, when you hear the sound of the meditation bell, bring your awareness to your breath and wait for further instructions.

[Ring bell]

Begin by simply breathing in, and breathing out, just letting your awareness settle into your breath . . . Notice what it feels like to breath in and breath out through your belly and chest, the sensations associated with breathing . . . Feel the chair supporting you, the floor under your feet . . . Now take another breath in, and, on your next breath out, I want to invite you to bring all of your attention, all of your awareness, to your feet . . . You might notice any sensation you can feel in your feet: tingliness, tension, the shoes on your feet, the floor under your feet, anything . . . Notice the heels, the toes, the tops, and the bottoms . . . Simply become aware of any sensations in your feet, that's all. Just observe whatever is there . . . Next, move your awareness to your ankles and lower legs, noticing any sensations: maybe you feel your pant leg, or maybe you feel a specific sensation. Anything you feel is okay, even if you can't feel anything at all—just keep your awareness on that area of the body for the next few moments—the ankles and the lower legs . . . Next, move your awareness into your knees: the fronts of your knees, the backs of your knees, and the sides of your knees . . . Just notice any sensations. You could feel pain, or aches, or anything. It's not about searching for any particular feeling, it's simply about noticing what's there . . . Moving your awareness into you upper legs; the quadriceps, hamstrings, and thighs . . . Simply scanning this area of the body for sensations . . . You might feel pleasant sensations, unpleasant sensations, or neutral sensations. Doesn't matter what you feel, just simply observe the sensation in this present moment . . . And if your mind wanders away from the area of the body we're focusing on, that's totally normal. No need to get frustrated or think you're doing anything wrong. Just simply redirect your mind back to the area of the body we're focusing on, in this case, the legs . . . Letting your awareness move up into your stomach and belly. Notice what it feels like to breathe in, and breathe out. Notice the sensations associated with breathing . . . Moving your awareness up into your chest, simply noticing any sensation in the chest . . . Shift your awareness to your lower back, and let your awareness slowly rise, from your lower back, to your middle back, to your upper back. Just as if a cup was filling up with water, your back is filling up with awareness. Noticing any sensations, strong sensations, soft sensations, pleasant sensations, and unpleasant sensations. You might have pain in your back from sitting up straight, or you might feel relaxed sensations. Whatever you feel, just notice, just observe in this moment . . . And, again, if the mind wanders away, just simply bring it back to the area of the body we're focusing on, in this case the core, the back, chest, belly . . . Shifting your awareness to your hands: your fingertips, knuckles, and palms—notice any sensation in your hands: tingliness, warmth, the configuration of your hands, anything, any sensation . . . Moving your awareness up through your wrists and forearms . . . your elbows and upper arms; biceps, triceps, and shoulders. Simply notice any sensations . . . Moving your awareness up into your neck; the front of your neck, the back, and the sides of your neck, just notice, just observe any sensation . . . Noticing your jaw: notice if it's hanging loose or clenched. If it's clenched, just let it hang loose . . . Letting your awareness bathe across your face: your cheeks, nose, eyes, eyebrows, mouth, and forehead; just noticing any sensations in the face . . . Your ears and the sides of your head . . . And the back of your head . . . And the very top of your head: just noticing, just observing any sensation, noticing whether you can feel your hair in this moment . . . And next, expand your awareness to your whole body, from the top of your head to the tips of your toes, from the tips of your toes to the top of your head, just noticing, just observing any sensation in this moment. Notice what it feels like to breathe in and breathe out. Notice the abundance of sensations in the body in this moment . . . And in a moment I'm going to ring this bell, and, when I do, I want to invite you to shift your awareness to your ears and hearing sense, and, when you hear the sound of the bell, try to listen to it until it's no longer there or you can't hear it any longer . . .

[Ring bell]

When you feel comfortable, you can slowly open your eyes, if they were closed, and come out of the formal meditation.

Spend a few minutes processing this new meditation with the youth prior to closing out for this group. Ask how this meditation differed from the others, whether they liked it better or thought it worse, whether it was easier or more difficult, and any other questions you find relevant.

7. Homework and Close-Out

Encourage the youth to practice this new meditation technique. It can be especially beneficial for those having problems with sleep and can be practiced at night while lying down before falling asleep. Make sure to ask at least one volunteer youth to be ready to lead the introductory centering meditation for session 6.

SESSION 4 HANDOUTS

Discussion Key for "The Perfect High"

Discussion Questions	Answer Key
What happened when Roy finally reached Bubba Fats?	Bubba Fats told Roy the high was "within himself."
Why do you think Roy got so offended by Bubba Fats's answer?	He had searched for 14 years only to hear that the high wasn't actually an external drug, but an internal search for happiness. He was also frustrated because the high he was educated about wasn't something that was a quick high, it would have to be obtained by years of meditation practice.
What did Bubba Fats ultimately do at the end of the story?	Fearing for his life, he told Roy a lie to send him away.
What was the main, take-home point of the story?	That the perfect high is something that's found within. That it's easy to get hooked on searching for the perfect high, or happiness, through external sources.
Who knows what a delusion is? And how it played a part in this story?	A delusion is generally defined as a false belief that one has a strong conviction about. It kept Roy in the mindset that the perfect high, or true happiness, was something to be found outside of himself when in fact it was really something that he should be looking for within.

Personal Pros and Cons of Drug Use Contemplation

Example Script

Facilitator: For this contemplation we're going to start with some mindfulness of the breath. And then I'll guide you in some specific things to think about. It's good to let your eyes close, so you can visualize with your imagination, but, if you don't feel comfortable, it's okay to keep them open. When I ring this bell, just start off by taking a few deep breaths in and a few deep breaths out.

[Ring bell]

Breathing in, and breathing out. Let your awareness rest with your breath . . . You might notice that your mind takes a while to settle down, or sometimes it doesn't settle down at all . . . That's okay. If the mind wanders away from the breath, just simply bring it back, breathing in, and breathing out . . .

I want to now invite you to start contemplating your own drug use. We debated about the pros and cons of substance use on a general level, but what are your personal pros and cons? Do you smoke weed to have fun? Do you smoke to relieve stress? Think of the drug that you most often use and then think of all the pros and cons for using that drug. Maybe one pro is that the drug helps you relax, and maybe one con is that it's against the law and gets you incarcerated when caught. Maybe a pro is that it makes you feel positive, and a maybe a con is that it makes you more temperamental, reactive, and quick to get in fights . . . Just visualize your past experiences. Think of the drug that you most often use. Remember the last time you used it and why you used it. Remember, whatever comes up is okay. No need to censor anything . . . All the while just keep breathing in, and breathing out, using your breath like an anchor, to not let you get too lost in imagination . . . When you really, really think to yourself: "What are the reasons I use this drug?" Just notice what comes up and be authentic with yourself. This contemplation isn't about shaming or finding anything wrong with you, it's about being real with yourself; it's about learning the nature of the delusions we hold ourselves under when it comes to drug use . . . In a few moments, I'm going to ring the bell and, when I do, you can slowly let your eyes open and come out of the formal contemplation.

[Ring bell]

Personal Pros and Cons of Drug Use Worksheet

What are your Personal Pros and Cons of Using Drugs?

Pros	Cons

Bodyscan Meditation

Bodyscan Script

Facilitator: *We'll start this meditation similarly to the way we've been practicing it up until this point. That is, get in a comfortable position, let your eyes close if you feel comfortable with that, and then, when you hear the sound of the meditation bell, bring your awareness to your breath and wait for further instructions.*

[Ring bell]

Begin by simply breathing in, and breathing out, just letting your awareness settle into your breath . . . Notice what it feels like to breath in and breath out through your belly and chest, the sensations associated with breathing . . . Feel the chair supporting you, the floor under your feet . . . Now take another breath in, and, on your next breath out, I want to invite you to bring all of your attention, all of your awareness, to your feet . . . You might notice any sensation you can feel in your feet: tingliness, tension, the shoes on your feet, the floor under your feet, anything . . . Notice the heels, the toes, the tops, and the bottoms . . . Simply become aware of any sensations in your feet, that's all. Just observe whatever is there . . . Next, move your awareness to your ankles and lower legs, noticing any sensations: maybe you feel your pant leg, or maybe you feel a specific sensation. Anything you feel is okay, even if you can't feel anything at all—just keep your awareness on that area of the body for the next few moments—the ankles and the lower legs . . . Next, move your awareness into your knees: the fronts of your knees, the backs of your knees, and the sides of your knees . . . Just notice any sensations. You could feel pain, or aches, or anything. It's not about searching for any particular feeling, it's simply about noticing what's there . . . Moving your awareness into you upper legs; the quadriceps, hamstrings, and thighs . . . Simply scanning this area of the body for sensations . . . You might feel pleasant sensations, unpleasant sensations, or neutral sensations. Doesn't matter what you feel, just simply observe the sensation in this present moment . . . And if your mind wanders away from the area of the body we're focusing on, that's totally normal. No need to get frustrated or think you're doing anything wrong. Just simply redirect your mind back to the area of the body we're focusing on, in this case, the legs . . . Letting your awareness move up into your stomach and belly. Notice what it feels like to breathe in, and breathe out. Notice the sensations associated with breathing . . . Moving your awareness up into your chest, simply noticing any sensation in the chest . . . Shift your awareness to your lower back, and let your awareness slowly rise, from your lower back, to your middle back, to your upper back. Just as if a cup was filling up with water, your back is filling up with awareness. Noticing any sensations, strong sensations, soft sensations, pleasant sensations, and unpleasant sensations. You might have pain in your back from sitting up straight, or you might feel relaxed sensations. Whatever you feel, just notice, just observe in this moment . . . And, again, if the mind wanders away, just simply bring it back to the area of the body we're focusing on, in this case the core, the back, chest, belly . . . Shifting your awareness to your hands: your fingertips, knuckles, and palms—notice any sensation in your hands: tingliness, warmth, the configuration of your hands, anything, any sensation . . . Moving your awareness up through your wrists and forearms . . . your elbows and upper arms; biceps, triceps, and shoulders. Simply notice any sensations . . . Moving your awareness up into your neck; the front of your neck, the back, and the sides of your neck, just notice, just observe any sensation . . . Noticing your jaw: notice if it's hanging loose or clenched. If it's clenched, just let it hang loose . . . Letting your awareness bathe across your face: your cheeks, nose, eyes, eyebrows, mouth, and forehead; just noticing any sensations in the face . . . Your ears and the sides of your head . . . And the back of your head . . . And the very top of your head: just noticing, just observing any sensation, noticing whether you can feel your hair in this moment . . . And next, expand your awareness to your whole body, from the top of your head to the tips of your toes, from the tips of your toes to the top of your head, just noticing, just observing any sensation in this moment. Notice what it feels like to breathe in and breathe out. Notice the abundance of sensations in the body in this moment . . . And in a moment I'm going to ring this bell, and, when I do, I want to invite you to shift your awareness to your ears and hearing sense, and, when you hear the sound of the bell, try to listen to it until it's no longer there or you can't hear it any longer . . .

[Ring bell]

When you feel comfortable, you can slowly open your eyes, if they were closed, and come out of the formal meditation.

SESSION 5

EMOTIONAL AWARENESS

Session Summary

As you near the middle of the curriculum, the goal has been achieved if some form of group cohesion has been developed. Session 5 has the potential to deepen group cohesion, as its activities involve emotionally charged scenarios that often result in an increased empathy among the youth. The session overviews emotions generally, presents the role gender norms play in emotional expression, offers opportunities for emotional experiences, and offers tools to help manage emotions. Because of the amount of activities and their content, there is no formal meditation practiced in this session.

Materials Needed

- ■ Meditation bell
- ■ Sticky notes
- ■ Poster paper
- ■ Markers
- ■ Session 5 Handouts (optional)

Formal Meditation (Time)

- ■ No formal meditation (except for centering meditation)

Learning Objectives

- ■ Review 3 basic categories of emotions
- ■ Discuss the role of gender roles in emotional expression
- ■ Discuss the role of empathy and compassion in drug treatment
- ■ Practice "stand if" and "deep disclosure" activities

Session Agenda (Chair Configuration)

1. Centering Meditation: Bodyscan (Circle)
2. Emotional Categories (Semicircle)
3. Emotional Expression and Gender Norms (Semicircle)
4. Stand If (Circle)
5. Deep Disclosure (Circle)
6. Game: Concentration (Standing in Circle)
7. Homework and Close-Out (Circle)

1. Centering Meditation: Bodyscan

Since the Bodyscan was introduced as a new technique in the previous group, use it as a centering meditation in this session; make it short, with a purpose to get youth to *arrive*. Bodyscans can be difficult to facilitate in a short period of time. Make sure you present a truncated version in which you're not going through every detail of every part of the body (consult session 4). This centering should last no longer than 3–5 minutes.

2. Emotional Categories

After the centering, rearrange the chairs from a circle to a semicircle facing the wall that you'll be using for the presentation of emotional categories. This exercise is similar to the drug classifications exercise in session 2 and is comprised of three steps: 1) brainstorming emotions, 2) defining emotional categories, and 3) discussing emotional categories.

Step 1: Emotions Brainstorm

Start this activity by letting the youth know that today's whole group is going to be tied to emotions, emotional awareness, or emotional regulation in some form. Tape a piece of poster paper to the wall and label it "Emotions." Next, remind the youth of the drug classifications activity from session 2 and state that it will be a similar activity, only with emotions rather than drugs. Instruct the youth to call out (either by raising hands or popcorn style) different emotions with which they're familiar.

As they state emotions, write them down on each sticky note and post them on the poster paper.

Step 2: Defining Emotional Categories

Next, ask the group if all the emotions can be classified into major categories. The idea of this step of the activity is to highlight that all emotions can be categorized as either pleasant emotions, unpleasant emotions, or neutral emotions. After years of facilitating this activity, it's been clear to us that most youth gravitate more to the terms positive and negative, rather than pleasant and unpleasant. Thus, we simply define the categories as positive emotions, negative emotions, and neutral emotions. As you ask what categories they think there may be, most youth will state the positive and negative categories, and may need some guidance on the neutral categories. Offering examples are a good tool. Asking the youth to contemplate and discuss prior emotional experiences is also a good way of getting them to reflect on major emotional categories.

As these three emotional categories come to light via discussion, write them on three sticky notes and place them at the top of the poster paper in column-like fashion. Rather than dividing the group into teams and having them place the emotions in the correct categories, simply discuss which emotions go into which categories. Once all emotions are placed in the correct column/emotional category, facilitate the final step of this activity.

NOTE

It's okay if the youth don't agree on where to place each emotion. Some will say that an emotion can be both positive and negative and you may have to place it in between two of the columns. This is normal and okay.

Figure 8.1

Step 3: Discussion on Emotional Categories

Use the questions below as a guide to facilitating discussion on the benefits of being aware of emotional categories.

Discussion Questions

- Why do you think it's important to know the major categories that emotions fall into?
- What are the benefits, if any, in being able to know the "base" feeling of your specific emotion?
- Do you all think it's possible to have greater awareness of and control over your emotions if you're aware of that underlying, base feeling tone?

As you facilitate the discussion, guide the youth toward the take-home point that being aware of base feeling tones gives one more of a *heads up* that a specific emotions is about to arise, or has arisen, and, in turn, gives one more of the ability to respond—rather than react—to it. Use the talking points and example script below as a guide to facilitating this discussion.

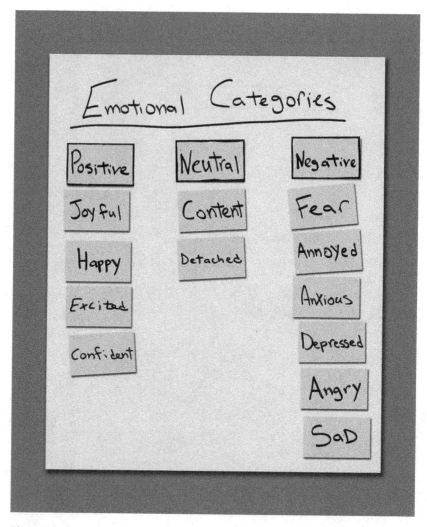

Figure 8.2

Talking Points

- Accessing base feeling tones leads to greater emotional awareness.
- Awareness of base feeling tones leads to greater emotional regulation.

Example Script

Facilitator: The reason we learn about these "bases" of emotional experience is because the greater our awareness of the major category in which a specific emotion falls, the greater our ability to have more control over that emotion. It works like this: If a strong emotion comes up, let's say anger, and you observe or think to yourself, "the base category of this emotion is negative, or unpleasant," you are mindfully putting some distance, even if it's a little bit, between yourself and the emotion of anger. That little space, the actual observing and your thinking "this is a negative emotion" gives you the ability to insert other thoughts into your awareness, as well: for example, "I'm hella mad right now so I need to *watch out because this is when I usually want to drink." Doing that makes it more possible for you to actually pay attention to yourself and not simply react from the anger, which awareness will give you a greater chance of not reacting and having an aggressive outburst or running to use drugs to neutralize your feeling. Does that make sense? . . . That's the power of being aware of these three major categories of emotions.*

3. Emotional Expression and Gender Norms

This activity incorporates a version of the "man box" and "woman box" created by the Oakland Men's Project (Kivel & Creighton, 1997) and has two steps: 1) the gender box, and 2) the *tree of emotions* metaphor.

Step 1: The Gender Box ("Man" or "Woman" Box)

The objective of this phase of the activity is to invite youth to contemplate the impact that gender socialization has had on emotional expression in their lives. This discussion can go in very different directions depending on whether you have a group comprised entirely of young women, one of young men only, or a coed group. The essence of this exercise is to draw a box and educate the youth about how society *boxes* them in, in terms of emotional expression, whether they're young men or young women.

Tape a piece of poster paper to the wall (next to the previous poster of emotional categories) and label the top of the box according to who's in the room ("Man Box" if only men, "Woman Box" if only women, both if coed). Draw a large box in the center of the poster paper. Start a discussion about how society influences emotional expression and gender norms by asking, What are some emotions that, if we express them as men/women, we get negative social feedback for doing so? Make sure to highlight a few examples yourself first, and then have a youth volunteer come up to the board and place the rest of the sticky notes from the last activity either inside or outside the box. Placing the notes inside the box suggests that it is societally acceptable to express that emotion, whereas placing it outside suggests that it is societally unacceptable and that negative social consequences could occur from our expression of them. If you have a coed group, do this twice—once for young men, and once for young women (each time with a representative from their respective genders). You can add a few other emotions/gender descriptors, as well, such as "weak," "strong," "vulnerable," "soft," "nice," etc., if they weren't already on the poster for the previous exercise.

After all sticky notes have been placed either inside or outside of the gender box, lead a discussion using the following questions as prompts:

- Even though society boxes us in emotionally, does it mean we don't feel those "outside of the box" emotions?
- What would social experience be like if we didn't subscribe to those gender norms for emotional expression?
- Whose rules do you want to play by? Did you agree to these publicly-exclusive forms of emotional expression when you were born?
- What is the cost of not expressing one's emotions? What is the cost of *bottling up* one's emotions?

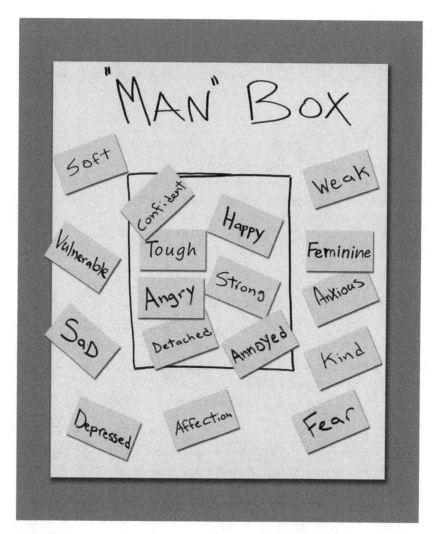

Figure 8.3

NOTE

Be clear and consistent about continually reminding the youth that you're not discussing personal feelings toward these behaviors, but rather how society as a whole looks upon them. We've often had youth put "sadness" or "crying" inside the man box because they feel that it's okay. We'd then ask them, if a bunch of young men saw another young man crying without knowing the reason, how do you think most of them would react? That often helps clarify personal vs. societal norms.

Step 2: Tree of Emotions

After facilitating the above discussion, tape the Tree of Emotions image (found also in the session 5 handouts) next to the gender-box poster paper or tape another piece of poster paper to the side and

Figure 8.4

draw the tree of emotions graphic yourself. Make sure, if you're taping up a scanned image, to have another piece of paper taped to it near the bottom, so that the youth cannot see the roots below the ground level. If you're drawing the picture by hand, simply do not draw the roots below ground level at this point. Ask the group what percentage of the tree is above the ground and what percentage is below the ground. Next, either draw the roots on the poster board below the ground or reveal the amount of roots that would be underground, if using the scanned image. Depending on the size of drawing of the tree and its roots, it's usually at least 50% in terms of actual wood that's below the ground.

Next, ask the group how this relates to emotional expression and how human beings behave in terms of emotional expression in society. Lead a discussion by asking the questions What do we show (in terms of emotional expression) to the public? And what do we keep private?" and have one of the youth come up and place a few of the sticky notes (or if you prefer you can place them yourself) in the appropriate places, with the above-ground sticky notes reflecting the *public* domain and the below-ground ones the *private* domain. The essence of this final visual is to suggest that, because society *boxes* people into either the man box or the woman box (or sometimes both or neither boxes, depending on orientation), that there is oftentimes an adverse effect for those either expressing or allowing the expression of emotions not associated by society with the gender of the person expressing them, as it leads to repression of healthy, though possibly uncomfortable, emotions. Use the talking points and example script below to facilitate this discussion.

Talking Points

- Ask, "How does the tree of emotions relate to human beings and emotional expression?"
- Ask, "Which emotions would we not show to the public, and which would we show?"
- Discuss experiences of emotional authenticity and inauthenticity.
- Present the metaphor of planting seeds in society.

Example Script

Facilitator: How does this tree, with about half of its wood above ground and the other half below ground, relate to emotional expression in human beings? If we think about what we show to the public, in terms of our emotional expression, what emotions or sides of ourselves do we show? Which ones do we not show? I like to think about what we show as our public self, and what we don't show as our private self? How many times has someone asked you how you're doing and you just say "good," "fine," or "cool" when you were actually going through something hard?

[Discuss]

The reason we use the tree of emotions metaphor is because of how the metaphor of a seed in a not-so-great, restrictive, repressive environment grows. Think about it like this: If society plants the types of seeds that will only grow within the bounds of society's visual comfort, just as it restricts certain emotions to being boxed away for each gender, what types of plants will grow? How will trees, for example, function in a world with pre-determined boxing-in of certain of their natural features to support societal tastes for pleasant appearances? It would result in trees not fully expressing their true being, and, with human beings, it results in many of us not fully expressing our hearts. And the cost? Bottling up of emotions, damaging outbursts, and emotional dysregulation—everything we discussed in the previous activity. All of these things come about from accepting these social restrictions and, thereby, not properly being aware of and true to our feelings and our inner world.

4. Stand If

The start of this session educated youth about major emotional categories, gender socialization as it relates to emotional expression, and the cost of not being emotionally expressive. This has all been done on primarily a didactic level, with some discussion. The next activity, *Stand If*, moves the youth from a cognitive to an experiential level. Because this can be an emotionally charged activity, it is appropriate to let the group know that you're shifting gears and prep them for the activity. When introducing the program in the first group, you already set the tone for the curriculum as a whole (e.g., "sometimes it will be fun, sometimes informative, sometimes serious and deep . . . "). You should, at the very least, reference this from the agreements, so that you can remind the group that everyone already agreed to keep an open mind to activities such as *Stand If*. Use the following talking points and example script as a guide to prepping the youth for the potential of the emotionally charged activities to follow.

Talking Points

- Remind youth about the agreements.
- Remind youth about the different levels of seriousness that the curriculum calls upon (games, fun activities, learning activities, serious activities).
- Invite youth to recommit to taking the following activities seriously and keeping an open mind.

Example Script

Facilitator: *The next couple of activities are going to be a little bit different than the ones in all the sessions we've done so far. They're going to have a little bit more of a serious tone, but they have the potential for some really positive outcomes. Remember, on the first day, when I was talking about how this program overall would have a lot of different aspects? That it would sometimes be really fun and we'd play games, other times it would be really informative, and other times it would be serious and deep? . . .* **[Get acknowledgement.]** *Well, these next few activities are going to be some of those potentially deep activities. We're going to do some activities that involve sharing about ourselves—and don't worry, we can share just as much as we feel comfortable sharing. But I really want to invite each and every one of you to take the activities as seriously as you can. Remember that one of our group agreements was to keep an open mind to all activities. That's what I want to encourage you to do for today. Is that cool with everyone? . . .*

The Stand If activity is an incarnation of an exercise that has been around for a very long time: its genesis (as for as we know) coming from the Oakland Men's Project's *Making the Peace* curriculum (Kivel & Creighton, 1997), and variations have been used with Challenge Day and the MBA Project among other programs. This activity has three steps: 1) explaining the instructions for Stand If, 2) the experience itself, and 3) processing of the experience.

Step 1: Stand If Instructions

Once the youth are rearranged in a circle and after prepping them regarding the seriousness of the activity, state that the Stand If activity involves the reading of approximately 10 statements. Instruct the youth to stand up if the experience from the statement has been true for them, and that this should be done in complete silence. Use the talking points and example script below to facilitate the first portion of the Stand If instructions.

Talking Points

- Stand if consists of reading approximately 10 statements.
- Youth should stand up if a statement is true to their experience.
- Activity should be done in complete silence.
- State that you'll participate, too (optional but encouraged for facilitator).
- State that, just because someone doesn't stand up, that doesn't mean they haven't had the experience.

Example Script

> *Facilitator: For this activity, which is called "Stand If," I'm going to read about 10 statements. I'm going to say, "Stand if" and then read a statement that has to do with predominantly with drugs, and if that experience is true for you, if you've had that experience, I want to invite you to stand up silently and slowly, and notice who else is standing. I'll let you know when to sit back down, and then I'll read another statement. So if the statement is true for you for any drug you've ever done or had experience with, either directly or as related to another experience, then you can stand up. Make sense?*

Immediately after you complete the general instructions, re-emphasize that the activity should be done in silence, that youth should not engage in communication of any kind (even nonverbal), and that they can notice who else is standing via peripheral vision only:

> *Facilitator: I know I just said this but I'm going to say it again to emphasize it. Please when you stand up, do so in silence. This activity works best when we stand up in silence and don't communicate with each other, even nonverbally. So that means try to avoid looking directly at each other—looking at others in the eyes, and just notice who else is standing only with your peripheral vision. Is that okay with everyone? . . .*

The final instructions are to state that you, the facilitator, will be participating (this is optional but highly encouraged) and that it is okay to not stand up if that's what one chooses to do:

> *Facilitator: Okay, I also want to let you know that I'm going to participate, too. Remember, I said that I wasn't ever going to ask you to do anything that I wouldn't do, so that's why I'm also participating. And the last thing is, it's okay to not stand up if you don't want to. When someone isn't standing, it could be because they didn't have that experience, or it could be because they just didn't want to share that during this activity. So let's not jump to conclusions and judge someone who either is or isn't standing. Cool?*

Step 2: Facilitate *Stand If*

Once you have gained acknowledgement of assent to these protocols, you can facilitate the activity using the *Stand If* statements below (also found in this session's handouts, for easy printing). The statements work in a progression from less intense to more intense statements. Depending on the gender and ethnic make-up of your group, it can be appropriate to edit these statements to reflect cultural and relevant experience. The statements below are what we've used with our groups, which are very ethnically diverse and have included both young men and young women.

Stand If. . .

- You've ever used drugs to deal with daily stress and to relax
- You've ever been peer-pressured, by people you knew, to do drugs when you really didn't want to
- You've ever wanted to quit—or reduce—your drug or alcohol use, and you couldn't
- You've ever seen an adult give drugs to a child or adolescent
- You grew up seeing drug deals consistently in your neighborhood
- You've ever had a police officer try to plant drugs on you and arrest you
- You've ever felt like you could not live without getting high at some point
- You've ever stolen money from a family member, or robbed someone, or sold your goods, to get money for drugs

- You grew up with a close family member who was addicted to drugs and/or alcohol
- You've used drugs to forget painful memories of traumatic events, like drinking to forget a friend who was killed or overdosed and died
- You've ever contemplated overdosing on drugs

IMPORTANT NOTE

It is imperative to think critically about the ethnic and gender make-up of your group. Being "pressured" by someone you know has very different connotations for young women than it does for young men. A lot of the young women we've worked with have been victims of sexual assault, and drugs have often played a role in both the abuse and the coping with the trauma that resulted. Further, if a youth stands for the statement about "ever contemplating overdosing," or anything close to suicidal ideation, it's imperative to check in with that youth at an appropriate time and potentially refer her or him to the appropriate professional.

Step 3: Processing *Stand If*

After the final statement has been read and all the youth have sat back down, instruct them to take a few deep breaths and just to notice what thoughts, feelings, and images arose during the activity. Use the discussion questions below to process the activity:

- What is the experience like for you?
- What was it like to see others standing with you? What emotions/feelings did it bring up?
- Were you surprised when certain people were standing? When certain people weren't standing?
- How did it make you feel to know that you're not alone in those experiences? That others have been through and felt similar things?
- What is empathy and how does it relate to this activity?
- What would be the benefit, if any, of being more empathetic in daily life?

Finish the exercise by discussing how empathy relates to the *Stand If* activity and how empathy might affect the youth's daily lives.

5. Deep Disclosure

The deep disclosure experience is designed for youth to disclose something that people or society have been unable to see about them (i.e., the roots of the tree under the ground). This activity is facilitated immediately following the *Stand If* activity, given that youth have already been taken in this exercise from a head (i.e., cognitive) level to a *heart* (i.e., emotional) level. This activity is a rendition of the Oakland Men's Project's (Kivel & Creighton, 1997) and Challenge Day's *If You Knew Me* exercise that was publicized by the MTV show "If You Knew Me." The exercise has three steps: 1) the prep, 2) the facilitation of the activity, and 3) a brief compassion meditation.

Step 1: Prep

It's necessary to give the youth some extra prepping instructions so they understand what's expected of them for this exercise. Use the following talking points to set the stage for this deep sharing:

Talking Points

- This is an opportunity to share something about yourself that others may not know.
- It could be about drugs, or just life in general.
- It could be deep, but doesn't have to be (just needs to be meaningful).
- You start by saying, "If you knew me, you'd know . . . " or "Something I've been holding in is . . . "
- Don't have to share if you don't want to.
- Re-invoke agreements of skillful speech, skillful listening, and one mic.

Example Script

Facilitator: *Coming from the Stand If activity, we're now going to have an opportunity to share something about ourselves, maybe things that came up during that activity, with others in the group. Just a while ago we were talking about that gender box, and looking at the image of the tree. This is an opportunity to share some of the things we've been holding onto and get them off our chest. It's one of the things in the healing process that needs to happen. What we're going to do is, and we don't need to do this in a circle, it can be popcorn style, but someone is going to share something from the heart. A deep truth about themselves—something about themselves that maybe others don't know, that they've been holding. It can be about drugs, or anything else. It doesn't have to be super deep, it just has to be meaningful, and that's all. And, of course, you don't have to share if you really don't want to, but I really encourage you to do so. There may be a difference in how we all view each other after this experience. And again, since I wouldn't ask you to do something I wouldn't do, I'm going to start by example. After I go, someone else just hop in after a few seconds if you feel called to, and we'll stop when it feels appropriate. You can start off by saying, "If you knew me, you'd know . . . " or you can just say "Something I've been holding is . . . " and then talk about what you want to talk about. Remember, as we each share, please practice mindful listening and the one mic agreement as we don't want anyone to feel disrespected. Okay? This is a time for us to share some truths about ourselves and let the world see us as we really are. Let me take a breath and we'll begin.*

Step 2: Facilitate Deep Disclosure

Facilitate deep disclosure. Don't worry if, after you've shared first, it takes a few moments for someone else to speak up. If you have a group of 8–12 youth, this activity could take upwards of 20 minutes.

NOTE

What makes this activity go deep? What contributes to it being facilitated effectively? The answer: the first person that shares will set the tone. There are a number of options for addressing the tone-setting: 1) you could share first, as we stated in the script above (which is the highest recommendation), 2) you could have a youth with whom you've created a relationship start (and prep them a few minutes before a session), or 3) you could have any youth start first (by volunteering). Because the level of depth in this activity depends on who sets the tone, you have an opportunity to give them an example and actually set that tone, which is very important.

After a number of youth, or all of them, have shared, and when it feels appropriate, stress the take-home point of this activity: That all human beings deal with distress and suffer, and, when we are aware of each other's suffering, we have the chance to practice empathy and compassion. Use the talking points and example script below as a guide.

Talking Points

- All human beings experience suffering.
- It's that common suffering that ultimately binds us together as human beings.
- When we remember that we all suffer, there is more of a chance to send each other empathy and compassion.

Example Script

Facilitator: What's one thing that everything that everyone shared has in common? . . . They were all emotional experiences. All of us, all human beings, have something in common: We all suffer. We all go through hard times. Sometimes the suffering isn't that intense, other times it's really intense. The reason why we all shared with each other here, why we all shared some of the below the dirt roots that we're carrying with us, is because, when we're aware of each other's suffering, we can choose to send one another love, compassion, and empathy, or at least just not be a jerk to one another. That's what this is about: being able to come together as human beings and recognize suffering for what it is and hope that it decreases. Does that make sense? . . . Anyone have anything else they want to say? About themselves or to someone who shared something?

After relaying the take-home point above, let any of the youth say any final words prior to transitioning into the brief compassion meditation.

WHAT IF?

Very strong emotions and/or trauma gets triggered by the activity? The first thing to consider is time. Make sure that this activity isn't facilitated toward the end of the group so a situation might arise where the group ends right after this activity. If a youth is visibly hyper-aroused, and you cannot wait until next activity's game (which is designed as a de-escalator), have the youth engage in taking some deep breaths. If you are cofacilitating, you can take the triggered youth to the side. If you are the only facilitator, or there are more than one youth triggered, have the whole group engage in deep breathing.

Step 3: Brief Compassion Meditation

This brief compassion meditation is something that will be highlighted and developed in the final third of this curriculum. However, given the nature of the previous two activities, we've found it skillful to introduce this exercise here, at least briefly, to offer youth the opportunity to practice empathy and compassion. Use the talking points and example script below as a guide.

Talking Points

- Start with mindfulness of the breath.
- Direct awareness to the activity just facilitated.
- Send compassion to everyone in the circle (including yourself).

Example Script

Facilitator: Let's just take a few moments to acknowledge everyone in the room, for having the courage to share or to just hold the space for these last two activities. I want to invite you to close your eyes so I can lead you through a brief 2–3 minute meditation.

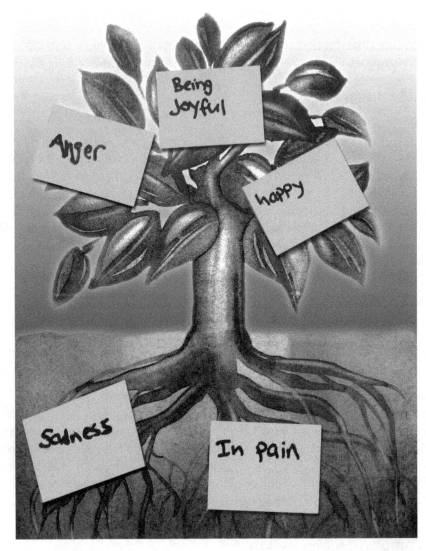

Figure 8.5

[Ring bell]

Take a few deep breaths in, and a few deep breaths out and just notice how that has a calming effect on your body, even if it's just a little bit. I want to invite you to think about how everyone in this room has been through something tough, and that some of us have shared those experiences today. I want to invite you to wish everyone in this room to be peaceful, free from pain and suffering . . . To find meaning from their hard experiences, and to grow from them—all the while just breathing in and breathing out . . . That emotion of feeling empathy for someone else's pain and wishing the pain to stop, that's called compassion. That's what I want to invite you to send to everyone else in the circle right now. Even yourself. Just continue to breathe in, and breathe out, and wish for your own and everyone's pain to subside, for all to be happy, healthy, and free from pain and suffering.

[Ring bell]

When you're comfortable, open your eyes, if they were closed, and expand your awareness to encompass the whole group.

IMPORTANT NOTE

If you feel like your group or class is not ready for the potential emotional intensity that might be elicited from the prior three activities, you can pass out a scanned version of the Tree of Emotions from the session's handouts and have the youth, while spread across the room, work on listing the emotions they feel are either acceptable in the public or preferred kept in the private domains, before circling back up to discuss. This allows for youth to go as deep or stay as surface level as they prefer and offers an alternative method to engage this content from a slightly less experiential perspective. This may also be appropriate in situations where emotionally charged activities may be contraindicated (i.e., very large classroom settings where trust hasn't been established). See figure 8.5 for an example.

6. Game: Concentration

As noted above, the game Concentration is a built-in de-escalator activity designed to help youth move from ruminating on the potentially tough experiences (i.e., strong negative emotions, trauma, etc.) that arose during the last two activities. It is essentially a game (adapted from infamous camping games) in which participants stand in a circle, a category is chosen, and then, on a clapping rhythm and beat, each participant has to say a specific thing from the category without hesitating or repeating something someone else said in that round. When someone hesitates or says something someone else said, they're *out*. This culminates with a final round of two participants until there is one victor. A number of rounds of this game can be played in which new categories are chosen for each round.

Concentration Game Instructions

Use the talking points and example script below as a guide for this activity.

Talking Points

- Have everyone in standing in a circle.
- There is a chorus/intro song that gives instructions:
  Concentration . . . (Three claps)
  Fifty-nine . . . (Three claps)
  No repeats . . . (Three claps)
  or hesitation . . . (Three claps)
  I'll start . . . (Three claps)
  category is . . . (Three claps)
- Everyone should follow your lead and clap with you.
- State that this is a category game: A category will be selected, the circle of respondents will proceed clockwise to the left, and each person will have to come up with something in that category (e.g., if I select the category of "emotions," everyone will have to name a specific emotion and, if you don't, you're out).
- Tell the youth, once you're out (i.e., if you hesitated or said something someone else had already said), you have to wait until the next round.
- Tell the youth everyone has to clap on beat, or they're out. That's why it's called concentration.
- Tell them that you'll start as an example, and, when someone's out, in the next round the next person to the left gets to pick a category.

Example Script

> ***Facilitator:*** *Okay, this game is called concentration. We're all standing in a circle because this is going to be a game based on categories, in which we all clap on a specific beat. The clap will go like this*

[Demonstrate three claps at a moderate-to-fast pace]

Everyone got that? Let's all clap like that together. We'll do a practice round, but basically I'm going to sing the chorus of the concentration song, after each pause we're going to do those three claps, I'll select a category, and then, after I state the first item from the selected category, the circle will move to the left and it will be on the next person to state something from that category. So if I say "emotions," the category is emotions. Then I'll go first, to give the person to my left some time to think, and then she'll go. Make sense? . . . Here's the thing, as you'll see in a moment, you can't hesitate, or you're out. You can't say something someone else has already said, or you're out. And if you don't clap or clap off beat, you're out. The objective of the game is to be the last person standing. After the first person gets out, the person to my left will get to pick a category and we'll keep doing that until there's only one person left. Make sense? . . . Any questions? . . . Okay, the chorus goes like this:

> *Concentration (clap, clap, clap)*
> *Fifty-nine (clap, clap, clap)*
> *No repeats (clap, clap, clap)*
> *Or hesitations (clap, clap, clap)*
> *I'll start (clap, clap, clap)*
> *Category is (clap, clap, clap)*

Then I'd state the category, we'd clap three times again, and I'd go first. Let's do a practice round.

Conduct a practice round with the youth; singing the intro and making sure everyone understands the premise of the game. If you get knocked out as the facilitator, help each person with the intro chorus and substitute "I'll start" with the name of whoever's turn it is to pick a category. Usually, by the end first round, youth who disclosed deep personal material from the previous activity are in a positive mood. Youth often have fun with this game, so play 2–3 rounds, depending on time that remains prior to closing the session.

7. Homework and Close-Out

Encourage the youth to continue to contemplate the activities of the session and to practice formally meditating. In your next session you'll have your first youth volunteer facilitate the opening centering meditation. Make sure to ask the youth in this group if anyone wants to volunteer to facilitate that meditation.

SESSION 5 HANDOUTS

Tree of Emotions

Figure 8.6
Courtesy of iStockphoto, reprinted by permission.

Stand If

Stand If. . .

- You've ever used drugs to deal with daily stress and to relax

- You've ever been peer-pressured, by people you knew, to do drugs when you really didn't want to

- You've ever wanted to quit—or reduce—your drug or alcohol use, and you couldn't

- You've ever seen an adult give drugs to a child or adolescent

- You grew up seeing drug deals consistently in your neighborhood

- You've ever had a police officer try to plant drugs on you and arrest you

- You've ever felt like you could not live without getting high at some point

- You've ever stolen money from a family member, or robbed someone, or sold your goods to get money for drugs

- You grew up with a close family member who was addicted to drugs and/or alcohol

- You've used drugs to forget painful memories of traumatic events, like drinking to forget a friend who was killed or overdosed and died

- You've ever contemplated overdosing on drugs

Session 5 Reference

Kivel, P., & Creighton, A. (1997). *Making the peace: A 15-session violence prevention curriculum for young people.* Alameda, CA: Hunter House.

SESSION 6

THE BRAIN AND DRUGS

Session Summary

Session 6 reviews the effects of drugs on the brain. We've found over the years that, after an emotional group (session 5), the youth would return the next session with high, playful energy and not delve deeply into emotionally charged activities. We started to become aware of a group defense/protective mechanism against the intensity of the last session. We piloted some of our drug education information at those times, which proved effective. Thus, this session covers the basics of brain physiology and the interaction between the neurotransmitter dopamine, the brain, and drugs. It also covers the role of mindfulness and meditation practice in executive function. This is the first session with a scheduled "youth-led" centering meditation. This passing of the torch serves the function of empowering young people. The Bodyscan is also practiced.

Materials Needed

- Meditation bell
- Slide show software, or,
- Session 6 Handouts (optional)

Formal Meditation (Time)

- Bodyscan (7–10 minutes)

Learning Objectives

- Review major areas of the brain
- Discuss the role of the frontal lobe in decision-making
- Discuss the interaction between dopamine and substance abuse
- Review neural pathways
- Discuss the relevance of mindfulness
- Practice the Bodyscan meditation

Session Agenda (Chair Configuration)

1. Youth-Led Centering Meditation (Circle)
2. Mindful Check-In (Circle)
3. Brain Presentation I (Semicircle)
4. Meditation Break (Circle)
5. Brain Presentation II (Semicircle)
6. Meditation: Bodyscan (Circle)
7. Homework and Close-Out (Circle)

1. Youth-Led Centering Meditation

The sixth session starts with a volunteer youth leading a brief centering meditation, either the Bodyscan or mindfulness of breathing. You will have already presented the idea of youth-led meditations in the previous groups, so this should be no surprise, but make sure you already have a volunteer from session 5 and have that person lead the centering meditation for approximately 2–3 minutes. The major point of this activity is for a youth to get the experience of being in the "facilitator" role. After she or he has finished, spend a few minutes processing his/her experience with the group.

Process Youth's Experience

Use the bullet points below as a guide to processing the youth's experience:

- First thank the youth in the group, possibly giving him/her a high-five or handshake and round of applause
- Then ask the youth, "How did it feel to lead the meditation?"
- Next ask, "Could you ever see yourself becoming a meditation teacher or something similar?" (e.g., counselor, teacher, healer)
- Next ask the group, "How was that meditation for you all? How was it when one of your peers was leading the meditation?"
- Finally, state to the youth that you'll be looking for someone to do the centering meditation (and possibly others) for the rest of the program, and that these are great skills to learn

Once finished with the centering meditation, proceed with the mindful check-in.

2. Mindful Check-In

Facilitate the mindful check-in with one major difference for this session: Simply state to the group, "Let's check in; who'd like to start?" That is, do not remind the group to take the deep breath or stay in the present moment. Because the group is halfway through the curriculum, use this time to assess to what level the group has integrated the mindful check-in into their experience. If they have, they will take the deep breath and start off with how they're feeling in the present moment without prompt. If not, that's okay, too. You can remind the group of the mindful check-in and its purpose, if need be.

3. Brain Presentation I: Major Brain Areas and the Role of Pleasure

If you have the ability to do a slide show, we recommend doing so, given that visual stimulation is always a welcome device with young people. If you don't have access to a projector/computer or cannot bring them into the institution you're working in, it is possible to do this presentation without a slide show; simply use the handouts located at the end of this session's chapter.

IMPORTANT NOTE

What's extremely important about this presentation is that it is catered to the specific needs of your group. Remember that, at the end of the first group, the curriculum directed you to ask the group what they were most interested in learning about. If any of the youth mentioned particular drugs there were interested in learning about (e.g., marijuana, alcohol, cocaine), then this presentation is the time to integrate that information. The slides below are general information, purposefully to encourage you to add and subtract information that addresses the specific needs of your group.

Slide 1: Four Brain Lobes

The slide show starts with a visual of the brain and its four lobes. Slide 1 is intended simply to educate the group about the four major lobes, with a focus on each one except the frontal lobe, given that Slide 2 is dedicated to that lobe.

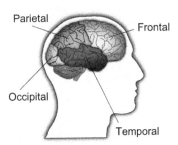

Figure 9.1

Use the talking points and example script below as a guide.

Talking Points

- Ask the question, "Who knows what these four major lobes of the brain are and what they do?"
- If no one knows, give a very brief, one-liner about the parietal, temporal, and occipital lobes. Make sure to give an example for each of them.

Example Script

Facilitator: The occipital lobe is here in the back. It's connected to the function of our eyes, so then what do you think its main purpose is? . . . Right! It generally governs our eyesight. What about this one on the side? Who knows what that is? . . . Yes, the temporal lobe. It has to do with our hearing. So our ability to hear is processed through this area of the brain. Anyone ever heard of the parietal lobe? It's this one here on the top. Who knows what that area of the brain governs? . . . Spatial awareness and orientation. So, when

I throw the football to you, your parietal lobe is the lobe that governs your ability to gauge where the football is in space and time and successfully catch it. We'll talk about this one **[point to frontal lobe]** *in a moment, but does anyone have any questions or comments about what we just covered? . . .*

Answer any questions or field any comments from the youth about the information on the first slide prior to moving on to Slide 2.

Slide 2: Frontal Lobe

Slide 2 focuses on the frontal lobe and its role in executive function and decision-making. There is an image of the frontal lobe as in human beings and also as in dogs for comparison.

Display Slide 2 and use the talking points and script below to present Slide 2.

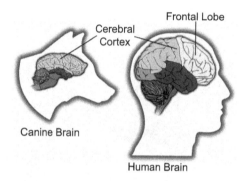

Figure 9.2

Talking Points

- State that the frontal lobe is the part of our brain that evolved the latest.
- Distinguish difference between the human frontal lobe and those of other animals whose frontal lobes aren't as big (e.g., dog).
- Point to the prefrontal cortex, state that this area is responsible for our *executive function*, and ask the youth what they think *executive function* means.
- Present the analogy of the brain's executive function with executives in the work force.
- Discuss the close relationship between mindfulness and executive function.

Example Script

Facilitator: *Who knows what this last part of the brain at the front is? . . . It's the frontal lobe. This is the part of our brain that evolved last, or, most recently in human evolution. The frontal lobe in human beings is bigger than most other frontal lobes for any other animal of any species. For example, the frontal lobe of a dog looks like this* **[point to dog's brain image]**. *See how much fuller ours is? What do you all think is the main role the frontal lobe plays in our lives, given the differences between our brain and a dog's brain? How does the way dogs think and react differ from the way we do as humans? Think about the ability to react vs. respond that we discussed a few sessions back.*

[Discuss]

Everyone's right. The dog's way of thinking is so much different than ours. They pretty much don't have as high an ability to think through how they're going to respond to certain situations, they just react. Like the lion mind vs. dog mind metaphor, the dog just sees the bone and goes after it. Doesn't think about it at all. Has anyone ever seen dogs go up and start humping someone's leg? Yeah? Well, I think you know that there'd be some hard consequences for us if we just went up to someone we liked and started humping the person's leg, right? We have the ability to think before we act, and that's what the frontal lobe's function helps us do. Specifically, this front part of the brain, the prefrontal cortex and frontal lobe, contribute to something called "executive functioning." Anyone know what that is? . . .

[Discuss]

What does "executive" mean? . . . What does an executive producer of a music album do? . . . What do an executive producer of a music album and an executive at a huge company have in common? . . . Right, they're both probably the bosses. They call the shots. That's basically the function of our prefrontal cortex and frontal lobe: it helps us control ourselves and tells us not to go hump the legs of people we like, as dogs do. It has the power, with training of course, to keep us out of a whole lot of trouble. And how do you all think mindfulness training plays a part in enhancing executive function? . . .

[Discuss]

Correct. The practice of mindfulness, at least some forms of it, provides, literally, the practice of being aware of what's arising inside us without being reactive to it. When we practice that, we're practicing executive function. And, as we keep practicing, our ability to regulate what arises in us—whether it be strong emotions, sensations, or disturbing thoughts—grows. That's why mindfulness has a close relationship with executive function. We'll come back to the role of mindfulness in the brain in a bit, but, any other questions or comments before the next slide? . . .

Slide 3: Dopamine, Pleasure, and Substance Use

Slide 3 overviews the role of dopamine and pleasure, and the role dopamine plays in illicit drug use: namely, that it is significantly increased by those particular substances and that there is risk for addiction because of this increased transmission of pleasurable sensations by dopamine. Slide 3 contains an image of the neurotransmitter dopamine and the rate of its increased activity as triggered by commonly used drugs.

Use the talking points and example script below to present this slide.

Talking Points

- Ask the question, "What are some things that you all do, besides using drugs, that make you feel good?"
- Ask, "How do you think dopamine is affected when you do drugs?"

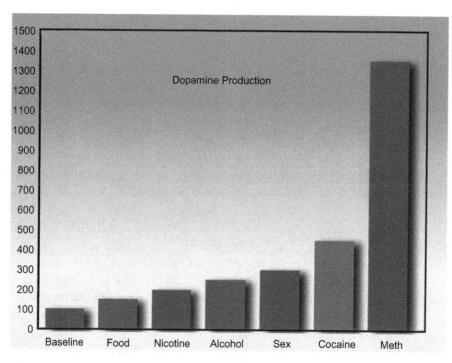

Figure 9.3

- Discuss the amount of dopamine that is increased in the brain by various drugs.
- Ask, "What do you think the effect of a huge increase in dopamine activity is, besides the sensation of feeling high?"

Example Script

Facilitator: *Before we cover this slide, I want to ask you all, what are some things you do that make you feel good? . . . Anything besides drugs? . . .*

[Discuss]

That's right. There are many things that make us feel good. Sex, food, working out—many things. Even hugs can make us feel good. Does anyone know what a neurotransmitter is? It's a chemical in the brain that transmits messages. See this? **[Point to image of the neuron on the slide.]** *This is a neuron. There are hundreds of millions, if not billions, of neurons in our brains. And the way they communicate with each other is through neurotransmitters. Anyone want to guess, if you don't already know, the neurotransmitter that is responsible for feeling pleasure? Every time you do something that feels good, this neurotransmitter communicates across millions of neurons in the brain, and that's what gives you the experience of feeling good. It's called Dopamine! You can remember it because, sort of like how dope gets you high, dopamine makes you feel good. So, every time pleasure, or that good feeling, arises in you, there are dopamine neurotransmitters firing across your brain. That's the role of dopamine. What about with drugs? What do you all think happens with dopamine when you do drugs?*

[Discuss]

That's right. The dopamine gets skyrocketed in our brains. Every time you do drugs, you're actually artificially increasing the dopamine in your brain. It's not that the drug puts more dopamine in your brain, it's just that it prevents certain processes from happening and so more dopamine gets caught in between your neurons. We'll talk about that in a bit. What do you all notice about the difference between the amount of effect of these drugs when it comes to dopamine? That's right, generally the stimulants are the drugs that increase dopamine the most. But Meth, this one increases dopamine activity way higher than any other drug. What do you all think the result of that is? Yeah, a much higher potential for addiction. Let's take a short meditation break, and then we'll cover some more details about dopamine in the brain.

IMPORTANT NOTE

This is a generalization to dopamine and the brain in regard to drugs. We know that it's much more complicated than this and encourage you to discuss other neurochemicals (i.e., serotonin, etc.) as time permits.

4. Meditation Break

Take a break from the slide show (we don't want to overwhelm the youth with psycho-education) and lead a brief Bodyscan meditation with an emphasis on calming the body. Suggest that there are times when meditation can simply enhance dopamine levels. Use the talking points and example script below as a guide for the meditation during this break.

Talking Points

- Lead a short Bodyscan meditation.
- Emphasize relaxation and calmness.

Calming Bodyscan Script

Facilitator: *Let's take a break from this slideshow stuff before we finish it. I'd like for us to take a meditation break. So, sit somewhat upright in your chairs, let your eyes close, if you feel comfortable with that, and, when you hear the sound of the bell, take a few deep breaths in and a few deep breaths out . . .*

[Ring bell]

As you bring your awareness to your breath, notice how it feels in your body to breathe . . . Notice all the sensations associated with breathing; your belly expanding and contracting, your chest expanding and contracting, everything . . . let your awareness briefly scan your whole body, just noticing any areas of tension or stress. Breathe into those areas, with the simple intention of loosening those areas and relaxing . . . With each breath in, and each breath out, imagine your body getting more calm, more relaxed . . . if you've noticed that your mind has wandered away, if you've started to think about something other than the body in this moment, that's okay. Simply bring your awareness back to the body, breathing in, and breathing out . . . calming the body, relaxing the body . . . and, in a moment, when I ring the bell, see if you can listen to the sound of the bell until you can't hear it any longer.

[Ring bell]

When you feel comfortable, you can slowly open your eyes, if they were closed, and expand your awareness to the rest of the group and room.

Process the meditation with the youth for a few minutes prior to finishing the slideshow of the brain on drugs.

5. Brain Presentation II: Substance Use, Trauma, and the Mindful Brain

Slides 4–5: Dopamine in Synapses

Slides 4 and 5 detail what occurs between synapses in the brain when one experiences being high. Cocaine is used as an example. This is a place where you could insert other drugs in additional slides such as marijuana, alcohol, ecstasy, etc., as based on what the youth in your group asked for at the start of the curriculum. Slide 4 is an image of a synapse without cocaine molecules and Slide 5 includes an image of a synapse and how cocaine blocks the dopamine receptors from entering other neurons.

Use the talking points and example script below to present these slides and alternate between them as needed.

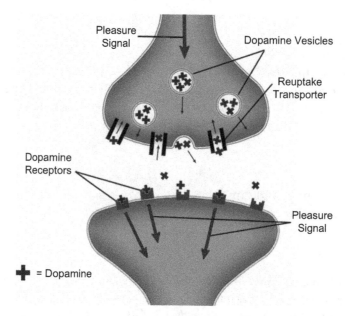

Figure 9.4

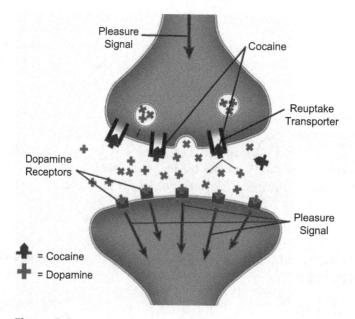

Figure 9.5

Talking Points

- Define synapses.
- State that cocaine molecules block dopamine from entering other neurons.
- State that dopamine gets caught in the synapse and the experience of being high arises.
- Present the musical chairs metaphor.
- State that different drugs work slightly differently depending on their components.
- Present information on other drugs in this respect, if need be.

Example Script

Facilitator: These two slightly round ends **[point to ends of neurons around the synapse]** *are the ends of neurons. As we said before the meditation break, this is how neurons communicate with each other. The space between them is a called a synapse. This is where all the magic happens when you get high. There are basically a bunch of pumps on the ends of these neurons. The ones on one neuron pump out dopamine and then the pumps on the other neuron suck the dopamine in. The thing is, when you add cocaine, for example, into the equation, the cocaine blocks the dopamine from going into the other neuron's pump. So there's a bunch of extra dopamine floating around in the synapse, and that's why, oftentimes, folks high off cocaine feel like they can run the world! Anyone here ever play musical chairs? In some sense it's like that, except that, instead of taking away a chair every time the music stops, think of it like you all got up to go to the bathroom, and, when you came back, some other people had taken your seats. And, with no other chairs in the room, you'd just be standing around. When cocaine enters the system, dopamine increases naturally because the pleasure center is activated, but the next thing those littler neurotransmitters know is that all these cocaine molecules have stolen their seats. And, instead of standing around, they run around frantically. That's what's going on in your brain when you're high off coke. Any questions? . . . Also, it's important to know that different drugs work slightly differently. All of them in some way activate dopamine and your pleasure center, but they work in different ways.*

[Present on other drugs if desired.]

Now that we've covered the experience of being high and what happens in the brain, let's circle back to the addictive process and how dopamine influences it.

Slide 6: Tolerance and Withdrawal

Slide 6 is an overview of the addictive process, presenting an analogy to tolerance and withdrawal. Youth are educated about the role dopamine plays in the addictive process via the thermostat metaphor. This slide has an image of a thermostat and the words "Tolerance" on it.

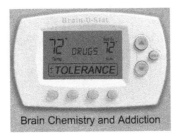

Figure 9.6

Use the talking points and example script below as a guide for presenting this slide.

Talking Points

- Define tolerance and withdrawal.
- Discuss the role of tolerance and withdrawal in addiction.
- Present the thermostat metaphor.

Example Script

Facilitator: *Who knows what tolerance is?*

[Discuss]

That's right. Tolerance is when you need more than the usual amount of the drug to get the same degree of high. So if you're smoking weed and usually one joint gets you high, you know you've developed some tolerance when one joint doesn't get you as high as it used to. What about withdrawal symptoms? Who knows what those are?

[Discuss]

Right again. Withdrawal symptoms happen when you don't have your drug any longer and start to feel the effects. Sometimes when alcoholics don't have alcohol for a while they get the "shakes." Has anyone ever seen that? Those are withdrawal symptoms. In another case, when people who've been on Opiates don't have them any longer, they get flu-like symptoms, sometimes worse. Those are also withdrawal symptoms. The key to withdrawal symptoms is that your body is telling you in one way or another that you need the drug and need it now. When you have an excessive amount of dopamine in your system, and then don't have it any longer, because you're not high any longer and have no more drugs, that's when withdrawal symptoms occur. Any questions about this? . . . Does this all make sense? . . . Let me explain this through a metaphor. Think about its being like a thermostat. When you want to feel warm, you turn up the heat. Let's say the regular setting is at like 69 degrees, but you want to feel even warmer, so you turn it up to 75 degrees, and you keep it at 75 degrees day and night for a week. Then let's say one day you just turn the heater back down to 69 degrees—to where it was before. How do you think you'll feel? Right, you'll probably feel cold. Even though, originally, before you had the heat on higher, you didn't feel cold. That's because you got used to the temperature at 75 degrees. It's similar with drugs and dopamine. Once your brain and body get used to a specific amount of dopamine from using a certain drug, when you don't have it any longer, you don't feel as good as you did without it before you used the drug. That's because your brain gets used to having that amount of dopamine available—in a way equivalent to the effect of changing the heat level over a long time in the thermostat metaphor—so it stops producing it. And, as you withdraw from the drug, with less dopamine, the pleasure chemical, available then, you then feel more depressed and in a bad mood than you would have before you began taking the drug. So, to not feel that way, what do you think most people do? . . . Right, they go back to the one thing that can restore that dopamine—the drug. Think of people who are really addicted to certain drugs as people who turned up their thermostats too long and, when trying to turn them back down, found life too cold. Any questions about this? . . . Does this make sense? . . .

Proceed with Slide 7 after answering any questions.

Slides 7–8: Drug Use and Bad Habits

Slides 7 and 8 provide an overview of the role neural pathways in the brain play in the forming of destructive habits (e.g., when anger or another strong emotion triggers drug use) that occur alongside consistent drug use. Slide 7 contains an image of a dirt path in an otherwise untouched grass field. Slide 8 contains a graphic of neural pathways in a brain.

Figure 9.7

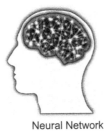

Neural Network

Figure 9.8

Use the talking points and example script below as a guide to the process arising from Slides 7 and 8.

Talking Points

- Define neural pathways using the grass path metaphor.
- Discuss habits and neural pathways.
- Discuss how solidified neural pathways of drug use lead to more drug use.

Example Script

> *Facilitator:* Who knows what a neural pathway is? . . . It's something that's formed in the brain after a behavior is repeated over and over. Think about its being like a short grass field between two synapses in the brain. Imagine if I walked from one side of the grass field to the other, every day for 6 months. Now imagine that I'd be tracing my footsteps exactly every time I walk across the path. What do you think would happen to the grass after 6 months? . . . Right, the grass would die, and a dirt path result. That's what's happening in your brain, for example, when you drink alcohol every time you start to feel depressed because your friend died, or even if you just smoke weed to deal with stress. The more you do it, the deeper the neural pathway will be carved. The result is that, when you don't have the drugs and those feelings of stress, or depression, or whatever arise, you'll want the drugs even more because unconsciously you'll know that's the antidote to those feelings. And that's another way to think about how addiction develops: over years of forming these neural pathways and developing a cycle of tolerance and withdrawal symptoms. Does this make sense? . . . Basically, the more you use drugs to cope with strong emotions, the more you'll crave drugs when a strong emotion arises. That's why people who have extensive trauma use drugs so often, because it numbs that emotional pain they feel. They use drugs to mask the pain, and, when they don't have the drug any longer, the pain comes back. Over time, the pain automatically triggers the craving to use drugs. The issue is that they get dependent on the drugs in order not to feel the pain, and they never actually heal their traumas. By show of hands, who here has ever used drugs to deal with emotional pain, be it something really intense or just simply using drugs to deal with stress? . . . Would anyone like to share the last time that happened?

Give the youth an opportunity to discuss the last time they used drugs to mask emotions. Spend a few minutes letting the youth discuss these experiences and ask whether they think the drugs they were using really healed their distress or whether those substances simply acted as a *band aid*.

Slide 9: Mindfulness and the Brain

The final slide of this brief slide show presents the idea that mindfulness practice can be used as a tool to *un-train* the neural pathways that have been created based on unskillful habits such as using drugs to mask strong emotions.

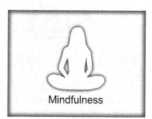

Figure 9.9

Use the talking points and example script below as a guide when presenting this slide.

Talking Points

- State that there are still ways for reversing neural pathways after habitual drug use as a painkiller.
- Define neuroplasticity.
- Discuss the role mindfulness plays in increasing neuroplasticity.

Example Script

Facilitator: Even though it can be depressing to think of those neural pathways we just talked about, especially if some of us deal with some of those issues, there's still hope. We wouldn't have you here in this program if we didn't have some tools for you to attempt to deal with strong emotions and drugs. Anyone want to guess what those tools might be? . . . Right. The mindfulness meditation training we've been doing for the last six sessions is the primary tool that can deconstruct some of those bad habits and neural pathways that were formed by using drugs to deal with distress. But it's more than just practicing meditation, it's really about developing that executive function, developing that ability to choose your response rather than simply reacting. We discussed the difference between a response and a reaction a few sessions back. Responding to our experience, rather than reacting to it, and choosing alternative and/ or healthier ways to cope will help deconstruct those negative neural pathways. Has anyone ever heard the term "neuroplasticity?" . . . What it basically means is that your brain actually does have the ability to unravel old unskillful neural pathways, bad habits, and create new ones. There used to be a bunch of scientists who thought that whoever you were when you reached your mid-twenties, that's who you were going to be for the rest of your life—meaning that your brain would become "set" and there was nothing that could be done about it. But that was all proved wrong by more recent and better research. And that's when the term "neuroplasticity" started getting thrown around the science community. And as we just said above, mindfulness is one way to increase neuroplasticity. Based on your meditation practice so far, why do you think that might be?

[Discuss]

Right. The way it works is that, when you're just observing the content of your minds, or the sensations in your body, without reacting, just being nonjudgmental, you're literally practicing another way to relate to whatever mental experience is arising in you. With a good amount of practice, you can apply that to situations that would normally be triggered by negative neural pathways. If you practice mindfulness or simply learn to become self-aware when feeling angry, there's more of a likelihood that you won't automatically use drugs to cope with that anger. Or at least you'd have more choice in that situation. And if you chose not to use drugs a number of times when anger came up in you, you'd be altering your behavior, which in turn would ultimately create new neural pathways in your brain. Does that make sense? . . . Any questions about this? . . . Okay, if nothing else comes to mind, let's stop talking about this and start practicing with our formal meditation for this group. Sound good? . . .

WHAT IF?

The youth start getting bored or less present during this primarily didactic presentation? First, continuously attempt to engage the youth on their personal experiences related to what you're presenting to keep them engaged. Second, it's completely okay to use multi-media platforms during this presentation. Remember, this is just a sample template for you. There are a number of ways and resources to present this information. For example, it is relatively easy to find an animation of the effects of Cocaine (and other drugs) in synapses of the brain on the Internet. If you feel like your group will be more engaged with video, by all means please incorporate.

6. Meditation: Bodyscan

Facilitate a Bodyscan meditation using the script from session 4. Encourage the group to meditate for a longer period (7–10 minutes).

7. Homework and Close-Out

Ask for another volunteer youth (preferably not the same one who volunteered for this session) to lead the centering meditation for session 7. Encourage the youth to think of themselves as *executives* of their own lives and to practice the Bodyscan at least three times prior to the next session.

SESSION 6 HANDOUTS

SLIDESHOW HANDOUTS

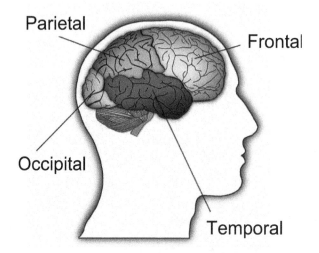

Figure 9.1

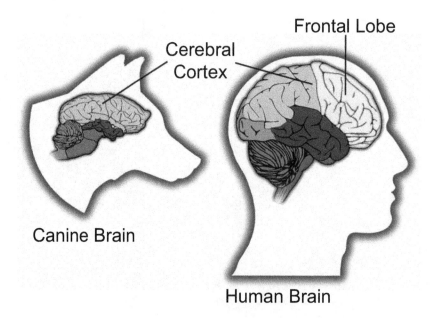

Figure 9.2

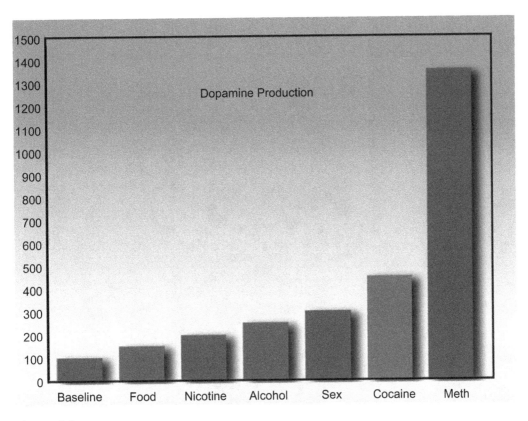

Figure 9.3

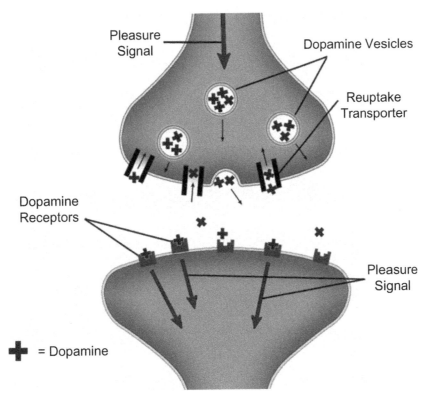

Figure 9.4

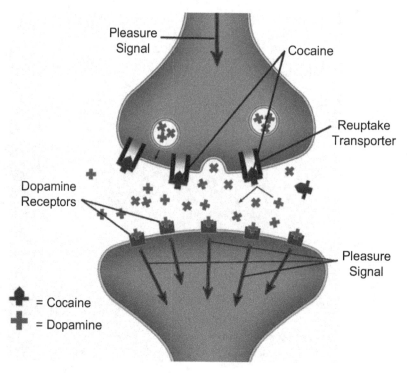

Figure 9.5

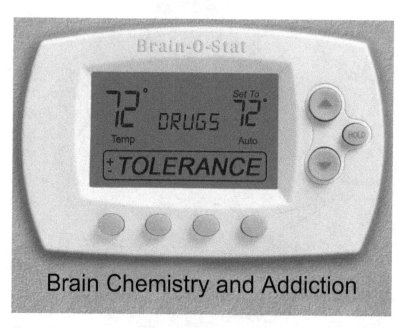

Figure 9.6

Figure 9.7

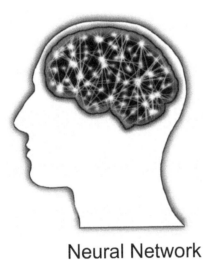

Neural Network

Figure 9.8

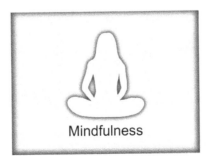

Mindfulness

Figure 9.9

SESSION 7

MINDFULNESS OF CRAVING

Session Summary

Session 7 covers one of the most important themes for how mindfulness can help prevent substance abuse: dealing with urges and cravings. This session reviews the role of urges and cravings in drug use, discusses the different types of cravings that lead to drug use, and teaches practices for effectively coping with such cravings. An advanced form of the Bodyscan meditation is taught with an emphasis on not giving in to one's desire to move while meditating.

Materials Needed

- Meditation bell
- Bite-sized chocolate bars (or other snack)
- Markers
- Poster paper and tape (or whiteboard)
- Writing utensils for youth participants
- Session 7 Handouts (optional)

Formal Meditation (Time)

- Nonmoving Bodyscan (8–10 minutes)

Learning Objectives

- Review the role of urges and cravings in drug use
- Practice awareness of urge/craving
- Present craving/urge flow chart
- Practice nonmoving Bodyscan meditation

Session Agenda (Chair Configuration)

1. Youth-Led Centering Meditation (Circle)
2. Mindful Check-In (Circle)
3. Mindful Eating Activity (Circle)
4. The Role of Craving in Drug Use (Semicircle)
5. Nonmoving Bodyscan Meditation (Circle)
6. Worksheet: The Roots of Craving (Spread Across Room; Circle)
7. Homework and Close-Out (Circle)

1. Youth-Led Centering Meditation

Once again, start with one of the youth participants leading a centering meditation (you should have asked for a volunteer at the end of the last session). Use the below discussion questions as a guide to processing the youth facilitator's experience:

- How did it feel to lead the meditation?
- Could you ever see yourself becoming a meditation teacher or something similar? (e.g., counselor, teacher, healer)
- How was that meditation for you all? How was it when one of your peers was leading the meditation?

2. Mindful Check-In

After the youth-led centering, facilitate a mindful check-in using any of the previous sessions' mindful check-ins as a guide. (Consult session 2 for the full exercise.)

3. Mindful Eating Activity

For this exercise you'll need snacks (i.e., bite size chocolate bars, strawberries, etc.) handy at your side. It's important that you have a small snack, as the point of this exercise is for the youth to slow down as they attempt to eat mindfully. Make sure you have enough snacks to provide two to each youth, as the first part of this exercise is to learn and practice mindful eating (with the first snack), while the second part is to elicit and be mindful of craving (with the second snack).

NOTE

We usually bring bite-sized chocolate bars, given how much the youth we work with like them, but any small snack (e.g., strawberries, as a healthy alternative) would work as well.

This activity has three basic steps: 1) mindful eating instructions, 2) mindful eating exercise, and 3) the enactment of craving and practicing mindfulness.

Step 1: Mindful Eating Instructions

First, let the youth know that the next activity involves food and is a "mindful eating" activity. Briefly ask one of the youth to define mindfulness (based on memory) and instruct them to apply the definition to the experience of eating (e.g., what would mindful eating be?). Next, take out your small bag of bite-sized chocolates and place them on your lap in clear view (make sure that there are only enough bite-sized bars in the bag so that each youth participant would get one. You'll need to have another bag hidden somewhere with more bite-sized chocolate bars that they can't see for

Step 3 of this activity). Next, explain the instructions for mindful eating. Use the talking points and example script below as a guide.

Talking Points

- Take no less than four bites.
- After each bite, chew slowly.
- Observe the different textures and tastes in the mouth.
- Swallow fully prior to taking another bite.

Facilitator: So, we're going to try this mindful eating exercise. This will be sort of like a meditation but we'll be eating these bite-sized chocolate bars while doing it. I'm going to pass out these chocolate bars and each of you will get one. But when I pass them out, don't automatically open them and eat them. Wait for me to ring the meditation bell and tell you when to start. I know these things are really small, and they're called bite-sized so that you can take them down in one bite, but we're going to do the opposite of that. We're going to eat these really slowly and observe what it's like, how different it is from eating fast. The main instructions for this activity include you having to take at least four bites. For each bite, close your eyes and chew slowly, feel the different tastes and textures in your mouth. Then, fully swallow that bite before taking another one. Repeat that at least four times and then we'll talk about what the experience was like.

Step 2: Mindful Eating Exercise

Pass out the bite-sized bars and ring the meditation bell to being the activity. Every once in a while throughout the activity, remind the youth to chew slowly and mindfully observe their experience (e.g., the textures in their mouth, the tastes, etc.). After you've noticed that each one has finished the last bite, ring the meditation bell and process the experience.

Process Mindful Eating Exercise

Use the following discussion questions to process the experience:

- What was the mindful eating activity like for you?
- How was it to eat that slowly?
- Did you notice any tastes or textures that you hadn't before?
- Do you think there's any benefit in eating food in this way on a regular basis?

Step 3: Enactment of Craving and Mindfulness Practice

This is the most important step in this activity from a substance-abuse-treatment perspective. You'll be offering the youth a taste of what it feels like to crave, or feel an urge to satisfy, and teach them how to practice mindfulness with such an experience (which may be transferable to drug cravings, as well).

Start by taking out your second bag of bite-sized chocolate bars (the bag that has been hidden) and place it on your lap in clear view. You might do this in a nonchalant way, possibly even at the end of the discussion on mindful eating. Shuffle the bag through your fingers in clear view and ask, "*Does anyone want another one?"* As their faces light up, ask the follow up question. *"How much do you want another one? On a scale of from 1–10, 10 being you want another really badly."* Field a couple of youths' answers. Tell the group you'll give them another one after the next activity.

Mindfulness of Craving Meditation. Facilitate a brief mindfulness exercise in which they are directed to become aware of the physical sensation of craving. Use the talking points and example script below as a guide.

Talking Points

- Direct awareness toward the sensation connected with the urge.
- Present urge *surfing* metaphor.
- Observe sensation/craving and notice its impermanence.

Example Script

Facilitator: *I'm going to hand these out in a moment, and this time it's up to you whether you eat it slowly or quickly, but first I'm going to ask everyone to close their eyes, if comfortable with that, and practice a brief meditation with me.*

[Ring bell]

I want to invite you to notice where you feel that "want" for the second chocolate bar. Some of you might "want" it badly, others not so much. Just observe where you feel that "want." Sometimes we call that an urge, or a craving, because we crave more, in this case more chocolate bars . . . Notice whether you can feel any physical sensations associated with that craving or urge . . . Maybe you feel something in your stomach, maybe you feel something in your mouth . . . Just observe. Just notice. Breathing in, and breathing out, just noticing where you can actually feel the physical sensation of the craving . . . If you can't feel anything, that's okay, just feel your breath in your belly. But if you can, just keep your awareness on that craving. What makes up the sensations of that craving? Are there smaller sensations? Is it always the same? Or does it change? Just notice. Just observe the sensations in this moment. All the while breathing in, and breathing out. See if you can stay with the craving until it goes away. See if, when the urge and craving arises, you can surf it like a wave until it's gone. A wave develops speed and strength, gets big and has a peak, and eventually crashes. Imagine surfing that wave and not crashing, not giving in. Just notice the urge or craving until it's gone, until there are no waves and the water is still. If you said you felt like a 7, 8, 9, or 10 in wanting a second chocolate bar, see if you can observe that craving and just let it pass, and watch those numbers drop, until it's a 2, 1, or even 0 . . . Breathing in, and breathing out, as we come to a close, just listen to the sound of the bell as I ring it.

[Ring bell]

After finishing the meditation, briefly process the experience using the discussion questions below as a guide:

- How was that experience?
- Could you feel a sensation associated with craving?
- Did you have specific thoughts associated with the craving?
- Could you observe your thoughts and sensations changing?

- Were you able to *surf* the urge/craving and see it become lower?
- For what else, besides with food, could being aware of cravings (and not giving into them) be beneficial?

After completing the discussion above, pass out the second chocolate bar or snack at your own discretion. Oftentimes we'd give the youth the choice to either eat the second snack slowly and mindfully or at their own preferred pace.

4. The Role of Craving in Drug Use

Ask the youth to rearrange their chairs into a semicircle around the wall/board you'll be presenting on. The emphasis of this discussion will be on the idea that urges and cravings are often precursors to actual drug use. We will not be suggesting that it is only cravings and urges and not external forces that play a role in drug use, but will simply focus on the internal states of craving here (and the role of external forces later in the curriculum). This activity has two steps: 1) discussing the role of craving in drug use, and 2) presenting the trigger and urges flow chart.

Step 1: Discussion on Role of Craving in Drug Use

Start this discussion by asking the youth what they think is the role cravings have in drug use. Use the talking points below and the example script as a guide to building on the discussion and presenting the role cravings play in drug use.

Talking Points

- Start by asking of the group, "What role do cravings play in drug use?"
- Cravings are at the root of drug use.
- Sometimes we do the drug so much that, when we don't have it, we really want it.
- There are two forms of craving: 1) wanting something (desire), and 2) not wanting something (aversion), i.e., really wanting something to go away (e.g., a strong emotion, memory, etc.).
- If craving can be targeted, there is a higher chance that the behavior of drug use can be avoided.

Example Script

Facilitator: *What role do cravings play in drug use? . . . Just as with hunger, anger, and other strong emotions, urges and cravings play a central role in drug use. Remember, craving is that really strong urge of "I want," but it also takes the form of "I don't want," or craving for something to go away. It's like the same coin that has two different sides. We talked a little bit last session how some of us use drugs to cover up strong feelings, emotions, and hard memories. That's the "I don't want" side of craving. Some of us have had the experience of doing drugs so much that when we don't have the drug we're used to doing, we want it really badly. That's the "I want" side of craving. But just as we practiced a few minutes ago, cravings and strong urges are things that can be observed, watched, and not reacted to. We can train our minds to watch the craving and not react to it. That's what this mindfulness training is really about, whether we're talking about drugs, hunger, anger, or other strong emotions. If we can train our minds to be nonreactive, as we* *talked about in session 3 where we defined the difference between a reaction and response, and if we target the actual underlying urge or craving, we have a better shot at not being so reactive, not doing the drugs, or not reacting out of anger, or, at the very least, thinking about what we do before doing it, whether we actually do it or not. Does that make sense to everyone? . . .*

After setting the stage, present some discussion questions to the group and have a discussion amongst yourselves. Below are some questions we often use, but feel free to add to, subtract, and transform them to fit your group's needs:

- Do you think it's possible to control your urges when it comes to drug use?
- Do you think drug cravings are stronger than other types of urges and cravings?
- What is the difference between how mindfulness teaches us to deal with our cravings versus other approaches?
- What's one time in your life (if any) where you knew you should not have used drugs but you had such a strong urge that you did anyways?

Step 2: Triggers and Urges Flow Chart

On the wall behind you (or whiteboard/flip chart), draw—or post your pre-drawn—flow chart so that everyone can see it in clear view. The chart will include a *T* that stands for trigger, a *U* that stands for urge, and a *DU* that stands for drug use, with arrows between the T and the U, and between the U and the DU pointing in a circular fashion. Present the flow chart to the group and explain that you'll be discussing triggers in much more depth next group session.

Use the talking points and example script below as a guide to facilitating this step.

Talking Points

- Define the T (trigger), U (urge/craving), and DU (drug use) on the chart.
- Discuss the cycle of triggers, urges (cravings), and drug use.
- Ask the group which of the three elements on the chart an individual has control over.

Example Script

Facilitator: *This is called the Triggers and Urges flow chart. You can see the letters T, U, and DU. You know how some people have "to do" lists? Well, think of this as the "tu du" chart, a way to always remember the role of craving and urges in any of your behaviors. The T stands for triggers. We're going to spend the whole group on this next time, but just to prep you, a trigger is anything that "triggers" us, or has the chance of making us want to do drugs. These could include people, places, emotions, memories—you name it. We'll go into depth on this next week, but for now this is okay. The U stands for urge. As we've been talking about all during the session, urges and cravings are at the root of all drug use, or at least most of it. The DU stands for drug use. Just as I just mentioned, "a trigger makes you want to use drugs." The trigger occurs, and triggers your "want," and that's the urge, which then triggers the actual use . . . And you can think of this like a cycle too, it's not always linear. Sometimes continued drug use triggers craving for more drug use. I have a question for the group: Out of the three elements on this chart, what do we have control over? . . . The thing that we're focusing on here, because it's what we have control over, is the "U."*

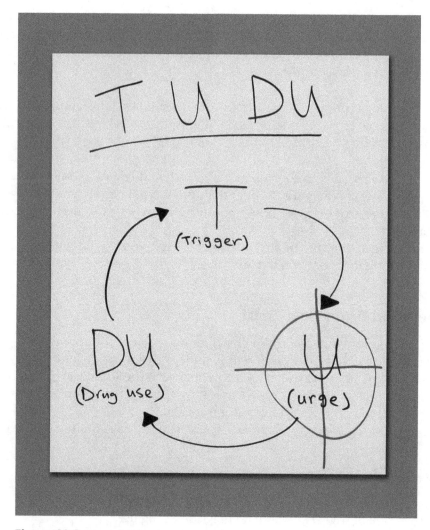

Figure 10.1

[Draw a target sign over the U.]

If we can target the urge and craving, we can stop the cycle of continued drug use, or stop the cycle of continued aggression, or anger, or whatever the unhealthy action is. That's what today's whole session has been about, being able to identify the underlying urge and cut it out before it grows. And how can we do that? How do we target those urges? Any ideas? . . . Mindfulness and meditation is a great way to deal with your urges because it trains us to relate to our urges differently, to watch them and not act on them. There is a lot of power in that. Let's practice.

5. Nonmoving Bodyscan

After the previous discussion, proceed directly into the formal meditation of the session. The primary difference between this meditation and its previous incarnations is that you'll be asking the youth not to make any physical movements for the duration of the meditation. That is, invite them not to move their hands, head, feet, and whole body (breathing is, of course, okay). This will train the youth to not immediately react to the desire to shift their bodies (and the transferable skill of nonreactivity has the potential to flow in to other areas of their lives, such as drug cravings and other undesired behaviors).

Use the talking points and example script below as a guide for facilitating this meditation (also find a printable version of this meditation in this session's handouts).

Talking Points

- Differentiate this meditation by prompting the youth to not move.
- Facilitate a nonmoving Bodyscan.
- Remind the youth every so often of the intention to not move and to be aware of the urge to move.

Example Script

Facilitator: *For today's group we're going to do a Bodyscan meditation like the one we've been doing for the past few sessions with one major difference: I want to ask you NOT to move during this whole medita-tion. You can breathe, of course, and, if you keep your eyes open, you can blink, but, other than that, try not to move at all. This is going to be difficult, and there are going to be many times when you're going to want to move to get more comfortable; if you learn to just observe the discomfort and that urge to move, without moving, you will learn how to conquer your urges to use drugs, or urges toward any behavior, for that matter. If, for some reason, you get too uncomfortable, it's okay to readjust. My invitation to you in those situations however, is to become aware of the urge to move first, observe it for a few moments, and then readjust your body. Can everyone give this a fair try? . . . Take a moment to stretch and loosen your body, since we'll be holding it in place for about 8–10 minutes. Sit in a posture you feel that you can hold for that amount of time and, remember, I invite you not to move outside of breathing for this whole practice. When you hear the sound of the bell, bring all of your awareness to the act of breathing and then wait for more instructions.*

[Ring bell]

Start by taking a few deep breaths in and out. Just notice your body as you breathe in and out . . . Notice your posture, the chair that's supporting you, the floor under your feet . . . On your next breath in and your next breath out, bring all of your attention to your feet. Become aware of any sensations in your feet. These could be positive sensations, negative sensations, neutral sensations. It doesn't matter, just become aware of them . . . When you shift your attention to your feet, you may notice an inclination or urge to move and adjust them. Simply notice that urge without actually moving them. Notice what it feels like—the different sensations that comprise that urge—and just maintain your posture . . . moving your awareness up into your ankles . . . and the lower legs, the shins and calves, just become aware of any sensations. They may be small sensations, or large sensations . . . you might feel tingliness, or the touch of your pant leg, it could be any sensation . . . and if you get that urge to adjust your body, wherever that may be, just shift your aware-ness to that urge, to that part of the body, observe it, dissect the urge, surf the urge to move, and then come back to the area of the body we're focusing on, in this case the lower legs . . . letting your awareness move up into the knees: the fronts of the knees, sides, and back of the knees . . . and up into your upper legs: the quadriceps, hamstrings, thighs, just scan this area of the body like an x-ray machine, scanning for differ-ent sensations . . . and again, when the temptation to move the body arises again, move your awareness to wherever you feel it strongest. Just observe that urge, surf that urge, and do not move the body . . . letting your awareness move up into your hips and belly: noticing your belly expanding and contracting with each breath, simply be aware of what it feels like to breathe right now. The sensations associated with breathing in, the stretchiness of the skin, the sensations associated with breathing out, the deflation of the belly. Just observe any sensations . . . moving your awareness into your chest, become aware of any sensations in the chest. Simply breathing in, and breathing out. Just noticing any sensations . . . shifting your awareness to your back. Let your awareness slowly rise up your back, from your lower back, to your middle back, to your upper back. Just as if a cup is filling up with water, your back is filling up with awareness . . . and again, if the urge to move arises, simply observe it, let it arise, let it pass, and don't react to it . . . moving your awareness to your hands: the configuration of your hands, your fingertips, knuckles, and palms . . . maybe you feel heat in your hands, or tingliness, or any sensation. Simply be aware . . . Letting your awareness rise up through your wrists into your forearms, scanning this area of the body like an X-ray machine, simply observing sensations . . . up unto your upper arms: the biceps, triceps, and shoulders . . . the neck: the front of your neck, the sides, and back of your neck . . . Letting your awareness rise up into your jaw and chin, and slowly expand across the face: the mouth, the cheeks, the nose, the eyes and eyebrows, and forehead. Just observe . . . you may feel an itch. Just observe that itch, try not to react to it. Observe the subtle sensations that make up the larger sensation of the itch . . . the ears and the sides of the head . . . the back of the head, and finally the top of your head. Just observing any sensation . . . and finally let your awareness expand to your whole body, from the top of your head to the tips of your toes, from the tips of your toes to the top of your head . . . just noticing any sensations that are happening right now . . . and again, when the urge to move, to readjust, to make your posture more comfortable arises, simply shift your awareness to where that sensation for the urge is strongest, observe the urge, and watch it change. Watch it arise, watch it pass . . . In a few moments, I'm going to ring the bell. When I do, shift your awareness to your ears and try to listen to the bell until it's no longer there. When you can't hear it any longer, you can open your eyes.

[Ring bell]

Discuss the experience of this advanced meditation using the below guiding questions:

- Was it difficult to not move? What was the experience like?
- What was the benefit of practicing the nonmoving meditation?
- How long do you think you could practice that meditation before "needing" to move?
- How does learning to not react to one's urge to move relate to learning how to not react to one's urges to use drugs?

WHAT IF?

The youth move around constantly or don't take the nonmoving aspect of this meditation seriously? Remind yourself that although the goal is to have youth do every meditation as instructed, this often-times isn't a reality. There's no need to become preoccupied or frustrated with a youth who isn't sitting still for this or any meditation for that matter. Youth will take care of themselves when needed and it's best to not take their lack of interest or ability to sit still personally. You can always inquire about how the meditation experience was for them afterwards to get more information.

6. Worksheet: Roots of Craving

To finish the session, have the youth spread out across the room to individually contemplate the root of their drug use. This activity is designed to start the process of insight in regard to youth understanding the nature of their craving for drugs (and other behaviors). Pass out the "Roots of Craving" from the session handouts at the end of this chapter and instruct the group in filling in the worksheet. The worksheet is categorized into two columns: the "want" column, and the "don't want" column. At the top it reads "I _____ because I want/don't want," and builds upon the personal pros and cons of substance use activity from session 4. Have the youth fill in the blank with their drug of choice, and lead by example. If it was alcohol, it would read, "I drink alcohol because I want/don't want." Then explain that the "want" column is the desire you were discussing earlier. Someone would want to do drugs to feel good, to feel cool, to feel that rush, etc. The "don't want" column represents wanting to get rid of something. Someone might want to do drugs to cover up hard memories, deal with trauma, get rid of the shakes, etc. State this to the youth with examples and then instruct them to write simple words or phrases in each column. Encourage them to contemplate both their "wants" and "don't wants" deeply. Give them 5–10 minutes for this activity prior to circling back up. Have the youth circle back up and give them an opportunity to share what they wrote.

7. Homework and Close-Out

Encourage the youth to practice the nonmoving Bodyscan at least three times prior to the next session. Also invite them to continue to contemplate the role of craving in, not only drug use but all behavior, as well. Ask anyone if s/he is willing to lead the centering meditation for the next session.

SESSION 7 HANDOUTS

Nonmoving Bodyscan Script

Talking Points

- Differentiate this meditation by prompting the youth to not move.
- Facilitate a nonmoving Bodyscan.
- Remind the youth every so often of the intention to not move and to be aware of the urge to move.

Example Script

Facilitator: *For today's group we're going to do a Bodyscan meditation like the one we've been doing for the past few sessions with one major difference: I want to ask you NOT to move during this whole meditation. You can breathe, of course, and, if you keep your eyes open, you can blink, but, other than that, try not to move at all. This is going to be difficult, and there are going to be many times when you're going to want to move to get more comfortable; if you learn to just observe the discomfort and that urge to move, without moving, you will learn how to conquer your urges to use drugs, or urges toward any behavior, for that matter. If, for some reason, you get too uncomfortable, it's okay to readjust. My invitation to you in those situations however, is to become aware of the urge to move first, observe it for a few moments, and then readjust your body. Can everyone give this a fair try? . . . Take a moment to stretch and loosen your body, since we'll be holding it in place for about 8–10 minutes. Sit in a posture you feel that you can hold for that amount of time and, remember, I invite you not to move outside of breathing for this whole practice. When you hear the sound of the bell, bring all of your awareness to the act of breathing and then wait for more instructions.*

[Ring bell]

Start by taking a few deep breaths in and out. Just notice your body as you breathe in and out . . . Notice your posture, the chair that's supporting you, the floor under your feet . . . On your next breath in and your next breath out, bring all of your attention to your feet. Become aware of any sensations in your feet. These could be positive sensations, negative sensations, neutral sensations. It doesn't matter, just become aware of them . . . When you shift your attention to your feet, you may notice an inclination or urge to move and adjust them. Simply notice that urge without actually moving them. Notice what it feels like—the different sensations that comprise that urge—and just maintain your posture . . . moving your awareness up into your ankles . . . and the lower legs, the shins and calves, just become aware of any sensations. They may be small sensations, or large sensations . . . you might feel tingliness, or the touch of your pant leg, it could be any sensation . . . and if you get that urge to adjust your body, wherever that may be, just shift your awareness to that urge, to that part of the body, observe it, dissect the urge, surf the urge to move, and then come back to the area of the body we're focusing on, in this case the lower legs . . . letting your awareness move up into the knees: the fronts of the knees, sides, and back of the knees . . . and up into your upper legs: the quadriceps, hamstrings, thighs, just scan this area of the body like an x-ray machine, scanning for different sensations . . . and again, when the temptation to move the body arises again, move your awareness to wherever you feel it strongest. Just observe that urge, surf that urge, and do not move the body . . . letting your awareness move up into your hips and belly: noticing your belly expanding and contracting with each breath, simply be aware of what it feels like to breathe right now. The sensations associated with breathing in, the stretchiness of the skin, the sensations associated with breathing out, the deflation of the belly. Just observe any sensations . . . moving your aware-ness into your chest, become aware of any sensations in the chest. Simply breathing in, and breathing out. Just noticing any sensations . . . shifting your awareness to your back. Let your awareness slowly rise up your back, from your lower back, to your middle back, to your upper back. Just as if a cup is filling up with water, your back is filling up with awareness . . . and again, if the urge to move arises, simply observe it, let it arise, let it pass, and don't react to it . . . moving your awareness to your hands: the configuration of your hands, your fingertips, knuckles, and palms . . . maybe you feel heat in your hands, or tingliness, or any sensation. Simply be aware . . . Letting your awareness rise up through your wrists into your forearms, scanning this area of the body like an X-ray machine, simply observing sensations . . . up unto your upper arms: the biceps, triceps, and shoulders . . . the neck: the front of your neck, the sides, and back of your neck . . . Letting your awareness rise up into your jaw and chin, and slowly expand across the face: the mouth, the cheeks, the nose, the eyes and eyebrows, and forehead. Just observe . . . you may feel an itch. Just observe that itch, try not to react to it. Observe the subtle sensations that make up the larger sensation of the itch . . . the ears and the sides of the head . . . the back of the head, and finally the top of your head. Just observing any sensation . . . and finally let your awareness expand to your whole body, from the top of your head to the tips of your toes, from the tips of your toes to the top of your head . . . just noticing any sensations that are happening right now . . . and again, when the urge to move, to readjust, to make your posture more comfortable arises, simply shift your awareness to where that sensation for the urge is strongest, observe the urge, and watch it change. Watch it arise, watch it pass . . . In a few moments, I'm going to ring the bell. When I do, shift your awareness to your ears and try to listen to the bell until it's no longer there. When you can't hear it any longer, you can open your eyes.

[Ring bell]

Roots of Cravings Worksheet

I _____ because I want/don't want

Want . . .	Don't Want . . .

SESSION 8

MINDFULNESS OF TRIGGERS

Session Summary

Session 8 overviews stimuli that *trigger* drug use. Building on session 7's emphasis on "craving," and its focus on the *result* of a trigger, session 8 focuses on the internal and external "*triggers*" themselves that result in the craving or urge to use drugs. Triggers are defined and then contextualized within three major influences on the individuals' life, and youth are invited to explicitly explore what major triggers have influenced their drug use and decision-making. Mindfulness practice is explicitly connected to the idea that more awareness of triggers, without judgment, can result in more responsive rather than reactive decision-making and, in turn, less drug use. Multiple educative mediums are used in this session and include discussion, didactic education, and other experiential activities. The noting form of meditation is introduced and practice in this session.

Materials Needed

- Meditation bell
- Handouts/poster board paper
- Sticky notes
- Session 8 Handouts (optional)

Formal Meditation (Time)

- Noting Meditation (8–10 minutes)

Learning Objectives

- Define triggers
- Review influences on drug use
- Review personal triggers/influences
- Practice noting meditation

Session Agenda (Chair Configuration)

1. Youth-Led Centering (Circle)
2. Mindful Check-In (Circle)
3. Mindfulness of Triggers (Circle; Semicircle)
4. Three Levels of Influence (Semicircle)
5. Meditation: Noting Awareness (Circle)
6. Homework and Close-Out (Circle)

1. Youth-Led Centering Meditation

Have a youth facilitate a centering meditation and use the discussion questions from the previous session to process his or her experience afterwards. Remember to ask for volunteers at the ends of all prior sessions and attempt to get new youth to access the experience of facilitating centering meditations.

2. Mindful Check-In

Facilitate a standard mindful check-in using the instructions from session 2. Remind the youth, if necessary, to take a breath and pause prior to speaking about their experience.

3. Mindfulness of Triggers

The relationship between triggers and cravings is key in mindfulness-based substance-abuse treatment. Mindfulness of triggers is critical for youth to learn about in order to successfully prevent relapse. This exercise has two steps: 1) a triggers visualization/ contemplation, and 2) defining triggers.

Step 1: Triggers Visualization

This visualization will prime the youth to think about their drugs of choice and how simply a memory can be a trigger. Use the talking points and example script below for this visualization.

Talking Points

- Ask, "On a scale of 1–10, 1 being no craving and 10 being the highest craving possible, how much are you craving the drug you most often use?"
- Direct the youth in the visualization below, prompting them to contemplate their drug of choice.
- Ask the same rating question.
- Discuss how simply thinking about drugs can sometimes be a trigger.

Example Script

Facilitator: I want you all to think about your drug of choice. If that's weed, think about weed. If alcohol, think about alcohol, and so on. Let's go around in a circle. What I want you to say is how much, on a scale of 1–10, you feel like using your drug of choice right now, in this moment. A "1" means you have no craving, a 10 means it's the highest possible craving.

[Facilitate this exercise and have each youth share.]

Now, we're going to take you through a visualization. Let your eyes close, if you feel comfortable with closing them. You don't have to close them if you don't want to, but it's usually a little easier to visualize with closed eyes. When you hear the sound of the bell, take a few breaths in and a few breaths out and wait for further instructions . . .

[Ring bell]

Start off by taking a few deep breaths in, and a few deep breaths out . . . Just let your awareness settle right here, right now, on the breath . . . I want to invite you to think about your drug of choice . . . Think about the last time you did that drug . . . Where were you? . . . Who were you with? Maybe you were at your favorite park, on the front porch of your house, or somewhere else. Just visualize it . . . Maybe you were with your best friend, a group, or alone. Just put yourself back there . . . Think about what happened next. You rolled up the weed, or cracked open the alcohol, or whatever the next step in your process was . . . Remember the smell, the emotions associated with that drug . . . Now you're actually using the drug. You're smoking, or drinking, or whatever. Experience that memory; think about what it feels like in this moment . . . Just stay with that memory for a little longer, and, when you hear the sound of the bell, you can slowly open your eyes . . .

[Ring bell]

Now, let's go around the circle again. I want you all to be honest, to say what you'd rate yourself at now for your craving level, after that visualization.

[Ask youth to rate themselves for a second time after the visualization above.]

Most youth will state that their rating was higher than before. The idea behind this activity is to highlight how simply a memory can trigger the urge to use drugs. After everyone shares his or her second ratings, proceed directly into the second step of this activity.

WHAT IF?

A youth states that the visualization has triggered him or her to the point that after the session they want to go out and use their drug of choice? First, acknowledge the power of memory with the young person: it was simply their memory and visualization that has triggered her or him to the point of wanting to actually use drugs. Then, contract with the young person to not use drugs by challenging him/her to learn and implement the techniques from this (and other) sessions. Finally, state to the youth that their urge to use may not last long, and make sure to check in with them before they leave group. Alternatively, if you simply aren't comfortable with the above activity (because you work in an educational or outpatient setting and are fearful of the very real risk that the youth may go out and use drugs), consult this session's handouts for an alternative "Triggers Contemplation" that is not as personalized. If you are working in an inpatient or correctional setting, the youth will (hopefully) not have access to drugs. This activity is also presented at the start of the session so that the craving may dissipate through time and the interventions presented.

Step 2: Defining Triggers

After finishing the triggers visualization, have the youth re-arrange their chairs into a semicircle. Use the sticky notes and ask the group to come up with triggers (based on what they contemplated) to write on each note and stick on the poster. As the youth are offering different types of triggers, write them down on your sticky notes and place them on the presentation poster to either the right or left side.

Next, tape a piece of poster paper on the wall and draw a decisional "T"—then, title one column *internal triggers* and the other *external triggers*. Ask someone to volunteer to define the difference between an internal and an external trigger. An **Internal Trigger** is defined as any part of one's subjective awareness that triggers one to want to use drugs. This refers to thoughts, memories, emotions, etc. An **External Trigger** is anything outside of one's subjective awareness (i.e., it is in their objective awareness) that either triggers a drug urge directly or triggers an internal trigger that then triggers the urge to use drugs.

Use the talking points and example script below as a guide.

Talking Points

- Triggers can be categorized as either *internal* and *external*.
- Internal triggers are parts of our subjective awareness; such as emotions, memories, etc.

Figure 11.1

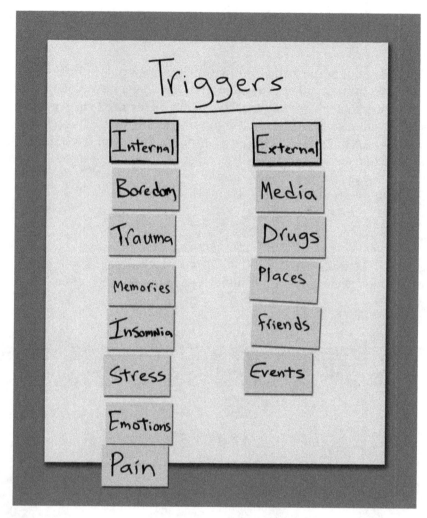

Figure 11.2

- External triggers are part of our environment; such as places, people, etc.
- External triggers can trigger an internal trigger (e.g., a really jerk person you see or hear can bring up emotions of anger or frustration).

Example Script

Facilitator: *Who knows the difference between an internal and external trigger? Who wants to try to define them? . . .*

[Discuss]

Right, an internal trigger is something that arises inside you. It's a part of your inner world. It could be something like a memory: just remembering good experiences could make us want to use again, just as it may have in the visualization we just did in this triggers visualization. Raise your hand if your rating increased just by remembering the last time you used drugs? . . . An internal trigger could also come from remembering a bad experience that could make us want to use in order to forget it; it could be an emotion, or even just a thought. An internal trigger is anything that comes up inside of us that makes us want to use. And an external trigger is something that's in the environment. It could be a person being rude to you, a place: as, for example, every time you walk by the park where you got high with your friends, just walking by that place could trigger you. And there's an inherent relationship between internal and external triggers: an external trigger can trigger an internal emotional state, say if a person comes up to you and is rude, and anger comes up within you, that could then trigger you to want to use. Remember that triggers and urges flow chart from last week?

[Draw Triggers Flow Chart on Poster Paper.]

It's like that: a trigger comes into your awareness, triggers an urge, which is really an internal trigger, and then drug use often occurs. Does that make sense to everyone? . . .

Finish this activity by having youth (or yourself via discussion with youth) place all the sticky notes in the correct columns as well as they can fit.

4. Three Levels of Influence

While still in the semicircle, move directly into the next activity on the three levels of influence on triggers and behavior. The essence of this presentation and discussion is to suggest that there are numerous forces that influence our behaviors; drug use being no exception. Working with those is not as simple as activating free will and free choice. There are personal, social, and environmental forces that influence our attitudes, opinions, and behaviors. Further, such influences that trigger drug use fall both within and without the bounds of our control. Because this is a mindfulness-based curriculum, our guiding principle is to help youth increase awareness of these factors so that they may have more autonomy and decision-making abilities, thus leading to a greater control over whether or not they use drugs. Knowing what one controls is essential in how one responds to the specific trigger, whether it be controllable or uncontrollable, internal or external.

Three Levels of Influence

The three levels of influence include personal, social, and environmental variables and this activity is loosely based on the work of Al Switzer (Patterson, Grenny, Maxfield, McMillan, & Switzler, 2011). What you'll be doing with the youth is delving deeper into the idea of what it is that "triggers" one to actually use drugs by reviewing the different triggers that can be placed within the personal, social, and environmental areas. This gives the youth an authentic view of what they'll be dealing with on a daily basis in terms of relapse and recovery. This activity has three steps: 1) presentation of the three levels of influence on drug use, 2) the personal triggers matrix worksheet, and 3) discussion of personal triggers and levels of influence.

Step 1: Presentation of the Three Levels of Influence on Drug Use

Start the activity by taking a blank piece of poster paper labeled "Three Major Levels of Influence" and taping it next to the "Internal and External Triggers" poster. Draw three rows from top to bottom starting with *Personal*, then *Social* under it, and, finally, *Environmental* at the bottom. The

Personal level of influence has to do with the individual's subjective awareness and level of motivation and will. The **Social** level of influence regards the person's social network. Does s/he hang around other people who constantly do drugs? Does s/he have supportive friends that don't use? Finally, the **Environmental** level of influence has to do with both the macro environment the individual is living within (e.g., living in a heavy drug neighborhood) and the microenvironment, as well (e.g., mother keeps prescription pills in the medicine cabinet and they're easily accessible to the individual). Use the talking points and example script below to present these concepts.

Talking Points

- State the three major levels of influence: personal, social, and environmental.
- Provide concrete examples for each level of influence.
- Distinguish the macro and micro levels of the environmental level of influence.

Example Script

Facilitator: What we're about to talk about has a lot to do with triggers, but we'll come full circle shortly. We want to discuss what are called the three major levels of influence on behavior, especially drug-use behavior because that's why we're here. You can see here on this poster paper **[point to three levels of influence poster]** *that we have three rows that all represent major levels of influence: personal, social, and environmental. Who wants to volunteer to state what they think these different levels are? Give specific examples.*

[Discuss]

The personal level has to do with you as an individual. That can be your level of self-awareness, abilities related to stopping or starting the targeted behaviors, and your relationship with triggering materials. Some people have a really tough time dealing with strong emotions; others don't. Some of us are really motivated to quit smoking cigarettes; others aren't. All of those variables would be placed under the personal level. The social level encompasses your social network: who you hang out with, what activities and interests they have, whether they do drugs, too, if you have strong support by them—all of that. Those are all social influences. If someone in your social network is pressuring you to smoke weed, versus someone else's friend trying to get them not to smoke weed, those are two very different factors but both are on the social level of influence. Does that make sense? . . . And finally there's the environmental level. There are two sublevels to this. The first is called the macro environment. That's like the neighborhood you live in, your city, your community, and the issues or lack thereof that come with it. So, for example, for someone who's trying to stop using alcohol and crack cocaine, do you think it would be easier or harder if they lived in a neighborhood with severe drug issues, where people were using those drugs all the time? . . . Right, it'd be harder. That's the macro level of the environment. There's also the micro level of the environment. That comprises the things you have direct access to, usually in your home or within close proximity. So, again, let's say you have an alcohol problem and your parents also drink. They have an alcohol cabinet in the home. Doesn't matter if you live in a really poor or rich area, like in the macro level of influence, if you know the combination to that lock on the liquor cabinet, which I'm sure wouldn't be hard to figure out for most of you, you'd have much more temptation to drink. So again, the macro level of the environment is made up of the large scale social issues that you're dealing with, such as poverty, drugs in the streets, relationship with police, etc., and the micro level are things in your home or very close by that you have direct access to. Does this make sense to everyone? . . . Any questions?

. . .

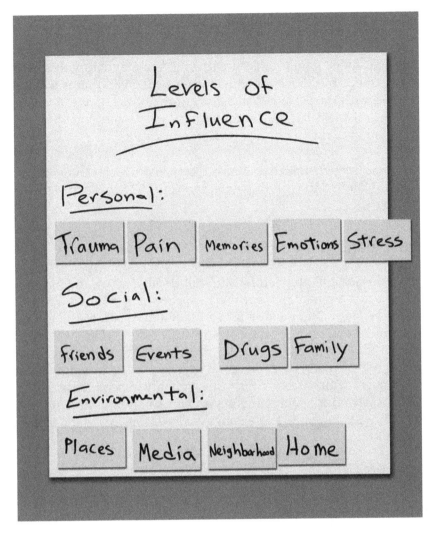

Figure 11.3

After presenting and discussing the initial material above, place (get input from the youth) all of the triggers on the sticky notes from the previous activity under the right realm of influence. Personal influences should include most internal triggers, such as strong emotions, memories, etc. Social influences should include peers, support networks, and access to drugs; environmental influences should include the socio-economic status of the individual and his/her community, the amount of illegal drug activity in the community, the amount of violence in the community, and factors related to an individual's microenvironment (e.g., pills in the medicine cabinet).

You can either go through each sticky note and take a quick poll with the group to determine which level of influence it should be placed under or select a youth volunteer to facilitate that portion.

Step 2: Personal Trigger Worksheet

Next, pass out the "Personal Trigger Worksheet" found in this session's handouts. This worksheet invites youth to fill in the personal triggers within the framework of the three levels of influence. Spread the youth across the room for privacy and allow about 7–10 minutes to complete the worksheet. Once finished, have the youth reenter the circle for discussion.

Step 3: Discussion on Personal Triggers Worksheet

The final step of this activity is for the youth to discuss their personal triggers within the three levels of influence conceptual framework. State that it is not mandatory that each youth share his or her personal worksheet, but that it's highly encouraged, given that it will help them develop an actual plan to deal with the personalized factors in their lives that lead to drug use (and other unhealthy behaviors, for that matter). Ask for a volunteer to start and, after he or she presents, make sure some variation of the following questions are asked:

- Which of these triggers/influences can you control? Which can't you?
- What is your plan to deal with those you can control? What about the ones you can't?

6. Meditation: Noting Awareness

The final activity of this session is the formal mindfulness meditation. You will be teaching a meditation that involves being aware of one's primary experience; whether it be a sensory, emotional, or thought-based experience. The premise for this meditation is that the more one can develop one's general sense of awareness of the moment, the more one can be aware of both internal and external triggers and all the sources of influence that are factors within one's life. The meditation starts with mindfulness of the breath, invites a brief sensory experience, and then invites the meditator to stay present with whatever his or her primary experience is. The noting technique is encouraged, alongside youth opening their eyes every so often to note what's in their external environment. Use the talking points and example script below as a guide (also find this script in this session's handouts).

Talking Points

- Start with awareness of breathing.
- Present brief Bodyscan.
- Direct awareness to primary experience.
- Invite the noting technique.
- Encourage the opening and closing of eyes every so often.
- Make sure to have an anchor to return awareness when it's wandered.

Example Script

Facilitator: *Find a comfortable position and let your eyes close, if you feel comfortable. This meditation will be a little different, and there may be some times where I encourage you to open your eyes for a few moments, as well. When I ring the bell, bring your awareness to your breathing as usual and then wait for further instructions . . .*

[Ring bell]

Take a few moments and just settle into your body, into your posture. Notice where it's easiest for you to sense your breath. Maybe that's in the nostrils, or the belly, or the chest. Wherever it's easiest, just let your awareness rest right there, breathing in, and breathing out . . . Breathing in and breathing out, you might notice that the mind wanders away from the breath. Remember, that's okay. It's normal for the mind to wander. Whenever you notice the mind wandering, simply redirect it to your breathing;

breathing in, and breathing out . . . Next, direct your awareness to the sensations associated with breathing in and breathing out . . . Notice the expansion and contraction of the belly or chest, the touch of the air on your nostrils. Notice any sensations associated with breathing . . . Do a brief scan of the sensations in your whole body. You can do a body scan from the top of your head to the tips of your toes, or the tips of your toes to the top of your head such as we've been practicing, or you can scan the sensations in your body in any way that feels comfortable for you . . . Just notice. Large sensations, small sensations, subtle sensations, everything. Maybe there's pain, or tingliness, or pleasant sensations, or unpleasant sensations, your job right now is just to notice them. All the while breathing in, and breathing out, just notice . . . As you're grounded in the body and with your breath, from here on out, I want to invite you to be mindfully aware of what your most prevalent experience is. It could be a sensation, it could be the breath, it could be an emotion, a thought, anything. Simply take note of what your experience is. If it's a painful sensation, you might note that to yourself as "sensation." If your mind wanders off and you start to think about what's for dinner, you might note, "thinking." Keep your awareness in the present moment and do your best not to get swept away in imagination. Simply observe whatever experience is most prevalent in this moment. If you find yourself swept away in imagination, just reset yourself by taking a few deep breaths in and a few deep breaths out, grounding yourself here and now in the moment . . . You might consider opening your eyes every once in a while. If you do, simply keep a soft gaze and just note what you see around you. Just like you note your internal experience, you can note your external surrounds and environment, as well. If you do so, don't look at any other person in the eyes and nonverbally communicate, just stay in the meditation and use the time to note what's around you. After a few moments, close your eyes again and note your internal experiences; thoughts, emotions, sensations, anything . . . Think of it like you're sitting next to a river and a bunch of leaves are coming down the river in the water. The leaves represent thoughts, emotions, sensations, any experience. Your goal is to simply watch those leaves come and watch them pass by in the river. You don't want to become one of those leaves by entertaining a thought or emotion too much. Next thing you knew you'd be swept up in the river of imagination and forget that you're meditating. That's not the goal, but, if that happens, not to worry, simply redirect your awareness to the here and now, taking a few deep breaths in and a few deep breaths out . . . Keeping your awareness here and now, just noting your primary experience, "thinking" "sensations" "emotion" whatever arises. Noting your external surroundings every once in a while, "people," "room," "chairs," whatever is around you . . .

In a few moments I'm going to ring the meditation bell, and, when I do, you can slowly open your eyes, if they were closed, and come out of the formal meditation.

[Ring bell]

After finishing the meditation, process the youths' experience and connect the noting of internal experience and external environment with the earlier triggers and sources of influence discussion. Use the below questions to guide this discussion:

- What was your experience like?
- Was it difficult or easy? Why/Why not?
- How does noting your experience relate to being aware of triggers?
- How does opening your eyes and closing them so often to observe both internal and external experience relate to the sources-of-influence discussion we had earlier?

Spend a few minutes discussing this prior to closing out for the session. Create enough space in the session time so that as many youth as possible can share their experiences and ideas.

7. Homework and Close-Out

After processing the meditation, ask a youth to volunteer for the next session to teach the centering meditation. Invite the group to continuously contemplate the three levels of influences and their relationship to triggers. If you're working in an outpatient setting or a school, invite the youth to label the different pressures they encounter in the world within the three levels framework. If you're working with youth who are either incarcerated or in inpatient drug rehabilitation, encourage them to continuously think about what they can and can't control; with an emphasis on the idea that trying to control something you can't control oftentimes brings about psychological distress.

SESSION 8 HANDOUTS

Alternative Triggers Contemplation

Step 1: Triggers Contemplation

This contemplation will prime the youth to think about different types of stimuli that have triggered themselves and their friends to use. You're not necessarily trying to *trigger* the youth in this contemplation (as opposed to as we did in the visualization) but rather inviting contemplation of the phenomena that triggers drug use. Use the talking points and example script below for this visualization.

Talking Points

- Center the youth with mindfulness of the breath.
- Prompt youth to think about what triggers drug use.
- State examples of people, places, things, emotions, etc.

Example Script

Facilitator: *Start by sitting in a comfortable position. Let your eyes close, if you feel comfortable with closing them. You don't have to close them if you don't want to, but it's usually a little easier to visualize with closed eyes. When you hear the sound of the bell, take a few breaths in and a few breaths out and wait for further instructions . . .*

[Ring bell]

Start off by taking a few deep breaths in, and a few deep breaths out . . . Just let your awareness settle right here, right now, on the breath . . . I want to invite you to think about what makes people want to do drugs . . . Think about people you know who do drugs. What do you think their reasons were? . . . Was it peer pressure? Was it a strong emotion? Was it a particular event? Did they just want to bring their mood up? Was there a particular place? A park, or a house? A place that in and of itself triggers them to want to use? . . . Think about your own drug use as well . . . What's triggered you in the past? Just search your memory and think about those moments before using . . . Think about the emotional factors, the social factors, everything . . . All the while just keep breathing in, and breathing out . . . In a moment I'm going to ring the bell, and when I do just simply bring your attention back to the present moment, open your eyes, and come out of the contemplation.

[Ring bell]

After finishing the above, proceed directly into step 2 of this activity.

Personal Triggers Worksheet

What Are My Triggers?

Personal Triggers	Social Triggers	Environmental Triggers

Noting Meditation Script

Talking Points

- Start with awareness of breathing.
- Present brief Bodyscan.
- Direct awareness to primary experience.
- Invite the noting technique.
- Encourage the opening and closing of eyes every so often.
- Make sure to have an anchor to return awareness when it's wandered.

Example Script

Facilitator: *Find a comfortable position and let your eyes close, if you feel comfortable. This meditation will be a little different, and there may be some times where I encourage you to open your eyes for a few moments, as well. When I ring the bell, bring your awareness to your breathing as usual and then wait for further instructions . . .*

[Ring bell]

Take a few moments and just settle into your body, into your posture. Notice where it's easiest for you to sense your breath. Maybe that's in the nostrils, or the belly, or the chest. Wherever it's easiest, just let your awareness rest right there, breathing in, and breathing out . . . Breathing in and breathing out, you might notice that the mind wanders away from the breath. Remember, that's okay. It's normal for the mind to wander. Whenever you notice the mind wandering, simply redirect it to your breathing; breathing in, and breathing out . . . Next, direct your awareness to the sensations associated with breathing in and breathing out . . . Notice the expansion and contraction of the belly or chest, the touch of the air on your nostrils. Notice any sensations associated with breathing . . . Do a brief scan of the sensations in your whole body. You can do a body scan from the top of your head to the tips of your toes, or the tips of your toes to the top of your head such as we've been practicing, or you can scan the sensations in your body in any way that feels comfortable for you . . . Just notice. Large sensations, small sensations, subtle sensations, everything. Maybe there's pain, or tingliness, or pleasant sensations, or unpleasant sensations, your job right now is just to notice them. All the while breathing in, and breathing out, just notice . . . As you're grounded in the body and with your breath, from here on out, I want to invite you to be mindfully aware of what your most prevalent experience is. It could be a sensation, it could be the breath, it could be an emotion, a thought, anything. Simply take note of what your experience is. If it's a painful sensation, you might note that to yourself as "sensation." If your mind wanders off and you start to think about what's for dinner, you might note, "thinking." Keep your awareness in the present moment and do your best not to get swept away in imagination. Simply observe whatever experience is most prevalent in this moment. If you find yourself swept away in imagination, just reset yourself by taking a few deep breaths in and a few deep breaths out, grounding yourself here and now in the moment . . . You might consider opening your eyes every once in a while. If you do, simply keep a soft gaze and just note what you see around you. Just like you note your internal experience, you can note your external surrounds and environment, as well. If you do so, don't look at any other person in the eyes and nonverbally communicate, just stay in the meditation and use the time to note what's around you. After a few moments, close your eyes again and note your internal experiences; thoughts, emotions, sensations, anything . . . Think of it like you're sitting next to a river and a bunch of leaves are coming down the river in the water. The leaves represent thoughts, emotions, sensations, any experience. Your goal is to simply watch those leaves come and watch them pass by in the river. You don't want to become one of those leaves by entertaining a thought or emotion too much. Next thing you knew you'd be swept up in the river of imagination and forget that you're meditating. That's not the goal, but, if that happens, not to worry, simply redirect your awareness to the here and now, taking a few deep breaths in and a few deep breaths out . . . Keeping your awareness here and now, just noting your primary experience, "thinking," "sensations," "emotion," whatever arises. Noting your external surroundings every once in a while, "people," "room," "chairs," whatever is around you . . .

In a few moments I'm going to ring the meditation bell, and, when I do, you can slowly open your eyes, if they were closed, and come out of the formal meditation.

[Ring bell]

Session 8 Reference

Patterson, K., Grenny, J., Maxfield, D., McMillan, R., & Switzler, A. (2011). *Change anything: The new science of personal success*. New York, NY: Business Plus.

SESSION 9

THE FAMILY SYSTEM AND DRUGS

Session Summary

Session 9 engages youth on the relationship between drug use and the family system. Family-based interventions have a large amount of empirical support for effectively reducing drug use among adolescents. Short of an actual family-based intervention, this session engages youth on topics related to their roles in their family systems, familial relationships, how drug use affects such relationships, and how mindfulness may help in building and rebuilding family cohesion. This session includes a number of group, individual, and meditative exercises to engage youth on the aforementioned topics. A compassion meditation is practiced in the context of promoting empathy toward family members.

Materials Needed

- Meditation bell
- Markers
- Poster paper or whiteboard
- Session 9 Handouts (optional)

Formal Meditation Time

- Compassion for Family Members (10–12 minutes)

Learning Objectives

- Discuss how drug use impacts family relationships
- Define intergenerational trauma and its role in drug use/addiction
- Practice compassion-based meditation

Session Agenda (Chair Configuration)

1. Youth-Led Centering Meditation (Circle)
2. My Children Contemplation (Circle)
3. The Effect of Drug Use on Family Relationships (Semicircle)
4. Addiction and Intergenerational Trauma (Semicircle; Spread Across Room; Circle)
5. Meditation: Compassion for Family Members (Circle)
6. Mindful Check-In (Circle)
7. Homework and Close-Out (Circle)

1. Youth-Led Centering Meditation

Have a youth facilitate a centering meditation and use the discussion questions from the previous sessions to process his or her experience afterwards. Remember to ask for volunteers at the ends of the previous groups and attempt to encourage new youth to get experience facilitating centering meditations.

WHAT IF?

The same youth keeps volunteering and no one else wants to? Start to give that youth feedback so that s/he actually gets more skilled at facilitating the meditation.

2. My Children Contemplation

The "My Children" contemplation is designed to guide youth to think about the impact their decisions have had on their parents/caregivers. In the activity you will guide the youth to imagine what it would be like to have children of their own engaging in similar behaviors they've engaged in (e.g., drug use, violence, illegal activities, etc.). The exercise is certainly NOT designed to guilt-trip the youth, but rather to build empathy toward their parents and/or caregivers. Use the talking points and example script below as a guide.

Talking Points

- Ask the youth, "Who thinks they want kids when they grow up?" (*Sometimes the youth may already have kids.*)
- State that the next activity involves imagining what it's like to have children that get into highly risk-taking behaviors.
- Facilitate the My Children Contemplation.
   - State that the exercise is NOT designed to guilt trip.
   - State that guilt may arise, and this is okay.

Example Script

*Facilitator: Anybody know if they want to have kids when they get older? Oh yeah? A few yeses, a few maybes, and a few nos. That's normal. This next exercise we're going to practice involves imagining that we have kids of our own that get into highly risk-taking behaviors, kind of like what some of you have been engaging in. I want to make this clear: **this isn't a guilt-tripping activity**, it's just designed to get you thinking about what it's like to have kids engaging in behaviors similar to your own, and to connect that with whoever your guardian is right now. Does everyone understand that? . . . Sometimes guilt will come up as a result of this activity, and it's okay. It's okay to feel guilty. It doesn't mean you're a bad person or something's wrong with you. If that's what comes up for you, we'll have a chance to talk about it after the exercise. Sound good? . . . Okay, sit in a somewhat upright position, and when I ring the bell, start by taking a few deep breaths in, and a few deep breaths out.*

[Ring bell]

I want you to start imagining yourself in the future, and let's just say that you really did want to have kids, even if you feel like you don't right now . . . You're in the future, and you have a child, 2 kids, maybe even 3 or more kids . . . Do you have a name? What would your kids' names be? When they're babies, they're so cute! You love them so much. All you want to do is protect them and raise them to be good people . . . Notice how it feels right now in your body. How does it feel to have kids? Positive? Negative? Neutral? . . . Fast forward in time and let's say they're 14, 15, or 16 . . . They have their own set of friends, maybe even girlfriends or boyfriends . . . They're still good people, but you've been stressed out lately. They've been coming home high and drunk, and hanging out with people who've tended to be in trouble with the law . . . Remember, this is your little boy or little girl . . . the same little boy or girl that you love so much, whose diapers you used to change. Who had been so dependent on you and did nothing but love you . . . how do you feel right now? That they're coming in late, drinking, smoking . . . Are you angry? Frustrated? Sad? Concerned? . . . Some nights they come home really late and you stay up worrying, just hoping they're okay. If you could just sit down and talk to them without yelling, what would you really want to say to them? How would you say it? What does it feel like when you ask them to do something and they don't do it? Does it hurt? Does it anger you? Just check in with yourself right now. What emotions, sensations, and thoughts are arising? . . . Take a few more deep breaths in and a few deep breaths out and, when I ring the bell, broaden your awareness to the whole of the group and slowly open your eyes.

[Ring bell]

Discussion: How Would You Feel as the Parent?

Use the following discussion questions to process the experiences of the youth. Use your best judgment to instruct the youth to share either in a circle or popcorn style:

- What was the contemplation like?
- How did it feel to visualize yourself as a parent?
- What was the main emotion that was coming up when you imagined your children doing drugs and engaging in other high-risk behaviors?
- Do you ever think about how your parents or caregivers feel about you using drugs? Or the other behaviors they might label as *high-risk*?
- What do you think their predominant emotions would be?
- How does contemplating your parents/caregivers' feelings affect you?

Do your best to get as many of the youth as possible involved in the discussion. The objective of this discussion is for the youth to get a glimpse into how their caregivers/parents are experiencing them.

WHAT IF?

A strong sense of guilt does arise? It's okay if a young person is feeling guilt. When a young person has been unaware of how they're negatively affecting people around them, a natural response is guilt. Some youth will take it harder than others and some will need to process and be supported in such moments. Take the time to create space to support them. Remind the youth that one remedy for guilt is to sit with it; really feel it, and make conscious decisions about how they want to behave in the future in order to prevent situations that may cause guilt.

3. The Effect of Drug Use on Family Relationships

After concluding the My Children Contemplation discussion, have the group rearrange their chairs into a semicircle positioned around a wall or easel. You'll be using a whiteboard or poster paper and need your markers for this activity. The essence of the activity is to brainstorm the major *themes* of the impact of drug use on the family system. The objective of this activity is for the youth to think about both the general and the specific consequences that drug use has on the family system and highlight the fact that, in most cases, one of the major themes is that relationships between family members suffer as a result of drug use. This activity has two steps: 1) brainstorming themes and 2) highlighting the core theme of strained familial relationships.

Step 1: Brainstorming Themes

The first step in this activity includes a brainstorming session in which you'll ask the group to state what they feel the impact of drug use is on a family system. Take a piece of large poster paper, tape it to the wall, and title the page "The Impact of Drug Use on the Family System." Next, ask the youth if they personally know anyone who struggles with drugs and alcohol (themselves included) and follow up with another question asking what they believe to be the impact of drug use on their or their friends' families. Inevitably, the major theme of *relationships* will arise in some way (usually from the youth), and that's what you want to highlight in this brainstorming session.

As youth are stating ways in which drug use impacts the family system, scribe their words around the poster paper, leaving a large blank area in the center. If a youth suggests the major theme of relationships in some way (e.g., "drug use messes up your relationship with your mom"), simply write "Relationships" in the center of the poster paper. If, after the whole brainstorm session, this theme hasn't been suggested in some way (which is rare), write it out yourself and present its significance to discuss with the group.

Use the talking points and example script below as a guide for this step of the exercise.

Talking Points

- Ask the group: "Does anyone here know someone that's struggled with drug or alcohol problems?"
- Direct youth to contemplate issues that arise in the family as a result of drug use.
- Ask the group: What are some of the negative consequences of drug use on the family? If one person in the family does drugs, how does that affect the family?
- Write the youth's responses on the poster paper, leaving a large blank area in the center (this is saved for the *Relationships* theme).

Example Script

Facilitator: *Okay, we're going to have a discussion about what the impact of drug use on the family system is. The first part of the discussion is a brainstorming session, but I first want to know, do any of you know anyone, yourself included, who struggles with drug and/or alcohol problems? . . . I appreciate your sharing that. For a moment I want you to think about what the main issues are that arise in that person's family as a result of that continued drug use. So, for example, if you know someone who drinks a lot, and steals money from their mom to buy alcohol, trust and money would be two issues that come up because of that person's drug use. Take a few moments and just reflect . . . Okay, let's see some hands. What are some of the major impacts of drug use on the family system? What are some of the negative consequences?*

Figure 12.1

Step 2: Highlighting the Core Relationship Theme

Once you feel the brainstorming session has been exhausted, proceed with highlighting the core theme of strained family relationships as a result of continued drug use. Start by drawing a circle around the centralized theme of "Relationships" and asking the youth where they would rank this theme in terms of importance out of all themes on the poster paper. Next, begin to connect the relationship theme to other themes by drawing a line from it to the other themes, asking the group how family relationships are connected to the theme your connecting it with each time. Use the talking points and example script below as a guide for facilitating this discussion.

Talking Points

- Draw a circle around the "Relationships" theme.
- Ask the group "How high would you rank this theme in terms of importance compared to all the other themes?"

- Connect the Relationship theme to other themes by drawing a line and asking the group how the two themes are related, for some of the major themes on the poster paper (you don't need to connect this theme with every other theme, for time's sake).
- Ask the group: "Does anyone want to share how his or her drug use has negatively impacted his or her family life?"
- Toward end of activity, ask the group: What would a perfect family look like to you?

Example Script

Facilitator: Does it feel like we have enough themes up here? Good. I want to present one other, that you've all actually brought up in different ways. Family relationships.

[Write out *Relationships*, if not already on poster, and draw a circle around it.]

If you really think about it, your relationship with your family; your mom, dad, grandmother, brother, sister, whoever is in your family, oftentimes gets affected in some way when you use drugs. That's because, most of the time, family members, mainly caregivers, don't want to see their kids doing things that can harm them, even if it feels to the kid like she/he's just having a good time. The interesting thing about family relationships is that almost everything you all called out here can be connected to relationships in some way. Let's take "money," for example.

[Draw line connecting *Relationships* theme to *Money* theme.]

Who can tell me how family relationships are connected to money in terms of the impact of drug use on the family system?

Youth: People could steal money from their family to buy drugs.

Facilitator: That's right. If someone is addicted to alcohol or likes to drink a lot, but doesn't have that much money, s/he might resort to stealing from the parents or caregiver so they can buy alcohol. And what do you think the cost of that will be on their relationship with the ones whom they stole from? Right, obviously the relationship will get strained over time. Then all these other things come up, right? Trust, or lack thereof, anger, betrayal, and on and on.

[Connect themes as appropriate.]

It's easy to see how drug use disrupts family relationships at a core level, and that's why it's important to understand how your drug use is impacting your family life. Does anyone here want to share how his or her drug use has negatively impacted his or her family life? . . . I have one last question before we wrap up this activity, if you could wave a magic wand, and change your family dynamic between you and whichever family members you spend most of your time with, what would the perfect relationships look like to you? And, what is it that you think you could do personally to contribute toward that vision?

The above is a short script exemplifying the importance of the relationship theme to one other major theme. For the sake of brevity, we didn't include explicit scripts for connecting the relationship theme to other themes, given that the themes that are stated by the youth will vary from group to group. Make sure that when you facilitate this activity you connect the relationship theme to at least 3–5 of the other more prominent themes on the poster paper. See image 9.2 for an example of the completed (theme-connected) poster.

4. Addiction and Intergenerational Trauma

The previous activity contextualized the negative impact of drug use on the family system. This activity takes the concept one step further by educating youth about how addiction (and the issues that arise from it) can be passed down from one generation to the next. **Intergenerational trauma** (as related to addiction and drug use) is defined here as the cumulative psychological and emotional wounding as a result of addiction/drug use over the course of one's life and across generations. We believe this definition creates space for young people of any background.

The primary objective of this activity is to educate youth about the intergenerational trauma process, as it relates to addiction, and for the group members to contemplate the impact that their ancestors (up until their parents) have had on who they are. A secondary objective is for the youth to consider the impact they themselves will have on those that come after them should they or anyone they're close to decide to have children. The primary method you will use to educate the youth about this process is a basic genogram. The construction of a genogram requires an extensive training and is beyond the scope of this activity, but a basic understanding of it will help youth understand intergenerational dynamics. This activity has three steps: 1) introducing the genogram, 2) cycles of addiction and trauma, and 3) the personal genogram worksheet.

Step 1: Introducing the Genogram

Tape a piece of poster paper to the wall and label it *Genogram*. State to the group that a genogram uses circles and squares to represent people, and that squares represent men and circles represent women. You're going to educate the group through a basic genogram of a fictional person whose whole family for three generations struggled with alcoholism. By discussing the life circumstances of each generation, you'll be giving the youth a crash course in the cycle of intergenerational trauma as it is related to addiction and drug use.

At the bottom of the poster paper draw a circle if the group is a girls group, a square if it's a boys group, or choose one if it's a co-ed group. Next, draw family members representing the past three generations of a family. Draw two lines at 45-degree angles out from the top of the circle or square and draw another circle and square representing the parents of the youth from this generation. Repeat this process once more for each of the represented parents, so that a genogram with two sets of grandparents, two parents, and one young person is displayed.

Use the talking points and example script below as a guide to presenting this information.

Talking Points

- Ask the group: "Who knows what a genogram is?"
- Educate the group about the basics of a genogram.
- Draw a genogram representing three generations.

Example Script

> ***Facilitator:*** *In this next activity, we're going to talk about how past generations of our family can affect us, and how we can affect future generations. Does anyone here know what a genogram is? Yes! It's a visual representation of one generation to the next of someone's family. It's a great way to learn about your family and learn about yourself. We're going to draw one here together. Genograms can be very sophisticated and complex. For the purposes of this group, we're going to keep it pretty simple. See this square here? This represents the most recent generation on this fictional genogram we're going to do. In genograms, squares*

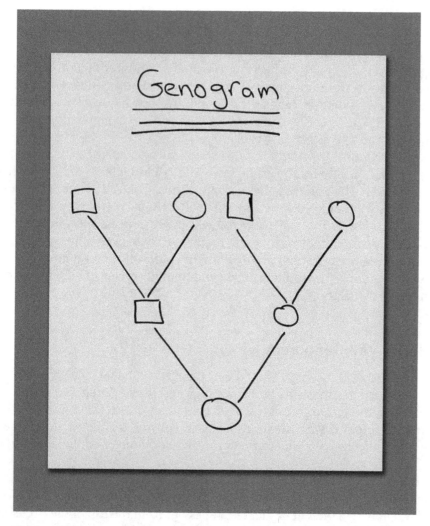

Figure 12.2

usually represent men, and circles usually represent women, so that's how we'll do it here, as well. Now, to be in this world, you know you have to have parents, right? Even if you never met your parents, we all know what biologically needs to happen for a child to be born. So we're going to draw two lines to another square, and circle. This represents this person's father and mother. And since we're going to do a basic genogram with three generations, we're going to do this one more time each for the father and the mother. We're just going to keep it simple and basic here. In a more unpacked genogram, we'd have brothers and sisters and aunts and uncles, really everything up here, and you'll have a chance to do a personal one in a bit, but for now we'll just keep it simple for time's sake.

Step 2: Cycles of Addiction and Trauma

The next step in this activity is to examine the life circumstances of each generation and how they influenced the next. We use a fictional family that represents pieces of many of our clients' experience over the years. Go to this session's handouts for the fictional family's description. This fictional family is comprised of seven people across three generations. There is the young man or woman, teen-aged, his or her parents, both middle-aged, and both parents' sets of parents (grandparents). It is important that you cater to the specific needs of your group. We often work with young people of color and will add details of experiences of racism, classism, and other *isms*. It's important that the youth in the group can relate to the experiences that are portrayed in the family. We've kept it somewhat general here so that it can be adapted to fit the needs of the specific subpopulation of youth you serve. Feel free to add or subtract details depending upon your group's subcultural make-up.

What you'll do to start this portion of the activity is explain the teenager's current situation (from the details above and/or from details you've added) and then work down from the grandparents on both sides of the family tree through the teen's parents, and back to the young person. Use the talking points and example script below as a guide for this discussion.

Talking Points

- Explain the young person's current situation.
- State that you're going to work your way down to the young person from both sets of grandparents.
- Explain one set of grandparents' history.
- Explain their son/daughter's (one of the parents of the young person's) history.
- Explain the other set of grandparents' history.
- Explain their son/daughter's (the other parent of the young person's) history.
- Highlight the process of intergenerational trauma/alcohol addiction.

Example Script

Facilitator: We're going to start with this person on the bottom. It's a circle, so that represents a young woman. Let's say she's 16 years old, and we'll just call her "T" for "Tanya." She smokes weed almost every day, but drinks twice as much. She's so mad all the time. She's mad at the world, mad at her mom, and tends to get in a lot of fights when she drinks. When she drinks, she connects with a deep rage that's inside her. Nothing is "fair" in her mind and she takes it out on the world. She drinks hard liquor, beer; any alcoholic drink. Sometimes even her friends get concerned for her because even they can't hang with her drinking. She's been in trouble at school, been suspended many times, and even has been in trouble with the law. Her relationship with her mom, whom she lives with in a two-bedroom apartment, is strained. Her dad and mom got divorced when she was too young to remember, and she has very limited contact with her dad . . . So, the first question I have for you all is, are there any reasons, besides simply the choices she's made in her life so far, that she is so angry at the world and could be considered an alcoholic at the age of 16? Could her upbringing, or even her parents' upbringing, have played a role in how she is today? What do you all think? . . . Yes. Her parents and even grandparents' upbringing could've played a role in all the issues she's having. That's what we're going to talk about during this activity. We're going to first skip her parents [point to parents on Genogram] *and start with her grandparents and work our way back down. By learning about and discussing the lives of her grandparents and parents, we'll get some insight into why she's behaving the way she does . . . Let's start with her mother's parents, this set of grandparents. Her father (the mother's father)* [point to Grandfather I] *was a very strict parent. In fact, any time she'd do something wrong, he'd punish her by beating her with this belt. He was also an alcoholic. He'd go to the local bar at least four nights a week, and, if he came home in a bad mood, his wife and daughter would get abused. And her mother, the grandfather's wife* [point to Grandmother I], *was emotionally absent. She never stood up for her daughter. She was very nonconfrontational and just wanted peace, but never got it. So, how do you think it was for this daughter* [point to the mother] *to grow up in this household? What do you think was the result of going through that constant abuse and witnessing her father drinking? . . . Right. It really affected her in a negative way. She grew up just trying to tip-toe around her violent and alcoholic father.*

She became severely depressed and began to drink to ease her emotional pain. She vowed to never be in a relationship like the one her mother and father were in, but she kept finding partners that reminded her of her dad, and always left them. She divorced her husband after a few aggressive and violent outbursts against her, and is still depressed to this day. She drinks hard liquor multiple times a day, and tries to hide it from her daughter . . . Before we connect her to her daughter, T, let's go through T's father's family line also. His dad, T's dad's father **[point to Grandfather II]**, *was extremely abusive all the time. He was an alcoholic and would routinely beat up his wife and son. It became so violent in that home that his son, T's dad, was removed from the home and lived in foster care for many years. T's grandmother on her dad's side* **[point to Grandmother II]** *dealt with her violent husband by numbing her pain, both physical and emotional, by drinking hard liquor and beer every day. She received the worst of the beatings from her husband, and, at times, this was witnessed by her son . . . So, how do you all think it was for T's dad growing up? What effect do you think all this had on him? . . . Right. He became very angry at a young age. He thought he was the reason that his dad was so violent and thought of himself as a failure. Like his dad, he turned to alcohol to deal with life. He also learned how to be violent with women from watching his dad, although every time he became violent with his now ex-wife, he despised himself for being like his father. He's divorced from T's mother and is in and out of jail. He is an alcoholic by every criterion . . . Now that you've got a sense of T's family lines, what do you think about her situation? Would anyone here be surprised if I told you this family's story, without first telling you about T, and then saying that T also struggles with alcohol? Why or why not? . . . Yes. There's a sense I have that I'd be surprised if she didn't struggle with alcohol. And we can all see that this isn't all her fault. We all make choices, we know that, but sometimes the options we get to choose from aren't that great. In the case of T, she had alcoholics on both sides of her family for at least two generations back. And we didn't even have time to go back further generations. Has anyone ever heard that phrase, "hurt people hurt people?" It basically means that those who get abused tend to also abuse others. When we look at T's family lines, we see that the trauma, abuse, and alcoholism were passed down from generation to generation. This is called intergenerational trauma, and basically occurs when things like addiction, oppression, or other deep traumas are present. It can be transmitted through learned behavior, like when T's dad learned about domestic violence by witnessing it, and also subconsciously, like how T drinks to deal with her rage but didn't know everyone in her ancestral line did, as well. There are also many other forms of intergenerational trauma, like the cultural transmission of trauma, when a whole group of people has been oppressed for generations. If we added the detail that T was from a nondominant culture and was very poor, that would be another factor influencing her. Does this make sense to everyone? . . . Does anyone have any questions or comments about this whole process? . . . Before we move into the next activity I want to make something clear. Just because we have intergenerational trauma doesn't mean we get a pass to keep using drugs or messing up in life. It just gives us some insight into why we might be doing what we're doing. We may not get to choose the circumstances that we must respond to, but at least this mindfulness practice gives us tools to choose how to respond to whatever circumstances we're in. Does this make sense to you all? . . . Does anyone have any other questions or comments?*

As you move down the ancestral lines and explain each of the family members' circumstance, write out some of the phrases that describe each family member's most prominent characteristics. That way the youth will have a better visual of all the factors that have influenced the young person from past generations. Give the youth space in the session schedule to discuss and ask questions. Sometimes youth will offer some of their own experiences from their family history. Make sure to re-invoke the agreements whenever necessary so that other youth understand the gravity of a young person disclosing her or his family's history.

Step 3: Personal Genogram Worksheet

Spread the youth across the room and have them begin to fill in the "Personal Genogram Worksheet" that's found in this session's handouts. This worksheet is designed to get youth thinking about their specific situations and if/how intergenerational trauma has affected them. Give them about 7–10 minutes to fill in as much as they know, including any pertinent life details. After calling the group back to a circle, discuss with the youth whether any of them has ever felt like they've been affected by intergenerational trauma. Make it clear that they shouldn't disclose anything they aren't comfortable disclosing about their family history, and that **they do not have to share it at all, if they so choose**. Finish the discussion/disclosure activity by presenting the idea that each individual can take control of his or her life by healing such trauma. Consult this session's handouts for talking points and an example script to use if desired.

WHAT IF?

You're working with foster care youth who may have estranged relationships with their families or no families at all? We recommend adding details of being part of the foster care system to the fictional family above. Most foster care youth we've worked with have suffered extensive intergenerational trauma and, as a result, have entered the foster care system. Talking about this process may be hard for some, but has also yielded great insights among some of our clients.

5. Meditation: Compassion for Family Members

After the genogram activity, disclose to the youth that the formal meditation for this session will involve focusing compassionate and positive energy on a family member and will be a bit different from the usual meditations. Use the talking points and example script below as a guide for this meditation.

Talking Points

- Focus on family member of choice.
- Imagine that person sending you love.
- You repay them by sending them love back.
- Present compassionate phrases.

Example Script

Facilitator: *This meditation is going to be a little bit different from the usual ones we've done. Oftentimes we're focusing on the breath, or the body, or something that's right here and right now. This new one we're doing today actually focuses on someone who's not here; a family member or someone that really cares about us. It could be someone who's alive or someone with whom you were close who's passed away. Go ahead and close your eyes and sit up somewhat straight, if you feel comfortable doing that, and, when I ring this bell, start off like we usually do and take a few deep breaths in, and a few deep breaths out.*

[Ring bell]

Breathing in, and breathing out . . . Just take a few moments and settle into your body, settle into your breath . . . Collect yourself by just bringing your full awareness to your body, to this present moment, just observing yourself breathe, breathing in, and breathing out . . . I want to now invite you to think about someone in your family who really cares about you, who really loves you. This could be a mom, dad, grandparent, sister, aunt, whomever. It could be someone who's alive or someone who's passed on. Simply think of someone in your family whom you know has been there for you . . . I want you to imagine that person loving you right now, in this moment. Imagine that he or she is wherever they are, thinking about you here, and thinking "I love him" or "I love her." Imagine that they're wishing you the very best; to be healthy, to be safe, to be happy, to be free from suffering . . . For some people it helps to even say, "May I feel love from _____" and then you add in their name . . . And repeat that phrase a few times . . . For others, it might help to visualize a beam of loving energy being projected from that person to you. Whatever feels best to you, go with that. Really feel the care from that person, really feel that love . . . Next, we're going to shift and repay that person for all the love he or she has sent our way; we're going to intentionally send that love back . . . Now, think of yourself sending that person love. You might say the phrases, "May you be peaceful, may you be happy, may you be free from suffering," while thinking of that family member, or, you might just imagine a beam of loving energy being projected to that person from you, or some combination of the both. Just send that love and compassion back to that person, because you know s/he feels the same way about you . . . If the mind wanders, it's okay, just come back to the breath for a few breaths and keep sending that love . . . all the while breathing in, and breathing out. In a moment I'm going to ring the bell, and, when I do, just slowly let your awareness come back to your breath for a few breaths, and you can open your eyes when you feel comfortable.

[Ring bell]

Process Meditation

After the meditation, take some time to process this experience with the youth. Use the discussion questions below as a guide, and feel free to customize this list to fit your group's needs:

- How was this meditation? What was it like?
- Was it difficult to imagine the person sending you love? If so, why? What came up?
- Could you imagine sending love/compassion? Was it difficult? Easy?
- What might be the effect of practicing this type of meditation consistently? And, is it something you'd be interested in?

6. Mindful Check-In

End this group with a mindful check-in. Have the youth engage in a normal mindful check-in and add the following question for them to answer once finished with check-in: "Is there anything you want to change about your relationship to your family? And, if so, what?" See example script below for a guide.

Example Script

Facilitator: *We're going to finish today's group with a mindful check-in. Sometimes it's good to do this at the end of a group, so we can check in about what the group content brought up. Also, given what we talked about today, everything from the effect of drug use on families, to contemplating your own children, to intergenerational addiction and trauma—I wanted to ask this question: "Do you want to change anything about your relationship to your family? And if so, what?" So, do the regular mindful check-in first, talking about how you feel in the present moment, and then answer the question. Sound good? . . .*

7. Homework and Close-Out

After concluding the mindful check-in, encourage the youth to continually contemplate the effect of drug use on the family system and to practice the compassion-based meditation. Ask if any youth can volunteer to lead next session's centering meditation. If you are the sole facilitator, ask a youth to volunteer to act in the role-play with you at the start of session 10.

SESSION 9 HANDOUTS

Fictional Family Description

The Fictional Family

- The **Young Person** (16 years old): S/he struggles with excessive alcohol and marijuana use. S/he also sometimes uses cocaine and ecstasy. S/he constantly struggles in school and her grades have been dropping for a few years now. When drunk, s/he becomes belligerent and can't control the deep rage that's inside him/her. S/he gets in fights constantly and "hates the world!" His/her dad wasn't in his/her life much and s/he is very resentful for that. S/he doesn't trust that any relationship s/he'll ever have will work.
- The **Mother** (40): Has suffered from depression for over 20 years. Her romantic relationships have been rocky, and she is currently divorced from her child's father. She's been depressed for the last two decades and usually has an annoyed attitude with her child. She deals with the depression by drinking whiskey a few times a day. She thinks her child doesn't know.
- The **Father** (43): Has struggled with alcohol and other drugs for the better part of his life. He's never held a job for more than a year, and was violent with his ex-wife on many occasions. She finally got the nerve to divorce him. He suffers from a deep rage toward the world and himself. He calls himself a *failure* and drinks away his sorrows. He fits the criteria for alcoholism.
- The **Grandfather I** (76; the mother's father): Comes from a very conservative background. He was extremely strict with his daughter and would punish her when she acted out by beating her with his belt. He struggled for years at finding steady work and would drink at the local bar at least four nights a week. If he was in a bad mood when coming home, he would beat the daughter and wife.
- The **Grandmother I** (74; the mother's mother): Was very absent emotionally and never stuck up for her daughter. She just tried to please her husband by not talking back or fighting back when her husband became violent. She drank occasionally, but not too often.
- The **Grandfather II** (79; the father's father): Was extremely abusive, both emotionally and physically, to his son and wife. He drank excessively and told his son he would never amount to anything. His episodes of violence became so intense that his son was removed from the home and lived in foster care for many years. The father, disgruntled and angry, has never apologized to his wife or son.
- The **Grandmother II** (78; the father's mother): Suffered the worst of the violent episodes from her husband. She would drink beer and hard liquor every day to deal with her emotional and physical pain. She attempted to leave her husband on many occasions but always ended up coming home, drinking herself to sleep, and staying at home.

Personal Genogram Worksheet

Genogram

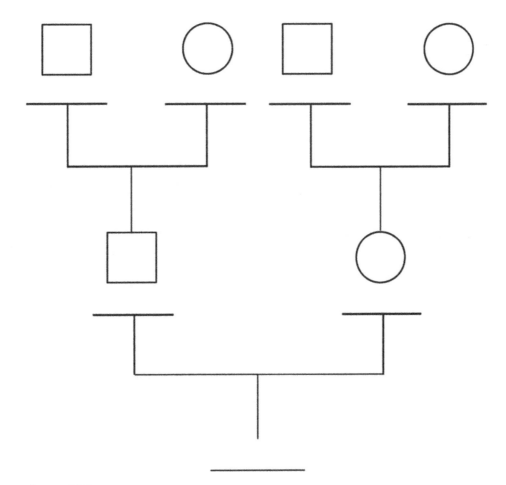

Figure 12.3

Healing Intergenerational Trauma

Talking Points

- Ask, "Can intergenerational trauma be healed? How?"
- State (if not already stated by youth) that healing starts with themselves.
- State that healing oneself can stop the trauma transmission process from you to the next generation.
- State that healing oneself can also affect past generations.

Example Script

Facilitator: *We've been talking about intergenerational trauma for a little while now. I know it can be tough so I can't tell you how much I appreciate everyone's willingness to talk about this. This conversation wouldn't feel complete to me, however, if we didn't talk about the process of healing intergenerational trauma. Can intergenerational trauma be healed? What do you all think? And if so, how? Any ideas? . . . I really believe that, in order to heal the trauma that's been passed down to us, we need to focus on and start with what's right in front of us, and that's ourselves. That's where the healing starts. By embarking on this path of healing, of growing, of becoming more self-aware, we start the process of healing the trauma that's been transmitted from generation to generation, and that's a powerful thing. And if we do stop that process, or at least start the path of our own healing, what do you think happens? How does that affect our current family? How does that affect future generations? . . . Yes. We can stop the cycle of transmission from ourselves to the next generation. Even if you don't choose to have kids, your brothers or sisters or close friends might have kids, and your experiences, the experiences of people from your community, have the potential to affect that next generation. I also believe that by healing ourselves we can heal our ancestors, as well. Because of how intergenerational trauma works, there are parts of my ancestors that are still living. They're living inside me right now. If I heal the trauma, they get healed, as well. They may still be living in me but be free from trauma, and that's a powerful way to think of the healing process; that it's not just for you but for your past and future generations, as well. Anyone have any thoughts on that?*

Compassion Meditation for Family Members Script

Talking Points

- Focus on family member of choice.
- Imagine them sending you love.
- You repay them by sending them love back.
- Present compassionate phrases.

Example Script

Facilitator: *This meditation is going to be a little bit different from the usual ones we've done. Oftentimes we're focusing on the breath, or the body, or something that's right here and right now. This new one we're doing today actually focuses on someone who's not here; a family member or someone that really cares about us. It could be someone who's alive or someone with whom you were close who's passed away. Go ahead and close your eyes and sit up somewhat straight, if you feel comfortable doing that, and, when I ring this bell, start off like we usually do and take a few deep breaths in, and a few deep breaths out.*

[Ring bell]

Breathing in, and breathing out . . . Just take a few moments and settle into your body, settle into your breath . . . Collect yourself by just bringing your full awareness to your body, to this present moment, just observing yourself breathe, breathing in, and breathing out . . . I want to now invite you to think about someone in your family who really cares about you, who really loves you. This could be a mom, dad, grandparent, sister, aunt, whomever. It could be someone who's alive or someone who's passed on. Simply think of someone in your family whom you know has been there for you . . . I want you to imagine that person loving you right now, in this moment. Imagine that he or she is wherever they are, thinking about you here, and thinking, "I love him" or "I love her." Imagine that they're wishing you the very best; to be healthy, to be safe, to be happy, to be free from suffering . . . For some people it helps to even say, "May I feel love from _____" and then you add in their name . . . And repeat that phrase a few times . . . For others, it might help to visualize a beam of loving energy being projected from that person to you. Whatever feels best to you, go with that. Really feel the care from that person, really feel that love . . . Next, we're going to shift and repay that person for all the love he or she has sent our way; we're going to intentionally send that love back . . . Now, think of yourself sending that person love. You might say the phrases, "May you be peaceful, may you be happy, may you be free from suffering," while thinking of that family member, or, you might just imagine a beam of loving energy being projected to that person from you, or some combination of the both. Just send that love and compassion back to that person, because you know s/he feels the same way about you . . . If the mind wanders, it's okay, just come back to the breath for a few breaths and keep sending that love . . . all the while breathing in, and breathing out. In a moment I'm going to ring the bell, and, when I do, just slowly let your awareness come back to your breath for a few breaths, and you can open your eyes when you feel comfortable.

[Ring bell]

SESSION 10

MINDFULNESS OF THE PEER SYSTEM

Session Summary

Session 10 engages youth on another important system that is heavily related to adolescent drug use: the peer group. The peer group is often an extremely influential system on youth using drugs, and most youth simply don't have the relationship skills to negotiate healthy boundaries with their peers. This session offers an array of activities that include role-plays, discussions, and tangible tools to build healthy relationships with peers. Another form of compassion meditation, directed toward peers, is taught and practiced.

Materials Needed

- Meditation bell
- Markers
- Poster paper or whiteboard
- Session 10 Handouts (optional)

Formal Meditation (Time)

- Compassion Meditation for Peers (10–12 minutes)

Learning Objectives

- Discuss the differences between friends and accomplices
- Discuss the role of leadership in relapse prevention
- Discuss the role of peer influence on relapse and relapse prevention
- Review leadership qualities necessary peer autonomy

Session Agenda (Chair Configuration)

1. Peer Pressure Role-Play (Semicircle)
2. Discussion: Friends vs. Accomplices (Semicircle)
3. Mindful Check-In with Prompt (Circle)
4. Mindful Communication (Semicircle)
5. Youth-Developed Peer Pressure Skits (Semicircle)
6. Meditation: Compassion for Friends and Accomplices (Circle)
7. Homework and Close-Out (Circle)

1. Peer Pressure Role-Play

This session starts with a role-play (as in session 3). Make sure the chairs are arranged in a semicircle prior to the youth entering the room. The essence of this skit will embody something that youth deal with constantly in relation to substance use and abuse: peer pressure. Most youth have experienced a friend or accomplice at some point attempting to get them to use drugs or engage in some behavior that may be harmful. The objective of this skit is to explicitly discuss these types of situations and set the context for teaching youth the skills necessary to make clear decisions when such situations arise.

The Role-Play

This skit will involve two people: the identified individual and the accomplice (something we'll define in-depth in the next activity). The identified individual will be trying to abstain from drug use because s/he has either a) gotten in trouble with his/her parents, b) gotten in trouble with school and/or the law, or c) needs to stay clean because s/he is on probation and gets tested regularly. Use the scenario that works best for your group, and feel free to use another scenario if you feel it's more culturally appropriate for your group. If you do not have a cofacilitator, make sure you partner with a youth participant (you should have asked for a volunteer at the end of the last session).

Below is an example of two young men who are on probation. Use the bullet points and example script below as a guide for facilitating this skit:

* The scene: two people hanging out in a room
* One is the identified individual, one is the accomplice
* The identified individual is on probation, and gets drug-tested regularly
* The accomplice peer-pressures the identified individual on a medium level

Scene Script

[Have one of the youth yell *Action!*]

Identified Individual (II): This probation thing sucks. I get drug-tested every week from my probation officer (PO).
Accomplice (A): Oh yeah. That sucks, bro.
A: Since you're on probation, you can't smoke weed, that's what you're saying?
II: Yeah, not cool.
A: What about all those pills you can take, and water you can drink, to get the weed out of your system?
II: That really works?
A: Yeah, I had some friends who did that.
II: But if I do it and get caught, fuck. I know my PO will lock me up.
A: Yeah I feel that. Well, I'm still gonna light up this blunt. You can hit it if you want; you know I got your back, right? It's some real good shit, too. Shit you might not want to pass up.

This short skit exemplifies medium-level peer pressure, in our opinion. Peer pressure can be overt (e.g., "if you don't smoke this shit you're a bitch!") to extremely subtle (e.g., simply the act of smoking weed in the vicinity of someone else). We wanted to start with a medium-level peer pressure situation so that youth can use it as a measurement to gauge the types of peer pressure they experience and/or perpetuate. Immediately following the skit, start a discussion with the group by asking:

"If you were the identified individual in that situation, what would you do?"

Then, use the following questions to facilitate further discussion:

- Have you ever been in a situation like this?
- If so, what did you do?
- Has there ever been a time when you gave in to peer pressure?
- How did you feel when someone was pressuring you?
- Have you ever been the person pressuring the other? If so, what was the underlying feeling you were feeling?
- Have you experienced more overt peer pressure? If yes, in what way?
- Have you experienced subtler peer pressure? If yes, in what way?

2. Discussion: Friends vs. Accomplices

For this discussion you'll need a large piece of poster paper, tape, and a marker. On the top left of the poster paper label write "Friends" and tape it to the wall in clear view. Then write "Accomplices" on the right side of the same poster paper. Next, ask the group to close their eyes (if they feel comfortable), and think of their closest friends and the people they care about most. Then have them call out the qualities that make their friends their true friends. You'll hear things like "respect," "caring," "love," and many others. Make sure you fill the poster paper with a number of qualities. A **friend** is someone who cares about you and has the ability to think about both his or her own interests, as well as yours.

IMPORTANT NOTE

Some youth we've worked with from very traumatized neighborhoods do not identify with the word "friend." In such cases, when youth report having no "friends," ask them what they call people outside of their family with whom they have real relationships and care about, and then use that word. If "family" is how they define them, then use that word.

Next, ask the group what they think the definition of an "accomplice" is. Engage the youth to think of multiple qualities and different scenarios in which accomplices may act. An **accomplice** is someone who's mainly self-interested. This is a broad definition, we know; however, the qualities that make up an accomplice can be complex. Sometimes an accomplice can be someone who is deliberately trying to get you to do something you shouldn't, because of negative consequences that will follow. Other times an accomplice might be someone who's actually a good friend, but who, in the moment, isn't considering the interest, wants, or needs of the other individual (e.g., smoking weed in front of someone who regularly gets tested). For the sake of this presentation, we keep it broad so that we can include many definitions from the youths' experiences. Make sure to engage the group during this portion of the activity to bring up many different and diverse ways in which accomplices enter their lives.

After writing down the qualities for both friends and accomplices on the piece of poster paper, summarize the definitions for each using the talking points and example scripts below.

Talking Points

- A friend is someone who cares about you and takes your needs and wants into consideration.
- An accomplice is self-interested and can present in many ways.

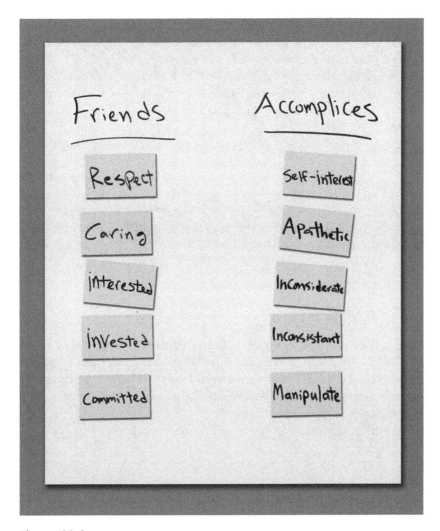

Figure 13.1

Example Script

Facilitator: So are we all on the same page about friends and accomplices? Remember, a friend is someone who really cares about you. S/he takes into consideration your wants and needs and doesn't try to
pressure you into things you don't want to do, especially after you've told them you don't want to do those
things. Those situations can involve drugs, sex, violence—many things. With a friend, you're in a real
relationship. They care about you, you care about them. It's a two-way street. It can also be that, sometimes, you really do want to do something you shouldn't be doing. For example, you might be on probation
and getting tested regularly for weed, and when presented with it you might really want to smoke weed.
A friend in that scenario will look out for you, and tell you not to do it. Does everyone agree with that? With
accomplices, though, they're different. An accomplice is mainly self-interested. It's not necessarily that s/
he doesn't care about you; accomplices can care, and they may not care, but the main thing is, they're not
looking out for your best self-interest. Sometimes accomplices will just hang out to get high, or hang out
because they know they can ask you to do things for them. Other times it may be a good friend who's just
acting as an accomplice in those moments. You might care about that friend, but s/he might not be the
best person for you to hang around. For example, has anyone ever been in a situation where they shouldn't

have used a drug, let's say weed, and when hanging out with a friend who also shouldn't have used the drug, maybe because both of you were on probation, you ended up smoking weed together? . . . In that situation, you're both friends, but acting as accomplices toward each other because you're not looking out for yourselves or each other's futures. You are just focused on the immediate gratification of smoking weed. So, accomplices are not necessarily bad people, but it's important to be aware when someone is acting as an accomplice because they probably won't have your best interest in mind. Does that make sense? . . . Any questions or comments? . . .

3. Mindful Check-In With Prompt

Facilitate a general mindful check-in and have the youth answer the following question after they've checked in: "How many of the people you hang out with would you consider accomplices? How many true friends?"

4. Mindful Communication

The crux of this session is the communication skills the youth will be learning so that they can use them when faced with the full spectrum of peer pressure situations from both friends and accomplices. You will be reviewing the STIC technique (from session 3) and then teaching youth how to set firm but respectful boundaries by bringing awareness to the present-moment relationship between the youth and her/his accomplice/friend and communicating skillfully about wants and needs. This activity has two steps: 1) review STIC and 2) mindful communication interventions.

Step 1: Review STIC

Take another piece of poster paper and post it to the wall. Write *STIC* on the top of it. Ask the group, Who remembers what this stands for? In this context, STIC is the foundation for setting boundaries with peers: mindful communication starts with mindfulness. Use the talking points and example script below as a guide for this activity.

Talking Points

- Review STIC.
- STIC is the foundation for mindful communication.
- Mindful communication is necessary for setting boundaries with friends/accomplices, and oneself when one really does want to do something that could have negative consequences.
- Mindful communication leads to deeper communication between friends and the possibility of transforming accomplices into friends.

Example Script

Facilitator: Who can tell me what STIC means? Who remembers? Right. S stands for stop, T stands for take a breath, I stands for imagine the future consequences, and C stands for choose. You probably noticed that today we're talking about peer pressure and situations where friends/accomplices don't necessarily have your best interest in mind; like smoking weed only because they want to smoke, not thinking about the consequences that may result for you. Today, we want to practice some skills to set some good boundaries those situations. STIC is important because it gets us grounded in the present moment and thinking about the future, so it will help us set appropriate boundaries with accomplices when they're trying to get something out of us, or with friends when they aren't thinking of our own best interest. Once we practice STIC, it gives us the foundation to think ahead and communicate skillfully to the person, or people, in front of it. It gives us the ability to practice skillful speech, like we talked about in the agreements back in the first group. Does that make sense? . . .

Step 2: Mindful Communication Interventions

Next, you're going to teach the youth some basic relationship-based interventions that fall within the realm of mindful communication. This comes out of the therapy philosophy of bringing awareness to the therapy relationship throughout the process and has the potential to bring folks closer, but mainly gets youth comfortable confronting others and asking for their needs with appropriate language. More importantly, it's a method youth can use to challenge those that are accomplices in their lives (friends, accomplices, family) to become true friends and supporters.

Figure 13.2

IMPORTANT NOTE

We have worked with many adolescent populations, and it's clear with many of them that simply asking them not to hang out with people they want to hang out with will only distance them from you as a facilitator. Rather than encouraging them not to hang out with someone (unless they've brought up that idea), we tend to tread softly in such conversations and invite the youth to consider whether they could challenge that accomplice into becoming a true friend. This conversation lends more to the youth making their own decision to either try to transform the accomplice into a real relationship, or, if after consideration, avoid that individual altogether.

On the same poster as above where *STIC* is in the top center of the paper, slightly below that, write "Q&A," also centered. Next, write, "Question: Whose interest is in mind right now?" And, finally, in a slight space below, write "Ask accomplices to be true friends and supporters."

Use the talking points and example script below as a guide to presenting this activity.

Talking Points

- STIC is necessary for mindful communication.
- Question whose interest is in mind in the situation.
- Ask the person to transform into a true friend/supporter.

Example Script

Facilitator: Okay, now we're going to talk about how to actually confront accomplices in a mindful, respectful way and get our needs met. We all remember STIC, since we just reviewed it. Why do you think STIC is necessary in a situation where you're going to confront an accomplice? Right, it helps us pause and think through whether or not it's worth it to have the conversation. Sometimes there may be people in your life about whom you feel it's not worth it or appropriate to even have the conversation, and we're going to take you through an exercise in a moment to think about those people. But in the meantime, STIC is a great tool to get us centered and really choose what we want to do next. Next we have "Q&A" up here. Who knows what that stands for? Yes, usually "question and answer." Here, we're using it as "question and ask," but if you just remember Q&A it will help you remember this in the moment. After completing STIC, the first thing you should do if you suspect you're in a peer-pressure situation, whether overt or subtle pressure, is ask yourself the questions, that's what "Question" stands for, "Whose interest is in mind right now?" Meaning that, when you ask yourself this, you contemplate whether the other individual or group you're with has your interest in mind, their interest in mind, or what's best for you in mind. Like we talked about before, sometimes you might want to smoke the weed, but it's not in your best interest. So that's what we mean when we say interest. After you ask yourself that question, which mainly happens on the mental level, or in your head, then you take it to the verbal level with the person you're with; you ask or challenge them to be a true friend rather than an accomplice in that moment. How do you think you could do that? . . . What words, phrases, or questions might you say to the other person to get them to be a true friend in that moment? Think of respectful, skillful, and mindful ways . . .

If necessary, tape another poster paper to the wall and write out the responses from the brainstorming session the youth present. Alternatively, if your original poster paper from this activity is large, you might write the youths' responses in any blank space. What we've found to be most important in these mindful communication interventions is that 1) youth speak from the heart, 2) youth modulate the volume at which they're speaking, 3) youth use "I" statements, and 4) youth are very clear in their requests. After the brainstorm session, either write out the above mindful communication points or distribute the "Mindful Communication Pointers" from this session's handouts.

Encourage the youth to develop their own personal scripts for situations in which peer pressure can arise. It's imperative that this comes from them and is not completely scripted by you. It's okay to share some examples; however, not every script will work for each individual. Encourage youth to share what they might say when someone is pressuring them to smoke weed. Below is an example of a script from one youth from our past groups that you might share, along with other language that encompasses the four points above:

If we're really friends, you'll respect my decision not to smoke right now. Just because I don't want to smoke with you right now, doesn't mean I don't want to be your friend, and I hope that smoking weed doesn't define our relationship. I hope we're real friends. I want to be cool with you, so, in this moment, can you support me in this decision?

5. Youth Developed Peer Pressure Role-Plays

After training the youth in mindful communication, state that you're going to ask a few volunteers to put those skills to practice in a skit similar to the one that was presented at the start of group. We have at times broken the group into pairs for dyad practice, and that works well when you have a large number of youth in the group. This activity has two steps: 1) peer pressure situation brainstorm, and 2) the skit itself. If you opt for dyads, you can pair the group up before proceeding with these steps.

Step 1: Peer Pressure Situation Brainstorm

Start a brainstorming session by simply asking the group to contemplate the most common peer pressure situations they've experienced, whether drugs are involved or not. Remind the group about the differences between subtle and overt peer pressure and the complexity of the qualities of accomplices. Develop a storyline involving 2–3 individuals where one youth is the identified individual (the youth who is dealing with peer pressure) and at least one (or more) youth is playing the role of the accomplice (the youth who is peer-pressuring). Next, co-develop (with the group) what each youth's role in the skit will be prior to acting it out. Help the identified individual figure out what s/he is going to say in the face of peer pressure using the mindful communication guide and reminding them that STIC is a large part of the practice.

Step 2: The Role-Play

Once a formidable skit has been developed, have the volunteers act it out. Get another volunteer to shout *Action!* to signify the start of the skit. The key is to have the identified individual literally practice STIC in the moment and then practice a personalized script (doesn't have to be an actual word-for-word script—some general guidelines will do) based on the mindful communication interventions that were taught in the previous activity. Have them practice the skit once and then switch the identified individual with the accomplice (and switch once more, if there are more than two people in the skit) so that everyone in the skit gets a chance to practice the mindful communication skills. Once the skit has been completed, process the experience with both the skit volunteers and the rest of the group. Use the discussion questions below as a guideline and add any others you think might be necessary:

- What was it like to practice the mindful communication and set healthy boundaries?
- Do you think you could do something like this in real life with your friends/accomplices? If yes, talk about with whom? If not, what do you think would get in the way?

Finish the discussion at an appropriate time and rearrange the chairs in a circle for formal meditation practice.

WHAT IF?

The youth in the group have extremely low energy and just don't seem to be into participating in a role-play? First, attempt to challenge the youth to raise their energy. It's important at times to not be too passive with youth in groups. It's okay to push gently as sometimes youth will actually respond and do what you're inviting (raising their energy). If, after pushing gently you intuitively feel it would be too much of a stretch for the youth to participate in the activity in a meaningful way, you might simply facilitate a discussion about peer pressure situations and what one might say in such situations. Facilitating a discussion about the content of an activity is always an option if you feel it aligns better with the group.

6. Meditation: Compassion for Friends and Accomplices

Once the chairs are rearranged in a circle, state to the group that you're going to start the formal meditation for this group. State that it will involve contemplating both friends and accomplices, sending them compassion similarly to the way they practiced that in the previous group, and that the meditation will be approximately 10–12 minutes long. Use the talking points and example script as a guide to facilitating this meditation.

Talking Points

- Start with mindfulness of the breath.
- Identify who in the youth's lives are friends and accomplices.
- Send gratitude and compassion toward the friends.
- Contemplate whether the accomplices can transform into true friends.
- Send compassion toward accomplices.

Example Script

Facilitator: We're going to practice our formal meditation for this group, and we'll start out as we normally do, practicing breath meditation. So then I want to invite you to get in a comfortable sitting position and close your eyes, if you feel comfortable doing so. If you don't, that's totally okay, just keep your eyes directed toward the floor a few feet in front of you. When you hear the sound of the bell, bring your awareness to your breath and wait for further instructions.

[Ring bell]

Breathing in, and breathing out, bring your awareness to where it's easiest to sense the breath . . . That could be the belly, the chest, or the nostrils . . . Wherever it's easiest to sense the breath . . . The mind may wander off, thinking about things other than the breath, like the future, or the past, or sounds in the present . . . That's okay, no need to think you're doing anything wrong, it's natural for the mind to wander. When you notice the mind has wandered, just gently bring your awareness back to the breath, breathing in, and breath-ing out . . . As we contemplate what we're about to contemplate, I'll invite you from time to time to remem-ber your breath . . . Next I want to invite you to start to think about all the friends you have in your life . . . Get a visual of their faces, think about how they behave, and consider who out of them behaves mainly like an accomplice toward you and who behaves like a true friend . . . Think about the different reason for why the accomplices are the accomplices, and why your true friends are your true friends . . . Family members can be true friends, as well, just as they can be accomplices . . . Really start to get a sense for who's who in your life . . . All the while, simply breathing in and breathing out. If the mind wanders off beyond the contempla-tion of friends and accomplices, simply take a few deep breathes, recentering yourself, and then continue to contemplate who are true friends and who are accomplices . . . Remember that sometimes true friends can act as accomplices. It can be complex. If that's the case for you within your circles, think about the specific qualities that and instances in which those friends behaved like accomplices . . . Next, I want to invite you to bring all of those true friends into your awareness. Those people you love, friends, family, whoever comes up for you in that category . . . We're going to send them gratitude and compassion in a similar way to what we did for our family members in the last group . . . I invite you to send that gratitude to them, thanking them for their support, for being a true supporter of you in your life . . . You might visualize their faces and send them love, compassion, and gratitude by reciting the phrases, "May you be peaceful, may you be happy, may you be healthy, may you be free from pain and suffering." Or you might send them that gratitude, love, and compassion in any way that feels right to you. It could be verbal or nonverbal. Just thank them for their support and send that compassionate energy . . . All the while, remembering your breath, breathing in and breathing out, recentering your awareness on the breath if it trails off beyond the contemplation . . . Next, I invite you to start contemplating all those folks in your life that came up when you thought of accomplices . . . Sometimes these can also be true friends, so that's okay . . . We're going to send them compassion, as well, because, with that compassion, we may be able to transform them from accomplices to true friends . . . Visualize all the accomplices in your life right now . . . Remember that sometimes, when accomplices peer-pressure you, they're doing it because they themselves are needing something in those moments. It could be a need to be appreciated, to be heard, to be loved, or a number of other things.

. . . That's a form of internal suffering, and we want to send them compassion, because, maybe if they knew that you were a true friend, they'd reciprocate that all the time toward you . . . You might visual-ize them and recite the phrases, "May you be peaceful, may you be happy, may you be healthy, may you be free from pain and suffering." Or you might send them that gratitude, love, and compassion in any way that feels right to you. It could be verbal or nonverbal . . . Consider what it would take for them to transform from accomplices to true friends. Would it be a conversation in which you're using the mindful communication skills we learned today? Or something else? . . . What would it take? How much would you want that to happen? . . . In a moment, when I ring the bell, bring all of your awareness to your ears and your hearing sense and try to listen to the sound of the bell until it's no longer there or you can't hear it any longer . . .

[Ring bell]

Once finished with the meditation, lead a brief discussion engaging youth on their experience and what they thought of the content. Use the discussion questions below as a guide:

* What was the experience like?
* How was it similar/how was it different from last week's meditation?
* Was it easy or difficult to determine which people were friends and which people were accomplices?
* Was there a lot of crossover? Accomplices who were also friends?

- What was it like to send compassion to both friends and accomplices?
- Is there any accomplice whom you'd really like to transform into a true friend? What will you do to make that happen?

7. Homework and Close-Out

After finishing the discussion above, encourage the youth to continue contemplating today's material and challenge them to *do* something (talk with an accomplices, use mindful communication) between now and next week. Ask for volunteers to lead next session's centering meditation and encourage the youth to meditate 4–5 times prior to the next sessions using a meditation of their choice.

SESSION 10 HANDOUTS

Mindful Communication Guidelines

- **Speak from the heart**
  - *Be authentic with yourself; speak from that place*

- **Be mindful of volume, tone, etc.**
  - *Do your best not to yell; stay calm and centered*

- **Use "I" statements**
  - *Instead of blaming or pointing the finger, speak from your own experience*

- **Be clear in your requests**
  - *Be as clear as possible. Be authentic with yourself and contemplate what you want from this individual (e.g., "to not smoke weed in your presence")*

Compassion Meditation for Friends and Accomplices Script

Talking Points

- Start with mindfulness of the breath.
- Identify who in the youth's lives are friends and accomplices.
- Send gratitude and compassion toward the friends.
- Contemplate whether the accomplices can transform into true friends.
- Send compassion toward accomplices.

Example Script

Facilitator: We're going to practice our formal meditation for this group, and we'll start out as we normally do, practicing breath meditation. So then I want to invite you to get in a comfortable sitting position and close your eyes, if you feel comfortable doing so. If you don't, that's totally okay, just keep your eyes directed toward the floor a few feet in front of you. When you hear the sound of the bell, bring your awareness to your breath and wait for further instructions.

[Ring bell]

Breathing in, and breathing out, bring your awareness to where it's easiest to sense the breath . . . That could be the belly, the chest, or the nostrils . . . Wherever it's easiest to sense the breath . . . The mind may wander off, thinking about things other than the breath, like the future, or the past, or sounds in the present . . . That's okay, no need to think you're doing anything wrong, it's natural for the mind to wander. When you notice the mind has wandered, just gently bring your awareness back to the breath, breathing in, and breathing out . . . As we contemplate what we're about to contemplate, I'll invite you from time to time to remember your breath . . . Next I want to invite you to start to think about all the friends you have in your life . . . Get a visual of their faces, think about how they behave, and consider who out of them behaves mainly like accomplice toward you and who behaves like a true friend . . . Think about the different reason for why the accomplices are the accomplices, and why your true friends are your true friends . . . Family members can be true friends, as well, just as they can be accomplices . . . Really start to get a sense for who's who in your life . . . All the while, simply breathing in and breathing out. If the mind wanders off beyond the contemplation of friends and accomplices, simply take a few deep breathes, recentering yourself, and then continue to contemplate who are true friends and who are accomplices . . . Remember that sometimes true friends can act as accomplices. It can be complex. If that's the case for you within your circles, think about the specific qualities that and instances in which those friends behaved like accomplices . . . Next, I want to invite you to bring all of those true friends into your awareness. Those people you love, friends, family, whoever comes up for you in that category . . . We're going to send them gratitude and compassion in a similar way to what we did for our family members in the last group . . . I invite you to send that gratitude to them, thanking them for their support, for being a true supporter of you in your life . . . You might visualize their faces and send them love, compassion, and gratitude by reciting the phrases, "May you be peaceful, may you be happy, may you be healthy, may you be free from pain and suffering." Or you might send them that gratitude, love, and compassion in any way that feels right to you. It could be verbal or nonverbal. Just thank them for their support and send that compassionate energy . . . All the while, remembering your breath, breathing in and breathing out, recentering your awareness on the breath if it trails off beyond the contemplation . . . Next, I invite you to start contemplating all those folks in your life that came up when you thought of accomplices . . . Sometimes these can also be true friends, so that's okay . . . We're going to send them compassion, as well, because, with that compassion, we may be able to transform them from accomplices to true friends . . . Visualize all the accomplices in your life right now . . . Remember that sometimes, when accomplices peer-pressure you, they're doing it because they themselves are needing something in those moments. It could be a need to be appreciated, to be heard, to be loved, or a number of other things

. . . That's a form of internal suffering, and we want to send them compassion, because, maybe if they knew that you were a true friend, they'd reciprocate that all the time toward you . . . You might visualize them and recite the phrases, "May you be peaceful, may you be happy, may you be healthy, may you be free from pain and suffering." Or you might send them that gratitude, love, and compassion in any way that feels right to you. It could be verbal or nonverbal . . . Consider what it would take for them to transform from accomplices to true friends. Would it be a conversation in which you're using the mindful communication skills we learned today? Or something else? . . . What would it take? How much would you want that to happen? . . . In a moment, when I ring the bell, bring all of your awareness to your ears and your hearing sense and try to listen to the sound of the bell until it's no longer there or you can't hear it any longer . . .

[Ring bell]

SESSION 11

MINDFULNESS OF THE EXTERNAL ENVIRONMENT

Session Summary

Session 11 engages youth about the impact of the environment on drug use. The exact tone of this session will depend on who's in your group. If you're working with lower socioeconomic youth of color, the ways in which the environment affects drug use may have a very different connotation than if working with White upper-class youth. The "environment" that youth reside in could mean living in impoverished conditions of a drug-ridden neighborhood and/or living in a wealthy home with constant access to a liquor cabinet or prescription drugs. Some youth will have lived through extreme poverty and will have seen firsthand severe drug addiction, and others will have not. Regardless, you can still present, discuss, educate, and learn about how the youth in your group perceive the role that the environment, both from a larger community and smaller family-home level, play on drug use. This is the last session with novel information to be imparted. The final group is a celebratory group that honors the youth for their committed engagement. Didactic, experiential, and discussion-based activities comprise this session, and a third compassion meditation directed toward community is taught and practiced.

Materials Needed

- Meditation bell
- Markers
- Poster paper or whiteboard
- Session 11 Handouts (optional)

Learning Objectives

- Discuss the multi-faceted environmental level of influence on behavior
- Discuss the impact of context for drug attitudes, cravings, and use
- Practice compassion-based meditation toward community

Formal Meditation (Time)

- Compassion Meditation toward Community (12–15 minutes)

Session Agenda (Chair Configuration)

1. Youth-Lead Centering (Circle)
2. Mindful Check-In (Circle)
3. Mindfulness of External Environment (Semicircle)
4. Transforming Systems of Influence (Spread Across Room)
5. Meditation: Compassion Meditation Toward Community (Circle)
6. Homework and Close-Out (Circle)

1. Youth-Led Centering

Once again, have a youth facilitate the centering meditation. Let the individual choose which meditation s/he'd like to facilitate. Give the leader approximately 3–5 minutes for the meditation, and then
process afterwards. If a new youth decides to facilitate the centering, use the process questions from the
previous groups. If a veteran youth facilitates the centering, give him or her feedback and thank the
youth for their continued commitment.

2. Mindful Check-In

For session 11, simply facilitate a standard mindful check-in. If the youth have been able to practice
taking the deep breath without your prompt, simply ask them to check in as in session 6. If they need
the extra instruction, use the guidelines for the mindful check-in from session 2.

3. Mindfulness of External Environment

This activity presents concepts that educate youth about the details of how an environment, whether it
be an impoverished community ridden with easily accessible drugs or a wealthy home with easy access
to a liquor cabinet, affects drug use. This activity is comprised of three steps: 1) a review of the three
levels of influence that were presented in session 8 2) education about an adapted ecological systems
theory, a theory that details how environments affect choices, attitudes, and behavior; and 3) how the
environment affects drug-craving and choices related to drug use.

Step 1: Three Levels of Influence Review

Have the youth re-arrange their chairs into a semicircle and ask the question, Who remembers the three
levels of influence from session 8? Who remembers what they were? Next, tape a piece of poster paper
to the wall and draw the three rows with a column to the left for the labeling of each of the three levels
of influence. Ask the youth to state the three levels of influence (either popcorn style or by raised hands)
and, if they need help, guide them and fill in the *personal, social*, and *environmental* levels of influence.
Next, review each level of influence by asking the group for examples from each category. Offer guidance as necessary and make sure that there is at least one concrete example for each level of influence.

Step 2: Ecological Systems Theory and the Environmental Level of Influence

The second step of this activity involves educating the youth about an adapted version of Ecological
Systems Theory, a theory developed by the famous psychologist Uri Bronfenbrenner. The conceptual
framework from this theory is highly applicable to the environmental level of influence and overviews
the different systems an individual interacts with in her or his environment that has both direct and
indirect influence on their lives. It is a great way to conceptualize the environmental level of influence
on a deeper level and pays homage to the complexity of influence that environments and communities
have on young people who use drugs.

Below is a summary of the systems within Bronfenbrenner's Ecological Systems Theory:

Microsystem: Entities with whom the youth interacts directly. For example, the family system,
school, people in the community, etc.

Mesosystem: The relationship the entities in the microsystem have with one another. For example, what value does a youth's family place on education? If a high value is placed on education, the interactions between the family and school systems are positive.

Exosystem: Entities that have an indirect but strong influence on the youth's life. For example, the mother's job, the neighborhood one lives in, etc.

Macrosystem: The major cultural influences, from both cultural heritage and current living culture (e.g., if one lives in poverty) that influence an individual's life.

Chronosystem: The major life events, transitions, and eras that influence an individual's life. This includes, for example, an individual whose parents have just divorced (major life event), the technological era, the war on drugs, the rates of incarceration in the United States (eras of strong influence on society), etc.

The adapted version of the above presents the theory in a simplified format: direct influences, indirect influences, and societal influences. For this step of the activity, tape a piece of poster paper to the wall and draw the adapted version of Ecological Systems Theory. This is an image of a solid circle representing an individual, with three concentric and large circles for each level of influence.

Next, educate the group about each system by giving concrete examples for how each of them affects an individual's life. Use the talking points and example script below as a guide.

Talking Points

- State that you'll be delving deeper into the environmental level of influence on behavior.
- Present the adapted Ecological Systems Theory.
- Present each system in the theory.
- Present example of an individual affected by different systems.
- Present examples of internal versus external locus of control and the impact of the environment.

Example Script

Facilitator: *We're going to go a bit deeper into the environmental source of influence. To do that, I want to present something that's an adapted version of Ecological Systems Theory. Anyone ever heard of that? This famous psychologist from a while back created it. Anyone ever heard of the Head Start program? Well, this psychologist was the co-founder of that, too. The theory is a way to think about the development of children as they grow and whether or not that development is psychologically healthy. It actually goes hand-in-hand with the environmental level of influence and plays a big role in the types of options we get presented with to choose from. This inner circle here* **[point to graphic on the poster]** *represents the individual, and all these circles around the individual represent the different levels, or "systems," of this theory. The innermost circle outside the individual represents direct influences on the individual's life. These are systems that an individual directly interacts with. So, what would be some examples of these? When you think of yourself, what "systems" do you directly interact with? . . . Right. You interact directly with the school system, the juvenile justice system, the family system, and so on. So your success in those systems at least in part would probably depend on how well those systems were run, right? For example, if you went to a really poor, underfunded school that didn't have high expectations for their students, how do you think that would affect your overall education? . . . Exactly. Your education would most likely suffer.*

The next circle out represents indirect influences on the individual's life. Think about your mom's, dad's, or caregiver's job. If they have a high-paying job that affects the community you live in, the house you live in, and, ultimately, your lifestyle. If they have a low-paying job or no job, the community you live in, the house you live in, your lifestyle—all that would most likely be different from that of an individual whose

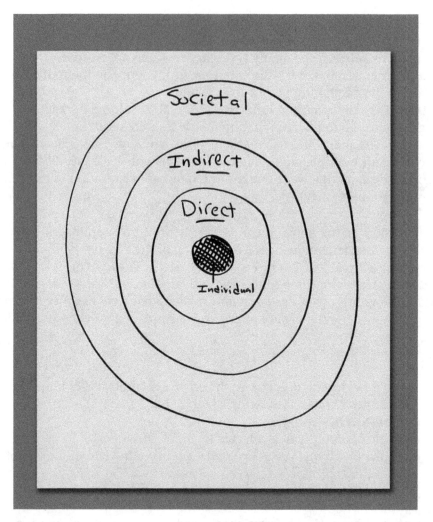

Figure 14.1

parent has a high-paying job. And growing up in a poor, violent, drug-ridden community is very different from growing up in a safe, middle- to upper-class community. Would you all agree? That's the indirect level of influence on our lives.

The last level or circle out is the societal level of influence. It is the major cultural beliefs of society, often disseminated through mass media, politics, and other channels. The societal level of influence in part represents things like poverty, ethnicity, racism, and so forth. Let's take a look at a specific example.

Take, for example, a young person of Mexican descent. She lives with her aunt and uncle. Her parents live in Mexico. Her family is filled with love, but she misses her parents. Why aren't her parents living here in the United States? Well, they can't get into the country because of their immigration status. What is immigration status related to on these three levels of influence? . . . Right. Societal thought. There are a bunch of politicians who want to create laws that don't let people from Mexico live here in the United States. Those ideas live in the societal level of influence in this theory. Politicians make up racist narratives to get people to vote and approve laws, an example of the indirect level of influence, which then doesn't let some people live in the United States. That affects the make-up of this young person's family and their lives in the direct level of influence/experience. That indirect level of influence affects this young person's attitudes, beliefs, and choices. Does that all make sense? . . .

Step 3: Environmental Influences on Drug Use

To start the final step of this activity, present the group with the *ice cream metaphor* to build upon the previous step and solidify the concept of the strong influence the environment has on one's behavior. The ice cream metaphor uses the analogy of losing weight and whether or not one has access to his or her vice—ice cream—on a daily basis. It is compared to the type of access one has to drugs and one's attempts to reduce or quit using them. Use the talking points and example script below as a guide to presenting this metaphor.

Talking Points

- Relate ice cream eating and weight loss to drug use and relapse.
- Access to ice cream and access to drugs have a lot to do with relapse.

Example Script

Facilitator: Before we move into this last discussion portion of this activity, I just want to drill home how much our environment can influence us when it comes to behavior, especially drug use. I'm going to use a weight-loss metaphor to illuminate the point. How many folks here have ever heard of those weight loss camps? . . . Yeah, well, there are these camps out there that people go attend to help themselves lose weight. How many of you all like ice cream? . . . Yeah, me, too. I love ice cream. Let's say that one of the people who attended one of these weight-loss camps also loved ice cream. He's living in this posh house on a ranch or in some serene location for a few weeks to a month for this program, and, of course, he's going get that urge to eat ice at times, because he loves it. Even with all the counseling and coaching, he's still going get the urge. But what do you think is going to happen when he walks over to the fridge and looks for some ice cream?. . . There's not going to be any ice cream in the fridge! One of the things that most of those camps don't tell you is that they control your whole environment. No ice cream, no pizza, not even any food like that to look at because you might relapse. That, coupled with exercise every day, means you will lose weight. But most of the folks that go to these camps ultimately gain all the weight back that they had lost at camp, because, when they go back home, into their regular environment, and go to their fridge, they will find the ice cream, and give in, and eat it, at times. That's the big difference. So think about it like this: if you live in an environment where drugs are easily accessible all the time, how do you think you're going to respond? Some of us do have a very strong will power, but that's a trap, because even those with the strongest of will power will, from time-to-time, give in and use, if they've used drugs before. That environment in which drugs are easily accessible could be an impoverished, drug-ridden neighborhood, or it could be the liquor cabinet in an upper-middle class family's home. What's most important is that, if you open up the fridge, metaphorically speaking, and there is a whole bunch of "ice cream" and "pizza" (that is, drugs), right in front of you in an uncontrolled environment, there is more of a likelihood that you're going to use. That doesn't mean you're weak or less than anyone else. It means you're a human being. This whole session is about learning to be aware of and not be controlled by one's urges, but it's also important to understand that there's a difference between being in a controlled and uncontrolled environment when it comes to drug use. Does that make sense to everyone? . . . Any questions or comments?. . .

After presenting and discussing the ice cream metaphor to the group, tape another piece of poster paper on the wall and label it *Environmental Forces on Drug Use*. Use the following discussion questions to start the dialogue about the environmental forces that affect drug use (write down thoughts on the poster paper):

- How does the ice cream metaphor relate to the systems from adapted ecological systems theory?
- What are some of the environmental forces that lead to addiction? (i.e., how do people become addicts?)

- Has anyone in this group either experienced these forces personally or known someone who's had these environmental forces play a vital role in their continuing drug use or another unhealthy behavior?
- How do biases/prejudices toward certain communities impact drug use in those communities? (e.g., the assumption that poor people use more drugs)
- What are some of the discrepancies in the laws that impact drug use in certain neighborhoods? (e.g., crack vs. cocaine mandatory sentencing laws) How does that contribute to different environmental forces influencing those who use drugs?
- Is there anything that can be done to combat some of these environmental forces of influence? If so, what?

NOTE

Add in any other questions that you think may pertain to the specific youth in your group.

The objective of this discussion is to engage the group about the larger role of drug use on a social, cultural, and even a societal level. Oftentimes, the conversation can run the gamut of discussing how poverty creates violence, which creates drug use and so on, to how there is a huge problem with alcoholism and other drug addiction in some of the wealthiest communities. This will be dependent on the experience and background of the youth in your group. This discussion should take anywhere from 20–30 minutes. As you wind the conversation down, go back to the poster paper and write the words *Environmental*, *Social*, and *Personal* in a triangle-type fashion below the previous graphic on the poster paper. Draw arrows between each source of influence and its neighbors in the triangle so that an image of a cycle is portrayed.

Finish this activity by discussing how environmental forces are at the base of a lot (not all, but a lot) of continued community drug use. Use examples for each stage and present how environmental issues lead to social issues which then lead to personal issues, and, that those personal issues all tallied up amongst a lot of individuals lead to more social and environmental issues, thus continuing the cycle of impact that drugs have on the community. Use the talking points and example script below as a guide.

Talking Points

- Review environmental, social, and personal issues.
- Discuss the cycle of drug use and community issues.
- Discuss how drug use in the community is a cycle that is non-linear and affects everyone.

Example Script

Facilitator: We've reviewed in this session and in session 8 the differences between these three main levels of influences: personal, social, and environmental. We've also discussed in detail in this group the role of environmental factors on drug use. Really, however, all of these levels of influence—environmental, social, and personal—affect us and are related to each other. You see this graphic here that reads "Cycle of Drug Use?" [point to graphic] Who wants to say how they think all these sources of influence affect each other? How do you think they relate to one another? . . . That's right. They're all connected. A person, who just lost his or her best friend to an overdose, might be prompted to use more drugs because of depression—the personal level. They may become reclusive and isolate themselves from their friends and family, straining those relationships—the social level. Then, this happens to a bunch of people, and, when tallied up, this snowballing of drug use affects the community as a whole—the environmental level. And then that environment of people who are all suffering, that affects the social level, cycling there again and influencing social

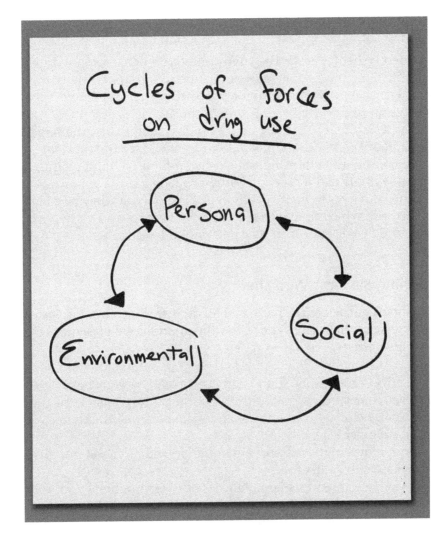

Figure 14.2

norms, which in turn influence individuals' psychology on the personal level—and round and round it goes in both directions. So it's not only a one-way cycle, all of these levels of influence affect each other in many ways. That's why it's so important, in our opinion, to discuss all three of these levels, because they all affect you. They all play roles in determining whether or not you'll be able to stay off drugs, if that's what you want—or, really, to achieve any goal. Can anyone think of a time in his or her life or an experience when it was apparent that the environmental level of influence contributed to your own drug use, or another unwanted behavior?

WHAT IF?

The youth in the group are having trouble grasping the concept, metaphor, or any other of the points you're trying to make? What's important in this activity, as in any activity you facilitate, is the underlying concept. If you have an alternative way to present the material, by all means please experiment with doing so, especially if youth are having trouble understanding. It's always good practice to disseminate information in a way that is most understandable for your audience.

4. Transforming Systems of Influence

After discussing in-depth the impact of the environment on behavior and drug use in the previous activity, devise a transition toward how one can influence and potentially transform the systems with which one interacts. We certainly aren't suggesting that one could solve all the problems with systemic oppression or poverty by engaging in the activities described below; however, we do take the stance of systems theory that, if one part of a system shifts, the larger system also shifts (even if by a small amount). This could mean an individual altering how s/he interacts with family, or an individual consciously choosing to bring awareness to—and relating differently to—the fact that his or her neighborhood has serious drug problems.

The premise of this activity is to invite youth to think about how they personally could have influence over the systems with which they interact. The activity involves two steps: 1) the "Transforming Systems" worksheet, and 2) a discussion of the content of the worksheet.

Step 1: Transforming Systems Worksheet

Invite the youth to spread out across the room and fill out the "Transforming Systems Worksheet" that can be found in this session's handouts. The following questions are presented to each youth to fill in to the best of her or his capacity:

1. Describe the environment that you live in. This could be your home, community, neighborhood; whatever comes up for you. Think about all the systems from the adapted ecological systems theory to help you contemplate and write about all the things you deal with in your immediate environment.
2. How does mindfulness of the external environment and its conditions help you to not become a passive recipient of its influence?
3. Given what you've learned this far about how the environment can influence drug use and behavior, how can you personally influence the environment? Write down at least 1–2 concrete things you can do to influence the environment around you.
4. Write down at least one thing about your environment that you commit to being mindful of so as to decrease the risk of your own drug use (or other unhealthy behavior).

Make sure when passing out the worksheet to state to the youth that, if they have any trouble understanding any portion of the questions, they should ask you to clarify. It should take approximately 7–12 minutes for the group to fill out the worksheet completely. Once they are finished, have the youth circle back up for discussion.

Step 2: Group Discussion

Once all are back in a circle, encourage youth to share what they wrote down on their worksheets. Use your best discretion on whether to go around in a circle or engage in popcorn-style sharing. Encourage each group member to share.

5. Meditation: Compassion Meditation Toward Community

The formal meditation for this session builds on the compassion-based theme of sessions 9 and 10 and invites youth to contemplate their community as a whole and send it compassion. Use the talking points and example script below and refer to this session's handouts for a printable version of this meditation.

Talking Points

- Start with mindfulness of the breath.
- Invite awareness to family-based compassion.
- Invite awareness to peer-based compassion.
- Invite awareness to community-based compassion.
- Present the Aspen Tree Interdependence metaphor.

Example Script

Facilitator: *We're going to build on the last couple of compassion meditations we've been practicing. I want to encourage you to find a comfortable sitting position, and, when you hear the sound of the meditation bell, simply start off as we usually do, taking a few breaths in and a few breaths out . . .*

[Ring bell]

Breathing in, and breathing out. Just let your awareness find where it's easiest to sense your breath . . . Maybe that's in the nostrils, feeling the touch of the air as you breath in and breath out . . . Maybe that's in the belly or chest, feeling the expansion and contraction of the core as you breath in and out . . . Wherever it's easiest, just let your awareness rest right there . . . I want to invite you to direct your awareness to your family. You could think of the family member you've been sending compassion to for the last few groups, or another family member . . . Get a visual of that person, and contemplate that person's love for you . . . Think about how much they love you and image them sending you that love . . . Let's repay them the favor and send them love back. You might utter the compassion phrases while imagining the person's face: "May you be peaceful, may you be happy, may you be free from pain and suffering." Or you might just send the person love and compassion in whatever way makes you feel most comfortable . . . Just really imagine that compassion and love going from you to him or her . . . If the mind wanders, that's okay, just take a few breaths in and a few breaths out and refocus on the compassion you were just contemplating . . . Next I want to invite you to think of those true friends you have, your peer group. Think about all the friends that really love you, that really support you and want you to do good in life. These could be close friends, or even people you know that are nice to you . . . Get an image of one or a few of them and then send them love and compassion . . . you might utter the phrases, "May you be peaceful, may you be happy, may you be free from pain and suffering." Or you might just send them love and compassion in any way that feels comfortable to you.

. . . Now I want to invite you to think about your true friends, your whole family, and everyone you consider to be a part of your community. Your community could be your neighborhood, it could be everyone you care about, or even something else . . . As we talked about in this group, the environment has an influence on how we behave. But we also can influence our environment. One way to do that is to send compassion to our entire community . . . Picture the members of your community all together in one place; maybe a gym or amphitheater . . . Send them love and compassion. Thank them for being your community and supporting you. You might utter the phrases, "May you all be peaceful, may you all be happy, may you all be free from pain and suffering." Or you might just send love, compassion, and gratitude in whatever way makes you feel most comfortable . . . As you send compassion to your community, think about everyone in your community like trees in a forest. The forest is your community, and each tree represents each individual. There is something very interesting about an Aspen tree forest, for example. Above ground the forest looks like a bunch of individual trees, but when you go below the dirt, each tree's roots are intertwined with all the other

trees around it. So, from above, the trees look like individuals, but below they look like one conglomeration of roots. That's how the community works, it supports itself as an organism . . . Whatever your community is, whether it is just your family, just your friends, or the entire planet, think of yourself as connected to that community, a part of it, just as the roots of an Aspen tree forest are intimately connected . . . All the while you're simply breathing in and breathing out . . . Breathing in and breathing out, as we start to close this meditation, bring your awareness back to your breath and body . . . Just notice what it feels like right now in your body after this meditation. Notice your emotional tone, the thoughts arising . . . When you hear the sound of the bell, you can slowly open your eyes, if they were closed, and expand your awareness to the rest of the group.

[Ring bell]

After finishing the meditation, take a few minutes to process the experience of the meditation with the youth. Use the discussion questions from the previous sessions to prompt the youth to discuss their experiences prior to closing out this session.

6. Homework and Close-Out

State to the group that the next session's final meditation will be at the start of the group and the longest meditation to date. You can use your best discretion on whether you or a youth will facilitate this meditation. We'd only let a youth facilitate this meditation if they had shown some skill in facilitating in the past and took those meditations seriously. The next meditation will be approximately 15–20 minutes long, depending on your group. Prompt the youth to think about this final question before the last group: What has been your experience in this program and what have you learned? Encourage youth to think about this and state that it will be discussed in the final group. Also encourage the youth to meditate every day prior to the next session using a meditation of their choice.

SESSION 11 HANDOUTS

Transforming Systems Worksheet

1. Describe the environment in which you live. This could be your home, community, neighborhood; whatever comes up for you. Think about all the systems from the adapted ecological systems theory to help you contemplate and write about all the things you deal with in your immediate environment.

2. How does mindfulness of the external environment and its conditions help you to not become a passive recipient of its influence?

3. Given what you've learned this far about how the environment can influence drug use and behavior, how can you personally influence the environment? Write down at least 1–2 concrete things you can do to influence the environment around you.

4. Write down at least one thing about your environment of which you commit to be mindful so as to decrease the risk of your own drug use (or other unhealthy behavior).

Community Compassion Meditation

Talking Points

- Start with mindfulness of the breath.
- Invite awareness to family-based compassion.
- Invite awareness to peer-based compassion.
- Invite awareness to community-based compassion.
- Present the Aspen Tree Interdependence metaphor.

Example Script

Facilitator: *We're going to build on the last couple of compassion meditations we've been practicing. I want to encourage you to find a comfortable sitting position, and, when you hear the sound of the meditation bell, simply start off as we usually do, taking a few breaths in and a few breaths out . . .*

[Ring bell]

Breathing in, and breathing out. Just let your awareness find where it's easiest to sense your breath . . . Maybe that's in the nostrils, feeling the touch of the air as you breath in and breath out . . . Maybe that's in the belly or chest, feeling the expansion and contraction of the core as you breath in and out . . . Wherever it's easiest, just let your awareness rest right there . . . I want to invite you to direct your awareness to your family. You could think of the family member you've been sending compassion to for the last few groups, or another family member . . . Get a visual of that person, and contemplate that person's love for you . . . Think about how much they love you and image them sending you that love . . . Let's repay them the favor and send them love back. You might utter the compassion phrases while imagining the person's face: "May you be peaceful, may you be happy, may you be free from pain and suffering." Or you might just send the person love and compassion in whatever way makes you feel most comfortable . . . Just really imagine that compassion and love going from you to him or her . . . If the mind wanders, that's okay, just take a few breaths in and a few breaths out and refocus on the compassion you were just contemplating . . . Next I want to invite you to think of those true friends you have, your peer group. Think about all the friends that really love you, that really support you and want you to do good in life. These could be close friends, or even people you know that are nice to you . . . Get an image of one or a few of them and then send them love and compassion . . . you might utter the phrases, "May you be peaceful, may you be happy, may you be free from pain and suffering." Or you might just send them love and compassion in any way that feels comfortable to you

. . . Now I want to invite you to think about your true friends, your whole family, and everyone you consider to be a part of your community. Your community could be your neighborhood, it could be everyone you care about, or even something else . . . As we talked about in this group, the environment has an influence on

how we behave. But we also can influence our environment. One way to do that is to send compassion to our entire community . . . Picture the members of your community all together in one place; maybe a gym or amphitheater . . . Send them love and compassion. Thank them for being your community and supporting you. You might utter the phrases, "May you all be peaceful, may you all be happy, may you all be free from pain and suffering." Or you might just send love, compassion, and gratitude in whatever way makes you feel most comfortable . . . As you send compassion to your community, think about everyone in your community like trees in a forest. The forest is your community, and each tree represents each individual. There is something very interesting about an Aspen tree forest, for example. Above ground the forest looks like a bunch of individual trees, but when you go below the dirt, each tree's roots are intertwined with all the other trees around it. So, from above, the trees look like individuals, but below they look like one conglomeration of roots. That's how the community works, it supports itself as an organism . . . Whatever your community is, whether it is just your family, just your friends, or the entire planet, think of yourself as connected to that community, a part of it, just as the roots of an Aspen tree forest are intimately connected . . . All the while you're simply breathing in and breathing out . . . Breathing in and breathing out, as we start to close this meditation, bring your awareness back to your breath and body . . . Just notice what it feels like right now in your body after this meditation. Notice your emotional tone, the thoughts arising . . . When you hear the sound of the bell, you can slowly open your eyes, if they were closed, and expand your awareness to the rest of the group.

[Ring bell]

CLOSING CEREMONY

Session Summary

The final session is reserved for reflection on the program and celebrating the participation of the youth. A focus group engages the youth to reflect on their experience in the program as a whole. Youth are encouraged to appreciate themselves and each other, and the final component of compassion meditation—self-compassion—is taught and practiced. Certificates can be awarded and a celebratory meal (e.g., pizza) can close out the program.

Materials Needed

- Meditation bell
- Audio recorder/microphone (optional)
- Session 12 Handouts (optional)

Formal Meditation (Time)

- 15–20 minutes

Learning Objectives

- To review the material taught over the whole course
- For youth to offer feedback on positive experiences and potential improvements for the program
- To appreciate the group as a whole
- To celebrate completion of the curriculum

Session Agenda (Chair Configuration)

1. Meditation: Final Practice (Circle)
2. Mindful Check-In (Circle)
3. Focus Group (Circle)
4. Group Appreciations (Circle)
5. Food Celebration (Circle; Semicircle; At Tables)
6. Certificates of Completion (Semicircle)
7. Closing Ceremony (Circle)

1. Meditation: Final Practice

For the final session, encourage the group to formally meditate for a longer period. This could be 15–20 minutes, depending on the interest and ability of the group. Let the youth choose a meditation from the previous sessions and facilitate accordingly.

2. Mindful Check-In

After the longer meditation, facilitate a mindful check-in and ask the youth about their experience meditating for the longer period of time.

3. Focus Group

One of the most important aspects of this final session is the focus group activity. Focus groups are a qualitative interview technique designed to gather rich descriptions, experiences, opinions, and attitudes from groups of participants. Focus groups have the potential to provide detailed quotes both for research and evaluation, data for funders, and, most importantly, provide youth a chance to reflect on their experience and facilitators a chance to get important feedback that could improve their programming. The primary purpose of the focus group is for the youth to reflect on their experience of the program. We found over the years via our research that the focus groups themselves became therapeutic because of the potential to solidify the experiences of the youth into their awareness. The secondary purpose of conducting focus groups in this program is so you can continuously improve this curriculum. As noted in the chapter on curriculum development and research, evidence-based practice is comprised of three components: 1) empirical research, 2) clinical expertise, and 3) client preference/value (American Psychological Association, 2005; Institute of Medicine, 2001). By conducting focus groups, you can continuously collect data related to client values and preferences about the program (and, of course, collect data for empirical research, if you conduct a formal study).

This activity has two steps: 1) defining focus groups, and 2) facilitating the focus group.

Step 1: Defining Focus Groups

Start this step by asking the group, "Does anyone know what a focus group is?" Field any answers and describe the essence of a focus group: a group interview to gather the thoughts, opinions, and preferences of the members of the group. It's also good practice to explain why it's important for making the group better for the next cohort of youth who will participate in the program. Use the talking points and example script below as a guide.

Talking Points

- A focus group is a way to collect continuous data to improve programming.
- A focus group is a good way to reflect on experience.
- It's a method where we'll ask you all a question, and then go around the circle and hear your answers.
- You can answer every question, some questions, or no questions.

Example Script

Facilitator: A focus group is a way for us, the group facilitators, to learn about what was good about this group, and what was not so good. It's a way for you all to share your experiences, attitudes, and opinions and reflect on how this group has been. It really helps us because we want to continuously make this group better for the youth we'll work with after working with you all. Your real opinions will help to continue that process. What we're basically going to do is ask you all a set of questions about your experiences in this entire program. After each question, we'll go around the circle and if you have something you want to share, you can do so. If not, you can pass. You can answer all the questions, some of them, or none of them. It's up to you. All we ask is that you just be honest. Does that make sense to everyone? . . .

If you are conducting formal research with the group and using a microphone to record the focus group (or simply using a microphone for program evaluation purposes), it is imperative to go over any research consent and confidentiality requirements.

NOTE

We actually found the microphone to be helpful in facilitating the focus group process. Rather than what we originally thought, which is that youth would be hesitant to get recorded, they were very forthright and interested in helping our research causes. In our groups, the microphone has acted as a "talking stick" in the use of which youth know their words, experiences, opinions, etc. will be heard and taken into account. Thus, if one is not doing formal research or evaluation, it still may be worthwhile to use a microphone or some form of a talking stick.

Step 2: Facilitating the Focus Group

In our focus groups we oftentimes utilize what's called the "hour glass method" for asking interview questions. This process starts with broad general questions, then moves into more specific targeted questions, and ends with general questions again.

The questions we use in our focus group are presented below:

1) What was your overall experience in this group?
2) What was the meditation portion of the group like? Did it help? Not help? If so, how?
3) What was the discussion portion of the group like? Those topics we discussed?
4) What was the substance-use education like? Helpful? Not helpful?
5) What was your favorite activity of the ones we did? Why?
6) What was your least favorite activity? Why?
7) Out of every experience, which experience in this group stands out the most?
8) Is there anything we didn't ask about in this interview that you want to add?

If there are other questions you feel you should add, given the sub-cultural make-up of your group, feel free to do so. This activity is about you getting feedback to continuously improve your program. Facilitate the focus group using the questions above. Encourage, but don't mandate, that each youth answer every question. Ask each question, give each youth in the circle an opportunity to answer, and then ask the next question on the list. With 8 questions, you should expect to spend approximately 15–20 minutes facilitating this focus group.

4. Group Appreciations

After conducting the focus group, have the youth re-arrange their chairs into a circle for group appreciations. This activity involves the youth appreciating others in the group for their participation in the program. This activity has two steps: 1) the explaining of group appreciations, and 2) the group appreciations themselves.

Step 1: Explaining Group Appreciations

Notify the group that the next activity involves verbally expressing appreciation of everyone in the group. The point of the activity is to say something positive, that you've appreciated, about one other person in the group. The person who gets appreciated then will appreciate someone else (not the person that appreciated them) who hasn't been appreciated yet. Further, youth are encouraged to contemplate what they'd want to say if they knew they were never going to see each other again. Use the talking points and example script below as a guide to facilitating this activity.

Talking Points

- This is a time to appreciate each other for the work you've each done in this program.
- Think of something positive to say about everyone in the group.
- Contemplate what you'd say if you knew you'd never see them again, ever!
- Once you get appreciated, you then will appreciate someone else.
- You can't appreciate someone who just appreciated you or someone who's already been appreciated.

Example Script

Facilitator: As this is our last session together, it's time to think about all the positive things we've done in here together. Each and every one of you has shown up and contributed positively to this group in your own ways. What we're going to do is appreciate each other in this circle by thinking of something positive that we appreciated from each and every one else in the group. I want to encourage you to also think about it as if you'd never see anyone else in the group ever again. Ever! Think about what positive thing you'd want to say from what you've seen of them in the group. You can only appreciate one person at a time, and only appreciate someone after you've been appreciated. You also can't appreciate someone who's already been appreciated, so make sure you have at least one appreciation for everyone in the group. Everyone got that? Okay, I'll start . . .

Step 2: Group Appreciations

Prior to starting the appreciations, give the youth 3–5 minutes to contemplate what they'd say to each individual in the group. Then start the group appreciations, led by you, the facilitator, appreciating one of the youth for his or her participation in the group. Make sure you state something unique and positive about the individual (you're setting the tone). Make sure everyone gets appreciated at least once prior to moving on from the activity.

NOTE

Another way to perform this appreciation activity is with a ball of yarn. The person who starts the first appreciation would start with the ball of yarn and toss it, while holding onto the end of the string, to the person that was just appreciated. The appreciated person would then appreciate a third person, toss the ball of yarn to the third person, and hold onto the yarn taut. This would be repeated until everyone had been appreciated and holding a piece of yarn. A "web of connection" would then appear symbolizing all the connections that had been made during the program.

5. Pizza Party/Food Celebration

After the focus group, reward the youth for their participation with a pizza party or other food you feel is appropriate. We often would throw a pizza party or bring some food as a way to appreciate the youth for their participation. Youth are often extremely excited and thankful, and it is a time to connect informally after delving into group appreciations. Manage time wisely and spend no more than 15 minutes eating and connecting informally.

6. Certificates of Completion

Once finished with group appreciations, distribute certificates of completion to the youth in the group. We like to individualize certificates and conduct a ceremony where one person gets up from the circle at a time while the rest of the group gives him or her a round of applause. See this session's handouts for a general sample certificate of completion. We highly encourage you to not simply scan the certificate of completion from this session's handouts, but rather to create and customize your own. However, if you do not have that luxury, use the certificate in this session's handouts at your leisure.

7. Closing Dedication and Ceremony

Finish the program by circling up one last time and practicing a compassion meditation. Encourage the youth to direct compassion to themselves and others in the group. Thank the youth for their participation and send them love, compassion, kindness, and gratitude for their participation in the program. Use the talking points and example script below as a guide.

Talking Points

- Practice one last compassion meditation.
- Compassion toward all members of the group.
- Compassion toward self.
- Send the youth love, compassion, kindness, and gratitude.
- Give them any other prep/inspiration you wish as you end the meditation and program.

Example Script

Facilitator: For our last meditation, we're going to build on the compassion meditations we've been conducting for the past few groups . . . Sit in a comfortable position, let your eyes close, if you feel comfortable doing so, and, when you hear the sound of the bell, simply bring your awareness to your breathing and wait for further instructions . . .

[Ring bell]

Start by breathing in, and breathing out . . . Notice where it's easiest to sense your breath. That might be in the nostrils, the belly, the chest . . . wherever it's easiest to notice your breath, let your awareness rest right there. Breathing in, and breathing out . . .

. . . Next I want to invite you to contemplate someone in your family, someone who loves you and you love back. Someone that brings you feelings of joy, compassion, and love . . . imagine that person loving you in this moment . . . really feel that love . . . return the favor by sending love, compassion, and gratitude to that person. You might utter the phrases, "May you be peaceful, may you be happy, may you be healthy, may you be free from suffering," while visualizing that person. Or you might say whatever words or phrases feel comfortable to you. All the while you're simply breathing in, and breathing out . . . Next, I want to invite you to contemplate your friends and accomplices, the ones we thought of a few groups ago . . . Send them love and compassion, kindness and gratitude. Thank your friends for being true friends; send compassion to your accomplices and wish for their transformation into true friends, if that's what you want. You might visualize them and utter the phrases, "May you be peaceful, may you be happy, may you be healthy, may you be free from suffering," or you might utter whatever phrases or words feel right to you . . . Next, contemplate your community, your environment. Send compassion to your community. Visualize them as a whole, filling a sports stadium or gathering in one place. You might utter the phrases "May you all be peaceful, happy, free from suffering," or you might send love and compassion in whatever way feels right to you . . . And, finally, think of yourself in this whole process. You've committed to this program and have grown. You deserve love and compassion, as well. You might utter the phrases, while visualizing yourself, "May I be peaceful, may I be happy, may I be healthy, may I be free from suffering," or you might send yourself love and compassion in whatever way feels right. Remember that you're the most important person in your life . . . your ability to do well for your family, to be successful, depends on your ability to practice self-care and continue on the path of personal growth and transformation. I want to end this meditation by sending each and every one of you love, compassion, gratitude, and kindness. May you all be peaceful, may you all be happy, may you all be healthy, and may you all be free from pain and suffering. May you all be successful and continue on the path of personal growth and transformation. May you remember your true nature as a beautiful, amazing human being. Never give up and never listen to anyone who attempts to break you down. You can be what you want to be in this life. Mindfulness and the path of transformation will help you achieve your deepest life aspirations. May you feel love, compassion, kindness, and gratitude. Thank you for your authenticity and participation in this program.

[Ring bell]

After the meditation is over make sure you say your goodbyes in a socially appropriate way. We usually give each youth a big hug!

Congratulations! You have completed this mindfulness-based substance abuse treatment intervention for adolescents. May your continued dedication to young people be acknowledged and appreciated. May you continue to progress down your own path of mindfulness and transformation and help facilitate that path for youth. May you practice self-compassion and self-care to continue this work for this much needed issue. We bow deeply to your continued efforts and humbly thank you for the continuous evolution of this work.

SESSION 12 HANDOUTS

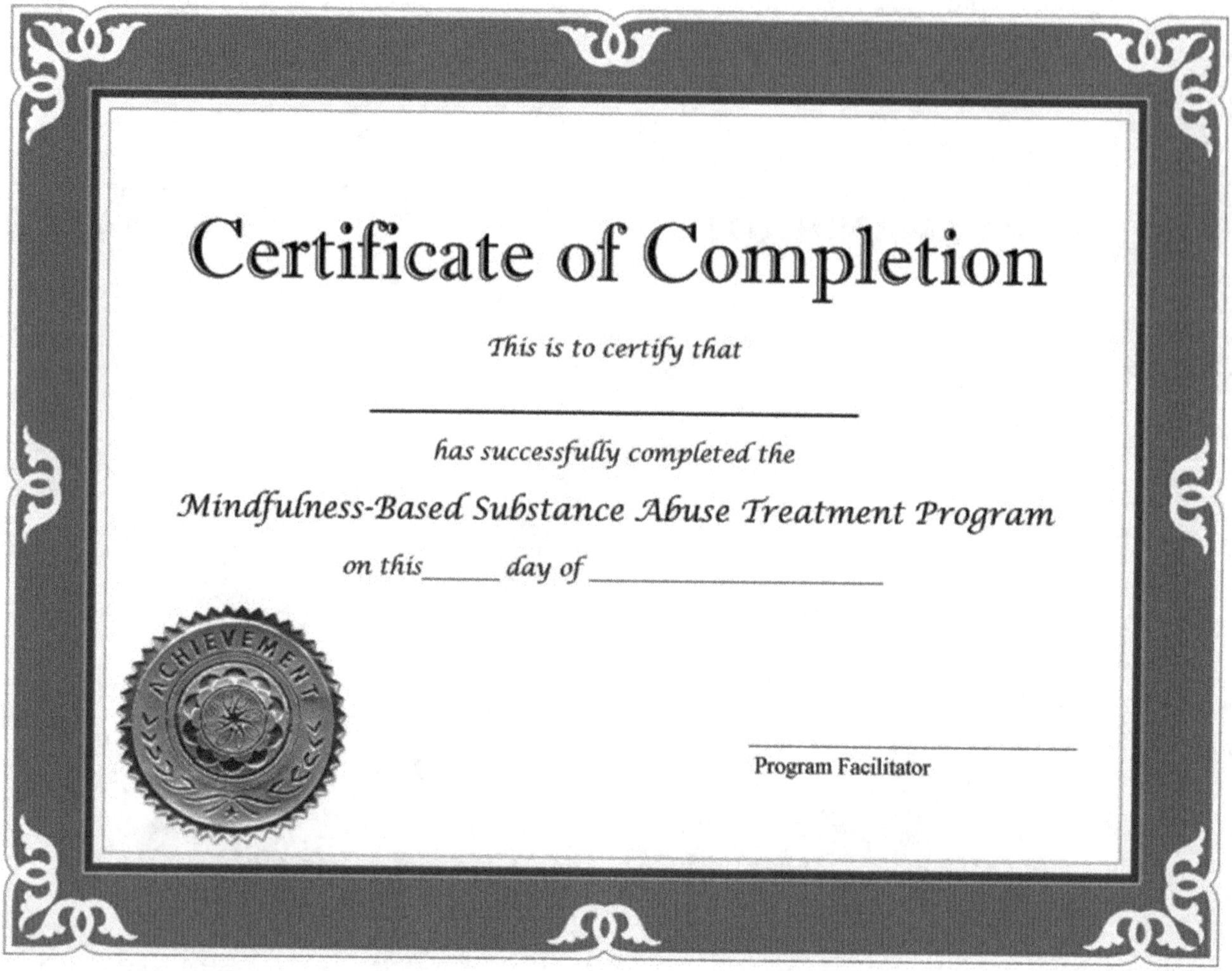

Certificate of Completion

This is to certify that

_____

has successfully completed the

Mindfulness-Based Substance Abuse Treatment Program

on this_____ day of _____

ACHIEVEMENT

_____
Program Facilitator

Figure 15.1

Final Compassion Meditation Script

Talking Points

- Practice one last compassion meditation.
- Compassion toward all members of the group.
- Compassion toward self.
- Send the youth love, compassion, kindness, and gratitude.
- Give them any other prep/inspiration you wish as you end the meditation and program.

Example Script

Facilitator: *For our last meditation, we're going to build on the compassion meditations we've been conducting for the past few groups . . . Sit in a comfortable position, let your eyes close, if you feel comfortable doing so, and, when you hear the sound of the bell, simply bring your awareness to your breathing and wait for further instructions . . .*

[Ring bell]

Start by breathing in, and breathing out . . . Notice where it's easiest to sense your breath. That might be in the nostrils, the belly, the chest . . . wherever it's easiest to notice your breath, let your awareness rest right there. Breathing in, and breathing out . . .

. . . Next I want to invite you to contemplate someone in your family, someone who loves you and you love back. Someone that brings you feelings of joy, compassion, and love . . . imagine that person loving you in this moment . . . really feel that love . . . return the favor by sending love, compassion, and gratitude to that person. You might utter the phrases, "May you be peaceful, may you be happy, may you be healthy, may you be free from suffering," while visualizing that person. Or you might say whatever words or phrases feel comfortable to you. All the while you're simply breathing in, and breathing out . . . Next, I want to invite you to contemplate your friends and accomplices, the ones we thought of a few groups ago . . . Send them love and compassion, kindness and gratitude. Thank your friends for being true friends; send compassion to your accomplices and wish for their transformation into true friends, if that's what you want. You might visualize them and utter the phrases, "May you be peaceful, may you be happy, may you be healthy, may you be free from suffering," or you might utter whatever phrases or words feel right to you . . . Next, contemplate your community, your environment. Send compassion to your community. Visualize them as a whole, filling a sports stadium or gathering in one place. You might utter the phrases "May you all be peaceful, happy, free from suffering," or you might send love and compassion in whatever way feels right to you . . . And, finally, think of yourself in this whole process. You've committed to this program and have grown. You deserve love and compassion, as well. You might utter the phrases, while visualizing yourself, "May I be peaceful, may I be happy, may I be healthy, may I be free from suffering," or you might send yourself love and compassion in whatever way feels right. Remember that you're the most important person in your life . . . your ability to do well for your family, to be successful,

depends on your ability to practice self-care and continue on the path of personal growth and transformation. I want to end this meditation by sending each and every one of you love, compassion, gratitude, and kindness. May you all be peaceful, may you all be happy, may you all be healthy, and may you all be free from pain and suffering. May you all be successful and continue on the path of personal growth and transformation. May you remember your true nature as a beautiful, amazing human being. Never give up and never listen to anyone who attempts to break you down. You can be what you want to be in this life. Mindfulness and the path of transformation will help you achieve your deepest life aspirations. May you feel love, compassion, kindness, and gratitude. Thank you for your authenticity and participation in this program.

[Ring bell]

Session 12 References

American Psychological Association. (2005). *American Psychological Association statement: Policy statement on evidence-based practices in psychology*. Washington, DC: Author.

Institute of Medicine. (2001). *Crossing the quality chasm: A new health system for the 21st century*. Washington, DC: National Academy Press.

INDEX

Note: Page numbers with *f* indicate figures; those with *t* indicate tables.

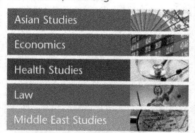